Florida Lawn Handbook

An Environmental Approach to Care and Maintenance of Your Lawn

Edited by

Kathleen C. Ruppert and Robert J. Black

D1413232

Second Edition

Contributors and Editors

Black, R.J., Consumer Horticulture Specialist, University of Florida, IFAS, Gainesville
Brown, S.P., Hillsborough County Extension Specialist, Seffner
Cisar, J.L., Turf Specialist, University of Florida, AREC, Ft. Lauderdale
Dunn, R.A., Nematologist, University of Florida, IFAS, Gainesville
Freeman, T.E., Plant Pathologist, University of Florida, IFAS, Gainesville
Holsinger, M.J., Sarasota County Extension Specialist, Sarasota
Kern, W.H. Jr., Urban Wildlife Ecology Specialist, University of Florida, IFAS, Largo
Koehler, P.G., Entomologist, University of Florida, IFAS, Gainesville
McCarty, L.B., Commercial Turf Specialist, University of Florida, IFAS, Gainesville (Former)
Nesheim, O.N., Pesticide Information Specialist, University of Florida, IFAS, Gainesville
Oi, D.H., Entomologist, USDA-ARS, Gainesville (Former)
Ruppert, K.C., Environmental Horticulturist, University of Florida, IFAS, Gainesville
Sartain, J.B., Soil Scientist, University of Florida, IFAS, Gainesville
Schaefer, J.M., Extension Wildlife Specialist, University of Florida, IFAS, Gainesville
Short, D.E., Entomologist, University of Florida, IFAS, Gainesville
Simone, G.W., Plant Pathologist, University of Florida, IFAS, Gainesville

Department of Environmental Horticulture
Institute of Food and Agricultural Sciences
University of Florida
Gainesville, Florida
1997

Cover Design and Illustration by Katrina Vitkus
Cover Photograph: IFAS Archive
Back Cover Photograph by Donna Mitchell

- of related interest

Your Florida Landscape: A Complete Guide to Planting and Maintenance. Written by over 30 faculty, this complete resource covers trees, palms, shrubs, ground covers, and vines. Includes the newest research-based information on topics such as how to evaluate your planting site, mulching, watering, fertilizing, pruning, common pests and beneficial insects. Over 240 color plates and 52 illustrations. 234 pp. Publication SP135.

Florida Guide to Environmental Landscapes. This package of research-based information helps a homeowner design and maintain attractive landscaping that saves energy. Site analysis, planning, design, planting and establishment, and plant selection and types are discussed. Color photographs and extensive designs are included. 32 pp. Publication SP114.

Troubleshooting Lawn Pests. Learn to recognize organisms commonly found in Florida's turf. Forty-six laminated identification cards identify and describe insects and the damage they cause. Excellent field resource for consumers, turf and garden managers. Publication SP180.

Beneficial Insects Poster. Should you spray or walk away? This colorful poster features fifteen of Florida's beneficial insects and invertebrates, and it helps you decide whether to spray or leave it be. Protect natural insect enemies and save time, money and energy. Wall poster is suitable for classroom, home, plant nursery or business. Originally produced in cooperation with the Florida Energy Extension Office. 17x21 in. Publication SP129.

Resources Catalog. Find out about all the books, manuals, videos, compact discs, flash cards and other media available from the University of Florida's Institute of Food and Agricultural Sciences. SP1.

These materials may be ordered by contacting:

Publications Distribution Center — University of Florida
P.O. Box 110011
Gainesville, Florida 32611-0011
1-800-226-1764

- about the cover...

The cover illustration shows a St. Augustinegrass lawn with a plug removed and enlarged to show what the lawn looks like from a "bug's-eye" view. Lawns are teeming with life — plants, insects, worms, bacteria — some of these are harmful and some beneficial. Each living creature plays a part in the life of your lawn. The environmental approach to lawn care takes these roles into account and seeks to use the least toxic method of control, if any is needed.

Use this key to the cover illustration to begin learning more:

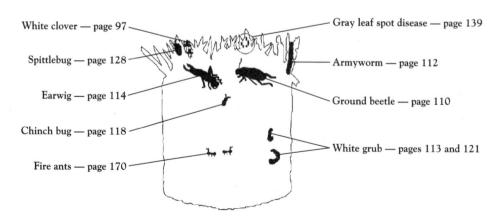

White clover — page 97
Spittlebug — page 128
Earwig — page 114
Chinch bug — page 118
Fire ants — page 170
Gray leaf spot disease — page 139
Armyworm — page 112
Ground beetle — page 110
White grub — pages 113 and 121

About the Editors

Kathleen Carlton Ruppert, a native Floridian, earned her bachelor's, master's and Ed.D. degrees from the University of Florida. She is an assistant professor in the Department of Environmental Horticulture. She teaches the use of ornamental plants, especially how people and plants interact by developing educational materials for gardeners, extension agents, teachers, volunteers, youth and advanced horticulturists.

Robert J. (Bob) Black grew up in Louisiana bayou country and received his bachelor's and master's degrees from Louisiana State University and his Ph.D. from the University of Tennessee. Before coming to UF in 1975, he spent two years as an Extension horticulture agent advising New Orleans gardeners. Now the UF/IFAS Consumer Horticulture Specialist, Black helps inform Florida landscape gardeners on how to select, arrange and maintain plants.

What is Extension?

The Cooperative Extension Service is a partnership of county, state and federal government which serves the citizens of Florida by providing information and training on a wide variety of topics. In Florida, the Extension Service is a part of the University of Florida's Institute of Food and Agricultural Sciences with selected programs at Florida Agricultural and Mechanical University (FAMU). Extension touches almost everyone in the state from the homeowner to huge agribusiness operations in such areas as: food safety, gardening, child and family development, consumer credit counseling, youth development, energy conservation, sustainable agriculture, competitiveness in world markets, and natural resource conservation.

What is a Master Gardener?

Master Gardeners are adult volunteers recruited and trained by County Extension Agents and UF specialists to provide assistance in Extension home horticultural programs. Through this program, enthusiastic gardeners study such areas as botany, horticulture, soil science, and plant and insect identification and management. After successfully completing the training program, Master Gardeners teach and promote environmental action—awareness and wise use of resources as well as reduced chemical, water and energy usage. They conduct gardening clinics at malls, write about gardening for local newspapers, speak in clubs, libraries and schools, answer phone questions, and conduct demonstration gardens at fairs. The Florida Master Gardener Program is administered by the Cooperative Extension Service, a part of the University of Florida's Institute of Food and Agricultural Sciences.

Visit our Web site!

The Institute of Food and Agricultural Sciences at the University of Florida has an extensive collection of information available online on the World Wide Web. Begin your visit with us at:

http://www.ifas.ufl.edu/

Foreword

This book is intended as a training guide for homeowners and lawn maintenance firms in their efforts to grow and maintain aesthetically pleasing and environmentally friendly lawns. The information enclosed is as complete and up-to-date as possible. However, management and pesticide recommendations are constantly being updated. New products continue evolving, while old ones disappear. Contact your county Cooperative Extension Service office annually (addresses included) for the latest recommendations.

The use of trade names in this publication is solely for the purpose of providing specific information. It is not a guarantee or warranty of the products named, and does not signify they are approved to the exclusion of others of suitable composition.

The pesticide recommendations presented in this publication were current with state and federal regulations at the time of publication. The user is responsible for determining that the intended pesticide use is consistent with the directions on the label of the product being used. Use pesticides safely. Read and follow label directions.

Acknowledgements

Any project of such magnitude is definitely the result of the efforts of many competent, dedicated professionals. Many of these chapters are revisions of previously published Extension fact sheets, circulars and bulletins by L.B. McCarty and J.L. Cisar. The editors wish to express their gratitude to typist Judy Wilson; illustrators Suzanne McCullough and Jane Medley; reviewers Sydney Park-Brown, Ed Freeman, Harold C. Jones, and Paul F. Ruppert; CD-ROM formatter Cheryl Alexander; and all the contributing authors. Special recognition should be extended to Julia Graddy, Billie Hermansen, Katrina Vitkus and Charles Brown of IFAS Editorial Department for their excellent technical and editorial reviews and assistance. We hope that no one has been omitted, but if they have, we apologize for our oversight.

Contents

❧ CHAPTER ONE ❧

Selection and Adaptability

Selecting a Turfgrass for Florida Lawns

L. B. McCarty

The lawn is an integral part of the landscape. It is the canvas on which the rest of the plantings are placed. A beautiful lawn will enhance any landscape, while a poor lawn will detract from the overall appearance. Not only do lawns increase the aesthetic and economic value of the landscape, but they also provide recreational surfaces, erosion control, and other ecological benefits. Choosing the proper grass is an important step and the decision should be made carefully. Table 1 provides information to assist in this selection process.

Some basic questions need to be answered before selecting a turfgrass for a Florida lawn. Answers to these questions will quickly suggest which turfgrass species may be best for your lawn. Avoid using the cost of installment and establishment as the major reason for choosing a grass. Instead consider the following questions:

❑ *What type of lawn is desired or expected?* Everyone would like a perfect green lawn that does not need to be mowed, fertilized, or irrigated, but that grass does not exist. For practical purposes though, decide if the lawn is to be a showplace, an average lawn, or just a cover to lessen soil erosion.

❑ *What level of maintenance will the lawn be given?* Most turfgrasses will respond to a range of maintenance levels; however, there is an optimum level for each grass. Levels of maintenance are closely related to cost and time, with high-maintenance turf costing the most and taking the most time to maintain.

❑ *Are there any physical or environmental limitations to the planting site?* Quality turf requires irrigation, so water quantity and quality are selection factors. Can the area be easily mowed? Soil type, pH, drainage, and other soil characteristics are important. The amount of shade the turf will receive can limit the selection of suitable grasses.

With answers to these questions in mind, use Table 1 and the following descriptions to select the proper turfgrass for your Florida lawn. The county Cooperative Extension Service office can help recommend turfgrasses best suited for your location.

REGION OF ADAPTATION

Environmental and soil conditions vary throughout the state and certain turfgrasses grow better in some locations than others. There are several turfgrass species and cultivars of each from which a selection can be made. Some turfgrasses can be planted statewide, while others perform best in the Panhandle and north Florida regions.

Note: Grasses grown in Florida are maintained in a totally different way from those grown in the northern regions of the United States. Northern-grown grasses (e.g., fescue, bluegrass, ryegrass) will grow in Florida only during fall, winter and early spring months, and will not survive year-round.

SOIL CONDITIONS

Several of the turfgrasses can grow in a wide range of soil conditions, including pH values of 5.0 to 8.5. Florida soil types in which most turfgrasses are grown include sand, clay, marl, or muck-type soils. For example, centipedegrass and carpetgrass grow best in acid soils. Iron chlorosis is a problem if they are grown in high pH (alkaline) soils. Carpetgrass grows best in wet soils, whereas an established planting of bahiagrass is more tolerant of drought and grows better in sandy soil than most other lawngrasses.

TOLERANCE

Turfgrasses vary in their ability to withstand stresses. Drought tolerance is a measure of how well the turf will survive extended dry periods without irrigation or rainfall. Turf can also be subjected to salt stress by water from an irrigation system or as spray from the ocean. Shade from trees or buildings is a common occurrence in most landscapes (Plate 1). Florida landscape turfgrasses vary in their shade tolerance. Wear tolerance is a measure of how well a grass continues to grow after being walked or played upon.

MAJOR PEST PROBLEMS

Each turfgrass has some major pest problem which could limit its use in certain locations. Major insect pests are chinch bugs, mole crickets, ground pearls, webworms, spittlebugs, and billbugs. Major disease problems are brown patch, dollar spot, Pythium, Helminthosporium, and gray leaf spot. Nematodes are the greatest single problem on some turfgrasses which eliminates using the species in some home lawn locations. Other pest problems can occur and cause severe damage. Proper management practices will keep most pest problems to a minimum.

LEAF TEXTURE

The categories of turf texture are coarse, medium, and fine. This is a relative measure of the leaf blade width. The choice of texture is merely a visual preference unless the grass is important for a sport such as golf. Most southern lawn grasses are coarser in leaf texture than those (e.g., fescue, bluegrass and ryegrass) grown further north. This is especially true of the three most commonly used lawn grasses in Florida (St. Augustinegrass, bahiagrass and centipedegrass).

TURF DENSITY

The number of leaves or shoots per area of the ground is a measure of turf density. Turf with high density and finer leaf texture generally produce better quality lawns. Turf with lower density and coarser leaf texture often require a higher mowing height to produce an acceptable quality lawn. Higher density varieties include hybrid bermudagrasses and zoysiagrass. Bahiagrass has a low stand density while other warm-season grasses have a medium density.

MAINTENANCE LEVEL

Each turfgrass grows at a different rate, and has optimum levels of fertility, mowing, and irrigation which produce a quality turf. Generally, as more water and fertilizer are applied to the turf, more mowing and pest control are required. Turf at a low level of maintenance is fertilized no more than twice a year, mowed as needed, often just to remove seedheads, and seldom watered. Moderate turf maintenance includes four times per year fertilization, weekly mowing, and irrigation as needed. High-maintenance turfgrasses require monthly fertilizing, twice-per-week mowing, and frequent irrigation during seasons of active growth.

MOWING HEIGHT

The growth habit of each turfgrass determines the mowing height for the best quality turf. Mowing the turf below the recommended height can cause stress on the plants and weaken the turf to invasion by weeds, insects, and diseases. By mowing as high as possible for a given species, the increased leaf surface for photosynthesis will result in a deeper root system, better drought tolerance, and healthier turf.

MOWING FREQUENCY

Turfgrass species and level of management determine how often a lawn needs to be mowed. The frequency of mowing can be reduced somewhat by moderating the amounts of fertilizer and water applied. Recycling lawn clippings also reduces the amount of fertilizer needed.

Table 1. Comparative chart of grasses grown for Florida.

Condition	Variety					
	Bahigrass	Bermudagrass	Carpetgrass	Centipedegrass	St. Augustinegrass	Zoysiagrass
Area Adapted	Statewide	Statewide	Wet areas	Panhandle & N.	Statewide	Statewide
Mowing Ht. (in)	3 - 4	$1/2$ - $1^1/2$	$1^1/2$ - 2	$1^1/2$ - 2	$1^1/2$* - 4	1 - 2
Soil Condition	Acid	Wide range	Acid	Acid	Wide range	Wide range
Texture	Coarse/med	Fine	Medium	Medium	Coarse-med	Med-fine
Drought Tolerance	Excellent	Excellent	Very poor	Fair	Good	Excellent
Salt Tolerance	Very poor	Excellent	Poor	Poor	Good	Good-Excellent
Shade Tolerance	Poor	Very poor	Fair	Fair	Good (cultivar dependent)	Fair
Wear Tolerance	Good	Excellent	Poor	Poor	Fair	Excellent
Nematode Tolerance	Very good	Poor to fair	Poor	Poor	Fair to good	Poor
Low Soil Potassium Tolerance	Good	Poor	Fair	Fair	Good	Poor
Maintenance Level	Low	High	Low	Low	Moderate	High
Major Use	Lawns	Athletic fields, golf courses	Wet areas	Lawns	Lawns	Lawns
Establishment Methods	Seed, sod	Sod, sprigs, plugs, seed	Seed, sprigs	Seed, sprigs, plugs, sod	Sod, sprigs, plugs	Sod, plugs, sprigs

*Dwarf St. Augstinegrass varieties only.

ESTABLISHMENT METHODS

Some turf species (e.g., St. Augustinegrass) are limited to vegetative propagation by sod, sprigs, or plugs because seed is not available or does not germinate true-to-type (see Table 2). Other turf species produce seed in sufficient quantity and trueness-to-type to allow establishment by seed (e.g., bahiagrass, centipedegrass, carpetgrass, common bermudagrass, and ryegrass). A quality lawn can be established by either method if the site is properly prepared and maintained.

Table 2. Reproductive and establishment methods of turfgrasses.

Turfgrass	Rhizome	Stolon	Tiller	Seed*
Bahiagrass	X	X	—	X
Bluegrass	X	—	—	X
Bentgrass	—	X	—	X
Bermudagrass				
–common	X	X	—	X
–hybrid	X	X	—	—
Buffalograss	—	X	—	X
Centipedegrass	—	X	—	X
Fescue	—	—	X	X
Ryegrass	—	—	X	—
St. Augstinegrass	—	X	—	—
Zoysiagrass	X	X	—	—

*All turfgrasses produce seed but some of these have low viability or do not remain true-to-type and therefore are not listed.

Bahiagrass for Florida Lawns

L. B. McCarty

Common bahiagrass (*Paspalum notatum* Flugge) was introduced from Brazil in 1914 and was originally used as a pasture grass on the poor sandy soils of the southeastern United States. Since 1914, several additional varieties have become available for use as lawngrasses (Plate 2). The ability of bahiagrasses to persist on infertile, dry soils and their resistance to most pests have made them increasingly popular with homeowners.

ADVANTAGES

Bahiagrass can be grown from seed which is abundant and relatively inexpensive. Once established, these grasses develop an extensive root system which makes them one of the most drought tolerant lawngrasses. Bahiagrass produces a very durable sod which is able to withstand moderate traffic. In addition, bahiagrasses have fewer pest problems than any other Florida lawngrass, although mole cricket can severely damage it.

DISADVANTAGES

The principle disadvantages of bahiagrasses are the relatively open growth habit and the tall unsightly seedheads that are produced continuously from May through November. The prolific seedheads, plus the very tough leaves and stems make bahias difficult to mow. Frequent mowing (e.g., weekly) with a heavy duty rotary mower is needed for best appearance. The coarse texture of several bahia varieties reduce their visual quality. Bahiagrasses are not well adapted to soils having high pH (alkaline soils) and grow poorly in areas subject to salt spray. They often appear yellow in spring and fall due to lack of iron and they can be seriously damaged by insects called mole crickets. Bahiagrass has low tolerance to most currently available postemergence grass herbicides. This makes weed control difficult in bahiagrass turf.

Note: Generally, bahiagrass will not provide as fine a lawn as St. Augustinegrass. St. Augustinegrass tends to produce a darker green, denser turf compared to bahiagrass. If a crab-apple-green colored grass with lower turf density is not acceptable, choose another lawn grass besides bahiagrass.

VARIETIES

Four varieties of bahiagrass seed or sod are sold for lawns: common, Pensacola, Argentine, and Paraguay. (Two other bahias, Wilmington and Paraguay 22, may also be used for lawns; however, commercial seed production of the former and sod production of both are very limited.)

Common

Common bahiagrass is the poorest type available because of its light green color, coarse texture, and prostrate, open-type growth habit which produces poor density turf. It has poor cold tolerance and is not recommended for use as a lawngrass.

Argentine

This variety is the best for lawns. Argentine has leaves that are wider than Pensacola but are longer, narrower, more numerous and hairier than those of common. Argentine forms a dense sod, has good color and cold-hardiness, responds well to fertilization, and is the least susceptible to dollar spot disease.

Pensacola

Pensacola bahiagrass was selected from plantings found in Pensacola, Florida in 1935 and has become the most widely grown variety. Pensacola is a long, narrow-leafed bahia used extensively along the roadsides in Florida due to its deep, fibrous root system and readily available seed. It is the second best lawngrass behind the variety Argentine, but is a very prolific seedhead producer.

Paraguay

Paraguay bahiagrass is also known as Texas bahia. Its leaves are very pubescent (hairy), giving them a grayish appearance, and they also are short, narrow, and tough. It has a low cold tolerance and is very susceptible to dollar spot disease. It is not as desirable a lawngrass as Argentine or Pensacola.

Bermudagrass for Florida Lawns

L. B. McCarty

Bermudagrasses (*Cynodon* species), also called wiregrass or devilgrass, are planted throughout Florida primarily on golf courses, athletic fields, tennis courts, and bowling greens (Plate 3). They are primarily used in areas where fine-textured, high quality turf is essential for sports activities, and maintenance budgets are adequate.

Bermudagrass is native to Africa where it thrived on fertile soils. Today, most of the bermudagrasses used for turf in Florida are hybrids of two different *Cynodon* species: *C. dactylon* and *C. transvaalensis*.

ADVANTAGES

Bermudagrass produces a vigorous, light to dark green, dense turf that is well adapted to most soils and climatic regions in Florida. Bermudagrass has excellent wear, drought, and salt tolerance and is a good choice for ocean front property. It establishes rapidly and is competitive against weeds and, depending on the variety, is available as seed, sod or sprigs.

DISADVANTAGES

Bermudagrass has a large number of cultural and pest problems which restrict its use in many Florida situations. It is not suitable for most home lawns because of the need for restricted use pesticides to control nematodes and insects. It also requires the most maintenance for an acceptable appearance of any Florida turfgrass.

In central and north Florida, bermudagrasses become dormant (turn brown) in cold weather. Overseeding in fall with ryegrass is a common practice to maintain year-round green color. Bermudagrasses are susceptible to several nematode, insect, and disease problems. Bermudagrasses also have very poor shade tolerance and should not be grown underneath tree canopies or building overhangs. They spread very rapidly by both above ground (stolons) and below ground (rhizomes) runners that are very difficult to control within flower beds, walks, and borders. Due to its rapid growth nature, thatch buildup can become a problem in bermudagrass. A reel mower should also be used to produce the highest possible quality turf stand.

CULTIVARS

There are several bermudagrass cultivars being used for turf in Florida (see Table 1). Currently, improved seeded bermudagrass varieties are being aggressively developed. Most seed is available with the hull removed (hulled) or with the hull remaining (unhulled). Hulled seed germinates faster but costs more; unhulled seed lasts longer during unfavorable weather before germinating. Only some cultivars are commercially available from turf producers. If your situation requires the use of bermudagrass, check with your county Cooperative Extension Service office for the best cultivar for your location and use.

Common

This is the bermudagrass traditionally available for establishment by seed. However, it generally produces a looser netted turfgrass with a coarse texture, low shoot density, and light green color and for these reasons is less desirable than other cultivars available (Plate 4). Common is often planted in seed mixes with bahiagrass for roadsides or reclamation sites.

Cheyenne, Sahara, Sundevil, Jackpot, and Others

These "improved" common type seeded varieties are darker green, deeper rooted, medium textured and moderately denser compared to common bermudagrass. They are general purpose, turf-type bermudagrasses used for lawns, parks, roadsides and sports turf. These should

Table 1. Characteristics of popular bermudagrass varieties.

Variety	Seeded	Texture
Cheyenne	yes	medium
Common	yes	coarse
FLoraTeX™	no	medium
Guymon	yes	medium
Jackpot	yes	medium
Midiron	no	fine
Midway	no	medium
NuMex Sahara	yes	medium
Ormond	no	medium
Quickstand	no	medium
Sundevil	yes	medium
Texture 10	no	medium
Tifdwarf	no	fine
Tifgreen (328)	no	fine
Tifgreen II	no	fine
Tiflawn	no	fine
Tifway (419)	no	fine
Tifway II	no	fine
U3	yes	medium

be used in areas where improved characteristics are desired when compared to common but quality and level of maintenance are lower than the Tif varieties.

FLoraTeX™

A variety jointly released in 1993 by the University of Florida and Texas A&M University. It is noted for its low maintenance inputs in terms of fertilizer and water, and extended fall color and earlier spring green-up. Its texture is medium and density moderate. It also appears to be much less susceptible to dollar spot disease and bermudagrass stunt mite. FLoraTeX™ must be vegetatively established and produces numerous seedheads in late spring. It should be used where desired turf quality is higher than common bermudagrass but level of maintenance and quality are lower than the Tif varieties.

Ormond

Ormond is a dark, blue-green bermudagrass with medium texture and density. Ormond was released in 1962. It is used on fairways and athletic fields where a higher mowing height is acceptable. Seedhead formation is minimal. Bermudagrass stunt mite and dollar spot disease are its major pest problems. Ormond is not commercially available.

Tifdwarf

This cultivar was released in 1965 and is used primarily on golf greens where a very low cutting height is desired for fast putting conditions. It is a very dark green turf with high shoot density and a low, slow growth habit. Tifdwarf has few seedheads, but it is susceptible to caterpillar and mole cricket damage. Tifdwarf turns a purple color in cold weather and normally requires overseeding on golf greens in the winter. Tifdwarf is a very high-maintenance grass and normally is not recommended for home lawns.

Tifgreen

This cultivar was released in 1956. It is a dark green bermudagrass with high shoot density, fine texture, and low growth habit. It has soft leaves and tolerates close, frequent mowing. Tifgreen produces few seedheads. This cultivar is the most commonly planted bermudagrass on golf greens around the world. Tifgreen is also popular for baseball and softball fields, tennis courts and lawn bowling activities. It requires a high level of maintenance in terms of irrigation, fertilizing, dethatching, mowing, and edging frequencies.

Tifgreen II

This cultivar is a mutant of Tifgreen which was released in 1983. It is a light green bermudagrass with vigorous, dense growth. Tifgreen II has better cold and nematode tolerance than Tifgreen. Excessive seedhead production and poor density at low mowing heights are problems with Tifgreen II.

Tiflawn

Tiflawn was released in 1952 and is noted for its medium dark green color; medium fine texture and shoot density; vigorous growth rate and establishment; and moderately low growing height. Tiflawn has excellent drought and wear tolerance as well as recuperative potential. It is widely grown on sports fields, recreational areas and lawns; however, it is susceptible to bermudagrass mites.

Tifway

Tifway is a dark green bermudagrass with medium texture and high shoot density. Tifway has better tolerance to pest problems than Tifgreen. Tifway is used in areas of moderate maintenance such as fairways and sports fields and higher maintained lawns.

Tifway II

Tifway II is a mutant of Tifway that was released in 1984 for its improved frost and nematode tolerance. It has a similar appearance to Tifway with increased shoot density and seedheads. Tifway II can be used in moderate maintenance situations. Tifway and Tifway II make beautiful yards if adequate time, machine, and labor resources are dedicated to their establishment and upkeep.

Buffalograss, Description and Use

L. B. McCarty

Buffalograss (*Buchloe dactyloides*) is a low-maintenance, perennial warm season species native to the subhumid and semiarid regions of the North American great plains. It spreads by stolons and seed and forms a medium to fine textured, relatively thin turf with a soft blue-green color that resembles common bermudagrass (Plate 5). The grayish-green color is due to the fine hairs that cover the leaves. Curling of the leaf blades also is a distinctive feature. It is the only dioecious turfgrass–there are separate male and female plants. The male flower is produced on the end of a stalk, while the female flower is produced at the base of the plant. Buffalograss is adapted for use on unirrigated lawns, parks, and roadsides in the warm zones of the subhumid and semiarid regions.

ADVANTAGES

Buffalograss spreads vegetatively by numerous stolons that branch profusely to form a tight sod. It has excellent hardiness to high temperature and tolerates fairly low temperatures in comparison to most warm season turfgrasses. It is adapted to a wide range of soil types with the possible exception of deep sands. It also appears to tolerate a wide range of soil pH. The spring green-up rate and low temperature color retention are intermediate to fair. The excellent drought resistance of buffalograss is one of its most outstanding characteristics. It has the ability to go dormant with the advent of severe drought and to initiate new growth after prolonged periods of moisture stress.

The main advantages of buffalograss are:

❑ seed (burrs) are available

❑ low maintenance in terms of fertilizer and water requirements, and

❑ drought/heat tolerance.

DISADVANTAGES

Several disadvantages are noted with buffalograss. It is naturally adapted to areas low in annual rainfall (10 to 25 inches per year). Higher rainfall areas, such as Florida, discourage buffalograss, and other plants such as bermudagrass often invade it. Diseases such as brown patch and leaf spot also become a problem when grown in high rainfall/irrigation areas and when over-fertilized. During extended dry spells, buffalograss will turn brown, which is a natural survival mechanism, but greens up

again with rain. Buffalograss also has very poor shade and traffic tolerance. Due to its open growth habit, weeds often invade when grown under higher rainfall or irrigations schedules. Buffalograss generally has poor tolerance to most postemergence herbicides; therefore, if used, herbicides must be applied before weeds emerge. As with most low maintenance grasses, buffalograss will not provide a dark-green, dense, aesthetically pleasing yard. Its appearance resembles a light green colored, thin, coarse common bermudagrass planting. It will not provide the quality of lawn that higher maintained grasses such as hybrid bermudagrass, zoysiagrass, or St. Augustinegrass will.

In summary, disadvantages of buffalograss are:

❑ excessive rainfall/watering (>25 inches/year total) weakens it,

❑ disease prone when grown under excessive watering or humidity,

❑ turns brown (dormant) during extended drought,

❑ very poor shade tolerance,

❑ very poor traffic tolerance,

❑ thin, open growth habit that weeds often invade,

❑ poor herbicide tolerance, and

❑ inferior stand density, color, and appearance.

ESTABLISHMENT

Propagation may be vegetative or by seed (burrs). Vegetative propagation by sodding has been the main method of establishment primarily because of a seed shortage. If vegetatively propagated, female plants are generally used since male plants produce unsightly seedstalks. When viable seed (or burrs) are available, seeding rates range from 1 to 5 lbs per 1000 sq ft. The higher rate is needed if seed are broadcast and/or if irrigation is not available or if a quicker establishment rate is desired. Lower rates (e.g., 10 to 20 pounds per acre or 0.2 to 0.4 lbs/1000 ft^2) may be used if the seed are drilled in rows.

Plugs ≥2 inches also may be used for establishment. These are spaced from 6 inches to 2 feet apart, depending on the desired establishment rate. Soil should be well watered before and after planting for several weeks to aid survival. Establishment rate using seed or plugs is generally slower than most other warm-season grasses.

MAINTENANCE

Buffalograss is somewhat pest-free in its native habitat but problems occur when grown in the warmer, more humid, and wetter southeast. Some authors even suggest the quickest way to thin a buffalograss stand is to start fertilizing and watering it. Therefore, only minimum maintenance practices should be used to keep a buffalograss stand. For lawn-type or golf course fairway situation, a cutting height between $3/4$ and 2 inches is preferred. For rough areas on golf courses, buffalograss is mowed between 2 and 3 inches and only as needed. The mowing interval is generally infrequent due to a slow vertical shoot growth rate. A dense stand requires minimum water, mowing, and weed control. Nitrogen requirements range from 0 to 1 lb N/1000 sq ft per year. Higher fertilizer rates encourage bermudagrass encroachment.

Supplemental watering normally is not advisable since overwatering can produce undesirable effects. If watered, apply only deep (e.g., $3/4$ inch), infrequent (weekly or longer) cycles.

AVAILABLE VARIETIES

Recently introduced varieties include Prairie and Oasis. They have better density, are lower growing, and have more competitive turf-type characteristics compared to older varieties. These were bred in Texas and Nebraska, respectively, and have not been shown to be long-term adapted to Florida conditions. Other varieties include Buffalawn, Sharp's Improved, Bison, Comanche, and Texoka.

With these considerations in mind, current varieties of buffalograss are not recommended as permanent turf in Florida.

Carpetgrass for Florida Lawns

L. B. McCarty

Carpetgrass (*Axonopus affinis* or *Axonopus compressus*) is a creeping, warm-season grass native to the West Indies which was introduced into the United States early in the 1800s (Plate 6). Carpetgrass is also called Louisianagrass and has become naturalized in the southeastern states, especially on poorly drained soils. Carpetgrass physically resembles centipedegrass in terms of leaf density and shape.

ADVANTAGES

Carpetgrass grows on wet soils where few other grasses persist, and has moderate shade tolerance. It is low-growing and produces a dense turf with good color when fertilized. Carpetgrass also can be grown from seed.

DISADVANTAGES

Carpetgrass will not survive on very dry soils unless irrigated frequently. Roots tend to be very shallow, so this grass has poor drought tolerance. During the summer, carpetgrass produces numerous tall, thin seedheads which make the lawn unattractive unless mowed frequently. It also has poor cold hardiness, turning brown with the first cold spell, and is slow to green up in the spring. The texture of carpetgrass is medium, the color light green and salt tolerance poor. It is also troubled by several insects, nematodes and diseases, especially brown patch disease. Carpetgrass is also recommended to be grown only in acid (pH: 5.0 to 5.5) soils.

Carpetgrass is not recommended for a high-quality lawn; however, it can be used in wet, shady areas where ease of maintenance is more important than quality.

VARIETIES

No named varieties of carpetgrass are available. The species A. *affinis* is sold as carpetgrass for lawn purposes.

Centipedegrass for Florida Lawns

L. B. McCarty

Centipedegrass [*Eremochloa ophiuroides* (Munro) Hack.] was introduced into the United States from southeastern Asia (Plate 7). It is well-adapted to the climate and soils of central and northern Florida. It forms a loose turf which is not very wear-resistant. Centipedegrass is the most common home lawn turfgrass in the panhandle of Florida.

Centipedegrass, low-growing and medium-textured, is a yellow-green colored perennial turf. Its low fertility requirements result in slow growth and reduced maintenance. Centipedegrass' natural color is crab apple green. Overfertilizing to obtain an unnatural dark green color reduces its cold tolerance and usually increases long-term maintenance problems.

ADVANTAGES

Centipedegrass is adapted to infertile soils. It spreads by stolons, producing a medium-textured turf. Maintenance requirements are low when compared to other turfgrasses. It has fair to good shade tolerance, good drought tolerance, and can be established from seed.

DISADVANTAGES

Centipedegrass is highly susceptible to damage from nematodes (especially ring nematodes) and ground pearl insects. Nematode damage limits centipedegrass' use in south Florida's sandy soils. It exhibits iron chlorosis (yellowing) and produces a heavy thatch if overly fertilized. It has poor salt tolerance and will not withstand heavy foot traffic.

Stolons from centipedegrass have a high lignin content and do not decompose readily, thus developing a thatch layer. The rate of thatch accumulation is a direct result of management practices which provide abundant vegetative growth. The subsequent growth of new runners are soon several inches above the soil surface and exposed to the wide fluctuations of temperatures as normally experienced in late fall and winter. Within several years, large brown dead patches form in early spring. This dieback is collectively referred to as "centipedegrass decline." This problem can be prevented by the following proper management:

❑ caution not to overfertilize,

❑ prevention of thatch accumulation,

❑ irrigation during drought stress, especially in the fall and early spring, and

❑ maintaining a mowing height of 1½-2 inches.

VARIETIES

Improved varieties of centipedegrass are available, including Oklawn and Centennial. However, these must be vegetatively propagated and are selected specifically for their improved cold tolerance. Centennial will perform a little better on alkaline soil than common centipedegrass. The centipedegrass seed and sod produced in Florida are a mixture of red- and yellow-stemmed grasses.

St. Augustinegrass for Florida Lawns

L. B. McCarty and John L. Cisar

St. Augustinegrass [*Stenotaphrum secundatum* (Walt.) Kuntze.], also called Charlestongrass, is a turfgrass widely adapted to the world's warm, humid (subtropical) regions (Plate 8). It is believed to be native to the coastal regions of both the Gulf of Mexico and the Mediterranean. In Florida, St. Augustinegrass is the most commonly planted turfgrass in urban, coastal areas. It can be grown in a wide variety of soils, but grows best in well-drained, fertile soils. To produce an acceptable quality lawn, St. Augustinegrass requires irrigation and moderate fertility.

ADVANTAGES

St. Augustinegrass produces a dark to blue-green, dense turf that is well adapted to most soils and climatic regions in Florida. It has good salt tolerance and certain cultivars will generally tolerate shade better than other warm-season turfgrasses. St. Augustinegrass establishes from sod quickly and easily. Several different cultivars of St. Augustinegrass sod and plugs are available from garden centers and custom sod installers throughout Florida.

DISADVANTAGES

St. Augustinegrass, like most turfgrasses, has certain cultural and pest problems which may limit its use in some situations. The coarse leaf texture is objectionable to some people. It requires irrigation to produce a good quality turf, and does not remain green during drought conditions without supplemental irrigation. Excessive thatch buildup can occur under moderate to high fertility and frequent irrigation conditions. It wears poorly, and

some varieties are susceptible to cold damage. The major insect pest of St. Augustinegrass is chinch bug, but cultivar resistance is available (e.g., Floratam and Floralawn). St. Augustinegrass Decline Virus (SADV) is a major disease problem in some parts of the United States but has not been a problem in Florida.

CULTIVARS

There are several cultivars of St. Augustinegrass available for lawns in Florida, and some make better lawns than others. Check with your county Cooperative Extension Service office for the best grass in your location. Table 1 lists some relative growth characteristics for currently available cultivars.

Common and Roselawn

Common and Roseland are pasture types of St. Augustinegrass that evolved in the 1800s. They produce a coarse, open turf that is susceptible to chinch bugs, herbicide damage, shade, and cold damage. They also have poor leaf color and are somewhat unresponsive to fertilization. Avoid planting these cultivars if the lawn appearance is important.

Bitterblue

An improved variety selected in the 1930s that has a finer, denser texture and darker blue-green color than common St. Augustinegrass (Plate 9). It has improved cold tolerance and good shade tolerance but is not resistant to chinch bugs or gray leaf spot disease. It tolerates

Table 1. Relative growth characteristics for St. Augustinegrass cultivars.

Cultivars	Mowing Ht. (in)	Cold Tolerance	Shade Tolerance	Chinch Bug Resistance	Green Color	Texture	Density
Normal Growth Habit Cultivars							
Common/Roselawn	3 - 4	poor	poor	poor	light	coarse	poor
Bitterblue	3 - 4	good	very good	slight	dark	coarse	good
Raleigh	3 - 4	very good	good	poor	medium	coarse	good
Floratine	2 - 3	fair	good	slight	dark	coarse	good
Floratam	3 - 4	poor	poor	good*	dark	very coarse	good
Floralawn	3 - 4	poor	poor	good*	dark	very coarse	good
FX-10	3 - 4	poor	poor	good	medium	coarse	good
Semi-dwarf Growth Habit Cultivars							
Delmar	1$\frac{1}{2}$ - 2$\frac{1}{2}$	very good	good	poor	dark	fine	good
Jade	1$\frac{1}{2}$ - 2$\frac{1}{2}$	good	good	poor	dark	very fine	good
Seville	2 - 2$\frac{1}{2}$	good	very good	slight	dark	fine	good
*Isolated evidence of a new chinch bug has been reported, which can feed on these cultivars.							

triazine herbicides (e.g., atrazine, simazine) less well than other varieties. Bitterblue can produce a good lawn under proper management practices and pest control.

Floratine

An improved selection from Bitterblue that was released in 1962 by the Florida Agricultural Experiment Station. It has finer texture, denser growth habit and lower growth habit that allows closer mowing than common St. Augustinegrass. It is not resistant to chinch bugs but tolerates light to moderate shade. Floratine's other characteristics are similar to Bitterblue's.

Floratam

An improved St. Augustinegrass, released jointly in 1973 by the University of Florida and Texas A & M, which has chinch bug and SADV resistance, and reddish colored stolons (runners). It grows vigorously in the warmer parts of Florida but has a very coarse texture (Plate 9). *It has poor cold and shade tolerance.* It will thin in direct relation to the amount of shade received. Its winter and early spring color is lower as it goes into a deeper semi-dormancy period and sheds its foliage more than other varieties. Spring green-up is also slow. Floratam is a preferred cultivar to plant in open sunny areas where chinch bugs are a problem; however, research has identified a strain of chinch bugs which can damage Floratam.

Raleigh

A cold-hardy cultivar released by North Carolina State University in 1980. It has a medium green color with a coarse texture (Plate 10). It is susceptible to chinch bugs, but due to its tolerance to lower temperatures, it is planted in northern Florida. It is also susceptible to brown patch disease. During peak summertime heat, Raleigh may yellow and not grow (spread) as aggressively as during cooler temperatures. Supplemental iron applications are needed to reduce this yellowing tendency. Raleigh is best adapted to central/north Florida in heavier, organic, clayey soils of medium to low soil pH.

Seville

A semi-dwarf variety with a dark green color and low growth habit (Plate 10). Seville is susceptible to chinch bug and webworm damage and is cold sensitive. Due to its compact growth habit, Seville tends to be thatch-prone and shallow rooting. It resists SADV and has finer texture than Floratam. Seville performs well in shade and produces excellent turf in full sun. Its cold tolerance resembles Floratine's. As a semi-dwarf variety, Seville's maintenance is different than taller growing varieties.

Floralawn

A cultivar released in 1986 by the Florida Agricultural Experiment Station which is resistant to SADV,

chinch bugs, sod webworms and brown patch. Floralawn is similar to Floratam in shade tolerance, coarse leaf texture and sensitivity to cold temperatures. Floralawn can be distinguished from other commercially available cultivars by morphological characteristics and by electrophoretic banding patterns. Floralawn should be grown in mild environments in full sun to moderate shade under low to moderate fertility.

Jade and Delmar

Two new releases which are commercially available as sod or plugs. Jade and Delmar have improved shade tolerance, shorter internodes, a semi-dwarf growth habit, darker green color, and better cold tolerance than Seville (Plate 11). Due to their semi-dwarf growth habit, these should be mowed at $1^1/_2$ - $2^1/_2$ inches. Jade has a finer leaf blade texture and better shade tolerance than Delmar. Delmar has enhanced cold tolerance; therefore, can be grown in cooler regions of Florida. Jade and Delmar are both susceptible to chinch bugs, sod webworms, and brown patch disease. These also have slow lateral runner growth, thus, require longer periods for grow-in from plugs or recovery from damage.

FX-10

A variety licensed in 1990 by the University of Florida Research Foundation, Inc. that is noted for its chinch bug resistance and deep root system. FX-10 has an open rosette appearance with gray-green to blue-green color (Plate 11) and is distinguishable from other varieties with hairs on young, upper leaves. Its cold tolerance, winter and spring performance and shade tolerance appear similar to Floratam's. FX-10's tolerance to atrazine is low. It appears best suited for sunny, warm, sandy areas that do not require a high maintenance variety.

Palmetto

Palmetto St. Augustinegrass is a selection from Florida noted for its rapid spread and dark green color. It has finer leaf blade density compared to Floratam and a lower growth habit. It appears to have good cold-tolerance. Palmetto St. Augustinegrass shows some resistance to gray-leaf spot disease, but it is not totally immune. It appears to have no notable chinch bug resistance. Little definitive research exists on its rooting, shade and disease tolerance, drought resistance and other characteristics.

Other Varieties

Several other lesser known and available St. Augustinegrass varieties have been released. These include FX-33, Sunclipse, Mercedes, Gulf Star, Emerald Blue, and others. Research performed on these varieties has been limited and generally these have not proven superior to older currently available varieties.

Zoysiagrass for Florida Lawns

L. B. McCarty

Zoysiagrasses (*Zoysia* spp.) are perhaps the most beautiful lawngrasses in the South. Several species and varieties of zoysias have been introduced from the Orient and have provided attractive lawns throughout much of the United States (Plate 12). An established, well-managed zoysia lawn is beautiful, but zoysiagrasses require a high level of maintenance and are not as trouble-free as often advertised.

ADVANTAGES

Zoysiagrasses are adapted to a wide variety of soils, have good tolerance to shade and salt spray, have good to excellent wear resistance, and provide an extremely dense sod, which reduces weed invasion. Once established, the slow growth of zoysia is an advantage because mowing is needed infrequently. The density of a zoysia lawn is second to none and the uniformity is excellent. When properly maintained, zoysiagrasses make excellent lawns.

DISADVANTAGES

Due to several overenthusiastic promotions and advertisements, the public has been misinformed on the merits of zoysiagrasses. Zoysias have advantages and disadvantages like all Florida lawngrasses.

The improved zoysias have to be propagated vegetatively and are extremely slow in becoming established. There is a push to produce seeded zoysiagrass. Several seeded sources of *Zoysia japonica* are currently being evaluated and may become commercially available. Two growing seasons may be required for coverage of the lawn when propagated by plugging or sprigging. All zoysias form a heavy thatch which requires periodic renovation. Other disadvantages include slow recovery from damage; poor growth on compacted soils; high fertility requirement; need for frequent irrigations; possible severe damage by nematodes, hunting billbugs; and several diseases. Zoysiagrass also tends to be shallower rooting and is weakened when grown in soils low in potassium levels. For maximum beauty, a reel mower must be used for cutting.

VARIETIES

There are several species and varieties of zoysiagrasses which can be used for Florida lawns. These varieties vary widely in color, texture and establishment rate. Only the common lawn types will be mentioned.

Zoysia japonica

This species is commonly called Japanese or Korean lawngrass. It has a very coarse texture, hairy, light green leaves, a faster growth rate than most zoysias and excellent cold tolerance. The hunting billbug and nematodes cause considerable damage to this lawngrass. *Zoysia japonica* is the only zoysia for which seed is commercially available. It can be used for lawns or general turf areas where convenience of establishment by seed is more important than quality. This species does not make as good a lawn as the other zoysias.

Meyer

Meyer zoysia, also called Z-52 or Amazoy, is an improved selection of *Zoysia japonica* released in 1951. Meyer has a deep green color, medium leaf texture, and spreads much faster than other varieties although it produces few rhizomes. Meyer makes an excellent lawn once established. Meyer is less shade tolerant than Emerald but is the most cold tolerant zoysiagrass. Hunting billbugs and nematodes are potential problems with Meyer. Meyer is the zoysiagrass often advertised as the "miracle" grass in newspapers and magazines.

Zoysia matrella

Also called Manilagrass, this species produces a finer and denser lawn than *Zoysia japonica* but is less winter-hardy. Manilagrass resembles bermudagrass in texture, color and quality and is recommended for a high-quality, high-maintenance lawn where a slow rate of establishment is not a disadvantage. *Zoysia matrella* appears to be highly susceptible to damage by nematodes.

Zoysia tenuifolia

Also call Mascarenegrass, this species is the finest textured zoysiagrass available. It has good wear tolerance but develops excessive thatch, giving it a puffy appearance. It also is the least cold hardy zoysiagrass, thus is best adapted to central and southern areas of the state.

Emerald

Emerald zoysia is a selected hybrid between *Zoysia japonica* and *Zoysia tenuifolia* released in 1955. This hybrid combines the winter-hardiness, color and faster growth rate of one parent with the fine texture and density of the other parent. Emerald resembles Manilagrass in color, texture, and density, but is faster-spreading and has wider adaptation. Emerald zoysia is highly recommended for top quality lawns where time and money allow an adequate maintenance program. Emerald may be the most beautiful of the zoysia lawngrasses, but it also is subject to thatch buildup and puffiness and is susceptible to dollar and leaf spot. Brown patch disease also can occur.

Belaire

Belaire is an improved *Zoysia japonica* developed in Maryland and released in 1985. It is noted for its excellent cold tolerance and medium green color. Compared to Meyer, Belaire has a more open growth habit, coarser leaf texture and faster establishment rate. Brown patch disease may be a problem.

El Toro

El Toro is another improved *Zoysia japonica* released in 1986 from California. It resembles Meyer but has a quicker establishment rate, improved cool-season color and less thatch buildup. El Toro is also reported to have early spring green-up and improved resistance to the rust disease.

Cashmere

Cashmere is a 1988 release from Pursley Turf Farms located in Palmetto, Florida. It resembles Emerald zoysiagrass in color, fine leaf texture and density but does not exhibit the stiff, bristle-like feel as does Emerald. Its shade tolerance is not fully known but lacks cold hardiness, thus is best adapted to the lower southern region. Pursley recommends Cashmere be grown in soil containing clay, shell, rock, marl, or sand.

CHAPTER TWO

Establishment

Preparing to Plant a Florida Lawn

L. B. McCarty and R. A. Dunn

Proper preparation of a lawn prior to planting is critical to ensure the establishment of a quality turf. Preparation will determine how quickly the lawn becomes established and its long-term maintenance requirements. Soil should be prepared whether you are planting a new lawn or replanting an old one, and whether you are seeding or propagating vegetatively. The following steps provide a general guideline for preparing an area for planting a lawn.

CLEAN AND ROUGH GRADE

Remove all construction debris, brush, large roots, rocks, weeds, and old tree stumps. If extensive grading is needed, remove the topsoil and stockpile it for replacement after the rough grade is established. The site should be gently sloped 1 to 2% (e.g., $1/2$- to 1-foot fall per 50 feet) away from the house. The rough grade should conform to the final grade after the topsoil is replaced. Swales or mounds with steep slopes more than 10% should be sodded and not seeded due to erosion problems.

Poorly-drained soil may require the installation of drainage lines. Tile drains are typically placed in rows 2 to 3 feet deep and 15 to 20 feet apart. These should be installed so at least a 1% fall for drainage is available. Seek professional advice if uncertain about the type and installation procedure. Steep slopes and most of the mounds currently used as catch basins around many condominium and commercial buildings should be avoided because grass is difficult to establish, proper moisture levels are difficult to maintain, and such conditions are dangerous to mow. If an area cannot be leveled, use ground cover plants other than turfgrass.

Control of perennial weeds, such as bermudagrass and torpedograss should be performed during site preparation. Several applications of a nonselective herbicide such as glyphosate (Roundup) or commercial fumigation may be necessary for complete weed control.

SOIL ANALYSIS

It is imperative to have a soil analysis made before planting. A representative soil sample can be obtained by collecting small plugs or garden trowels of soil at 15 to 20 locations around the yard from the top 6 inches of soil. Samples should be combined in a pan or bucket and thoroughly mixed. A portion of this can then be submitted to the Florida Extension Soil Testing Laboratory.

County Cooperative Extension Service offices can supply additional information on soil testing.

A soil test will determine the pH value and the report will indicate whether pH adjustment is necessary. If the soil is too acidic (pH too low), dolomitic limestone (dolomite) is recommended for increasing soil pH. Application should be based on a lime requirement which considers both soil buffering capacity and soil pH value. If the soil is analyzed by the Florida Extension Soil Testing Laboratory, a lime requirement determination will be provided. If the analysis is made at the local county Cooperative Extension Service office or by a commercial laboratory, this may not be included unless requested. In lieu of a lime requirement analysis, the application of 1 ton of dolomite per acre or 50 pounds per 100 square feet is sufficient to increase the pH of most Florida soils one pH unit, for example, from pH 5.0 to 6.0. A desirable pH range for most turfgrasses is 6.0 to 7.0.

Certain soils in Florida are basic, meaning that their pH levels are greater than 7.0. Turf grown on soils with pH levels greater than 7.0 often display deficiencies in minor nutrients such as iron and manganese. Further details on soil pH adjustment can be obtained from the Florida Cooperative Extension Service in your particular county.

Based on soil test analysis, fertilizer should be applied to correct nutrient level deficiencies in the soil. If phosphorus is deficient, a fertilizer high in phosphorus (for example 0-20-0) should be added and incorporated deeply by tilling into the soil prior to planting. Potassium also should be added, if needed, prior to planting. A starter fertilizer should be used at the time of establishment with vegetative plantings, but delayed until after germination if the area is seeded. Fertilization ratios and analysis used will depend primarily on soil test results and local product availability. A general recommendation is to use a turf-type fertilizer in 4-1-2 or 3-1-2 ratios with micronutrients. Apply at a rate of 1 pound soluble nitrogen per 1000 square feet. (See the section "Understanding Soil Analysis and Fertilization" in this publication for further information).

INSTALLATION OF IRRIGATION EQUIPMENT

If an irrigation system is desired, it should be designed by an irrigation specialist and installed according to design specifications. An irrigation system's capacity to perform properly is limited by its design, construction, and operation. A poorly designed or improperly installed system will never operate satisfactorily. Operation must be in a manner consistent with sound principles of turfgrass culture.

SOIL AMENDMENTS

Florida's sandy soils contain little organic matter and have very low water and fertilizer holding capacities. Addition of proper amendments to these soils can improve their physical and chemical properties. Amendments may be organic or inorganic; however, organic amendments like peat and compost are rapidly decomposed by soil microorganisms. Inert amendments such as colloidal phosphate are permanent. All organic materials should be sterilized to prevent incorporation of weed seed. A general guideline is to add 1 to 2 cubic yards of colloidal phosphate or organic material (5% by volume), such as peat moss, shredded pine bark, or rotted sawdust, per 1000 square feet of area. Two pounds of actual nitrogen for each cubic yard of sawdust should be added to the soil to aid decomposition and to ensure an adequate supply of nitrogen for the grass. Table 1 lists selective soil amendments and Table 2 lists commonly used peats for improving soils.

DEEP TILLAGE

Rototilling loosens compacted soil and improves the speed and depth of rooting. If soil amendments, lime, or a basic fertilizer have been added in the preceding steps, it is necessary to till the soil as deeply as possible, preferably 6 to 8 inches. A tractor-mounted or self-propelled rotary tiller will do an adequate job of tilling the soil.

FINAL GRADING

Final grading completed just prior to planting provides a smooth planting bed. The site can be hand-raked (Plate 13) and dragged with a hand-pulled drag like a metal door mat. Large areas can be smoothed by tractor-drawn equipment with a tiller rake or grading box, and

Table 1. Comparison of selective soils amendments.

Soil Amendment	pH	Water Holding Capacity	Cation Exchange Capacity	Resists Compaction	Durability
Peat Humus	acid	good	good	fair	5 yr.
Reed-Sedge Peat	acid	good	good	fair	4 - 5 yr.
Sphagnum Peat Moss	acid	excellent	good	fair	1 - 3 yr.
Sawdust	acid	fair	fair	fair	1 yr.
Sludge	acid	fair	good	fair	1 - 2 yr.
Calcined Clay	neutral	good	poor	good	>10 yr.
Colloidal Phosphate	neutral	good	good	good	>10 yr.
Perlite	neutral	fair	poor	good	>10 yr.
Sand	neutral	poor	none	good	infinite
Manure	neutral	good	fair	fair	$1/2$ - 1 yr.

Table 2. Characteristics of commonly used peats.

Type	Composition	Color	Level of Decomposition	Water Holding Capacity	Durability
Sphagnum Moss (top moss)	fluffy, fibrous residue of moss	yellow to tan	fresh	high	decomposes faster than peats
Remarks: Used more as a surface mulch and for packing boxes.					
Moss Peat (peat moss, Sphagnum peat, Highmoor peat)	fibrous	tan to brown	partially	high	intermediate
Remarks: Difficult to mix into soil.					
Reed-Sedge Peat (lowmoor peat)	semi-fibrous	reddish brown to dark brown	partially to substantially advanced	intermediate	high
Peat Humus (cultivated peat, black peat)	non-fibrous	dark brown to black		low to intermediate	extended (approx. 5 yr.)
Remarks: Longest durability of peats.					
Sedimentary Peat	non-fibrous	brown to black	—	low	—
Remarks: Contains silt and ash; least desirable; use with caution.					

then hand-finished. Soil particles should be no larger than golf ball size, and smaller is even better. To achieve a uniformly firm planting bed and to reduce erosion, loose soil can be compressed with a water ballast roller (Plate 14). Care should be taken not to add too much weight and cause soil compaction. Driveways and walks should be level with, or slightly above, the final grade. A good job of grading will result in a more level site and more attractive lawn which is easier to mow. Irrigation can be used to settle the soil before planting. Hand raking to break up a crusty surface is necessary prior to seeding.

SOIL FUMIGATION

Following raking, fertilizing, and incorporation of soil amendments, the planting area can be sterilized by soil fumigation, if desired. Fumigation is use of a chemical that generates toxic gases that spread through soil pores in the upper layers of soil to kill weed seeds, insects, disease organisms, and nematodes, and result in a nearly perfect planting bed for the turfgrass.

The soil fumigation product most widely available for preparing home lawns is dazomet (Basamid® Granular Soil Fumigant), which is a granular product that must be mixed uniformly into well-prepared soil several weeks before turf is to be planted. Further discussion of its use may be found in the section entitled *Nematode Management*.

Two other materials that are used in many commercial turf planting situations are methyl bromide (many brands) and metham sodium (Vapam® and other brands). Because of their toxicity and environmental risks connected with their use, these products are Restricted Use pesticides which must be applied by appropriately Certified Pesticide Applicators and can not be used in most residential lawn planting sites.

Methyl bromide usually provides the best control, but due to the need for a gas-tight polyethylene cover following application, costs are generally higher (Plate 15). Metham sodium does not require a cover, but a water source is necessary and control usually is not as good as with methyl bromide. As does dazomet, metham sodium requires a 2 - 3 week waiting period after application.

Establishing Your Florida Lawn

L. B. McCarty

Turfgrasses can be established by two methods, seeding and vegetative propagation. Vegetative propagation includes sodding, sprigging and plugging. Seeding is usually the easiest and most economical method of planting grasses, but requires a longer period of time to achieve a mature turf.

Not all turfgrasses are established from seed, and while planting sprigs or plugs is more laborious than seeding, rapid ground cover can be expected since most of our Florida turfgrasses grow quickly.

Tables 1 and 2 show the recommended planting rate for each turfgrass species.

Regardless of the method of planting, it is essential that a proper seedbed be prepared before planting. A healthy, attractive, long-lived lawn can be established only if you select high quality seed or planting material and select turfgrasses that are well adapted to the soil and climate.

Refer to the section "Preparing to Plant a Florida Lawn" for instructions on site preparation and planting lawns.

SEEDING

Seeding is the easiest and most economical way of establishing a lawn. Success depends on seed quality, proper seeding time, rate, and method of seeding.

Seed Quality

Successful establishment from seed depends on purchasing top quality seed. Law requires that each container of seed have a tag listing the turfgrass species and cultivar, purity, percent germination and weed content. Purity tells the amount (as a percentage) of the desired seed as well as other seed and inert matter. Germination percentage tells the amount of seed expected to germinate under optimum conditions. The quantity of weed seeds is also listed.

Read the tag thoroughly to be sure you are purchasing good quality seed. Try to purchase seed that has a purity of 90% or higher and a germination of 85% or higher. Always select the best quality seed of the cultivar you wish to plant. Many times contractors buy seed with poor (<50%) germination and poor purity (<80%) in order to save money. Usually this results in weed invasion and/or poor stand establishment. Text Box 1 is an example of a seed label.

Text Box 1. Example of a seed label.

Brand name: Centipedegrass Seed

98.75% Pure Seed

Other Ingreadients

0.00% Other Crop Seed
1.00% Inert Matter
0.25% Weed Seeds
85.00% Germination

Tested 12/94
LOT 0001-A

Seeding Time and Rate

The best time to seed is during the spring and summer months from April through July, since this permits a full growing season before cold weather. Seed may be planted as late as September or early October, but establishment is much slower because of cooler weather. In most instances a mature sod will not be formed when planted this late until the following summer. In north Florida, young seedling grasses may be winter-killed if they are planted too late in the fall. Spring and summer seeding also takes advantage of Florida's rainy season and may greatly reduce irrigation requirements.

Seeding rates are shown in Table 1. Rates vary with species and cultivar of grass. Economics must be considered since certain turfgrass seeds are quite expensive, and therefore optimum seeding rates are not always practical. The seeding rates suggested will give adequate coverage and produce a mature turf area with good postplanting care. Rates vary from 4 ounces per 1000 square feet for centipedegrass, which has a very small seed, to 10 pounds per 1000 square feet for bahiagrass, which has a large seed. Seeding rates can be reduced, but the trade-off is a more open turf area subject to weed invasion and erosion.

A hard, impermeable seed coat that restricts the entrance of water or gases into the seed can prevent or seriously delay germination even under favorable

Table 1. Seeding rates for Florida turfgrasses.

Turfgrass	Quantity (lb/1000 ft²)
Bahiagrasses	7 - 10 (scarified)
Bermudagrass (common)	2 (hulled) 4 (unhulled)
Carpetgrass	4 - 5
Centipedegrass	0.25

conditions. Seed germination is enhanced by scarification processes that disrupt the impermeable coat and permit the entrance of moisture and gases. Bahiagrass seed is often scarified either by soaking in a mild acid solution for a period of time or else physically abraded to help remove its impermeable seed coat. Bahiagrass seed which has been scarified increases the percent of germination and germination rate. It is recommended when available.

Many seeding methods are used, ranging from planting by hand to the use of mechanical equipment for large turf areas. Evenness of seed distribution is important from the standpoint of overall uniformity. The seedbed should be moist, well prepared, and leveled. Rake the entire area with a heavy garden rake to produce furrows into which the seeds are planted. Seed should be applied mechanically either with a drop-type or rotary spreader. Mechanical seeders provide a more uniform distribution of seed than hand seeding (Plate 16). For best distribution of seed, apply one-half the required amount in one direction and apply the remainder at right angles to the first seeding (Figure 1). For very small seed like centipedegrass and bermudagrass, applying the seed is difficult unless it is mixed with sand, topsoil, or another convenient carrier that adds bulk to the spreader. It is a good idea to buy some additional seed in case erratic establishment results. Refrigerate unused seed for longer storage life.

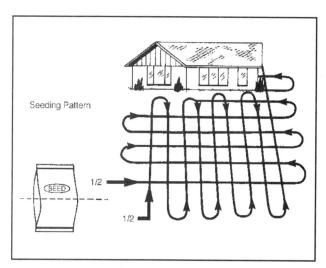

Figure 1. Seeding pattern.

After application, the seed should be lightly covered by working it into the soil with a rake. Ideally, topdressing the seed with $1/4$ to $1/2$ inch of soil would be the best method, but this is impractical for most home lawns. The seed can be covered reasonably well by raking. If the seedbed was furrowed before seeding, then raking or dragging with a board will work the seed into the furrows and adequately cover it. Roll the seeded area with a lightweight roller to firm up the soil and to ensure good contact between seed and soil. The area should then be mulched with weed-free grass hay or straw, so that 50 to

75% of the bare ground is protected (Plate 17). Mulching helps conserve moisture and prevents erosion of topsoil and washing of seed. As a general rule, one bale of hay will cover approximately 1000 square feet.

Proper watering is the most critical step in establishing turfgrasses from seed. The soil must be kept continuously moist but not excessively wet until the seeds have germinated. Supplying water two or three times a day in small quantities for approximately 2 weeks will ensure adequate moisture for germination. If the surface of the soil is allowed to dry out at any time after the seeds have begun to swell and before roots have developed, many of the seedlings will die. *Improper watering is the most common cause of seeding failure.* Initial watering should be from a fine spray if possible, or from sprinklers with a low precipitation rate. Coarse spray and high water pressure or high precipitation rates will wash the soil and uncover buried seeds. Avoid overwatering and saturating the soil. This can cause the seeds to float, and increases the incidence of disease which can kill the seedling plants. As the seedlings mature and the root system develops, the number of waterings can decrease, but the volume should increase so that the entire root zone is wetted, not just the soil surface. If water is not available, avoid planting in April, May and October since these are traditionally Florida's driest months.

VEGETATIVE PLANTING

Vegetative planting is simply the transplanting of large or small pieces of grass. Solid sodding covers the entire seedbed with vegetation. Plugging or sprigging refers to the planting of pieces of sod or individual stems or runners called stolons or rhizomes.

Sod

Sodding is more expensive than sprigging or plugging but it produces a so-called "instant lawn" (Plate 18). Without proper site preparation and post-installation care, however, the sod can die almost as easily as any other newly planted area.

Before buying the sod, inspect it carefully to guarantee the absence of noxious weeds and other pests such as insects and nematodes. Store the sod in a cool, shady place until used. Sod life on pallets during summer is less than 48 hours.

The area to be planted should be properly prepared (e.g., tilled and raked smooth) and moistened at the time of laying sod. Sod pieces should be fitted together as tightly as possible, but the sod should not be stretched to fit an area (Figure 2). If cracks are evident between pieces, they should be filled with topsoil. Tamp or roll the sod to remove air pockets and ensure good soil contact. If the roots are not in contact with the underlying soil, they

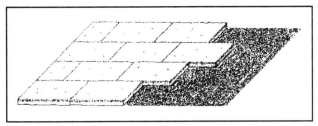

Figure 2. Start sodding from a straight edge and butt strips together in a brick-like pattern.

will dry and die. If the sod is wet but the soil below is allowed to dry out, the roots will not penetrate below the original layer of sod.

Do not let the soil dry out until a good union between the sod and soil surface has been achieved. Light, frequent applications of soil topdressing will help to smooth out the lawn surface.

Sodding is expensive, but is recommended where immediate cover is desired for an aesthetic reason or to prevent soil erosion.

Sprigs

Sprigging is the cheapest vegetative planting method. A sprig is an individual stem or piece of stem of grass without any adhering soil (Plate 19). Sprigs are also called runners, rhizomes, or stolons. Regardless of what a sprig is called, if it has at least one node or joint, it has the potential of developing into a grass plant.

Sprigging is simply the planting of individual grass stems at spaced intervals (Fig. 3). A suitable sprig should have two to four nodes from which roots can develop. Sprigs can be bought by the bushel, but more commonly sod is used and cut or pulled apart into sprigs.

There are several methods of planting sprigs. One method is to cut shallow furrows in the prepared planting area by using a push-plow or the edge of a hoe. Place the sprigs end-to-end or every 6 to 12 inches along the row and cover a part of each sprig with soil and firm by rolling

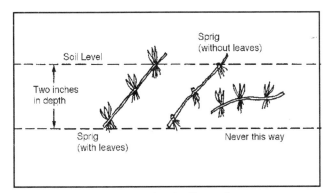

Figure 3. Suggested layout for planting springs.

or stepping on the furrow. The closer together the sprigs are planted, the faster the grass will cover the soil. Rows should be placed no more than 6 to 8 inches apart.

A second method is to place the sprigs on the soil surface at the desired interval end-to-end, about six inches apart, and then press one end of the sprig into the soil with a notched stick or blunt piece of metal like a dull shovel. A portion of the sprig should be left above ground exposed to light. Each sprig should have some leaves, but a joint (node) will do if the stolon has no leaves.

Regardless of the planting method, each sprig should be tamped or rolled firmly into the soil. This will help keep the sprigs from drying out and dying. As with seeding, the soil must be kept continually moist—not wet—until adequate rooting has occurred. Watering lightly once or twice daily will be required for several weeks after planting. Mulching can also be used in vegetative planting for moisture conservation and erosion control.

Another method of sprigging, which is used where rapid cover is needed, is *stolonizing, broadcast sprigging* or *shredding*. The sprigs are prepared by mechanical shredding or hand tearing of sod into individual sprigs, or purchased by the bushel (most commonly the bermudagrasses). The material is broadcast over the area by hand (like mulch). Sprigs are then cut into the soil with a light disc or covered with $1/2$ inch of soil topdressing. The area is then rolled and watered. This method will provide very fast coverage. Since the sprigs are planted at a shallow depth, they are very prone to drying out. Light, frequent waterings are necessary until roots become well established. This is the method often used to plant bermudagrass golf greens and fairways.

Plugs

Plugging is the planting of 2- to 4-inch circular or block-shaped pieces of sod at regular intervals (Plate 20). Three to ten times as much planting material is necessary for plugging as sprigging (Table 2). Several turfgrasses are currently available commercially as plugs in trays. These commercial plugs usually have well developed root systems and are treated as other plugs described in Table 2.

Square plugs can be cut from sod with a shovel, axe, or machete, while round plugs are cut with special steel pluggers similar to a bulb planter. The plugs are then placed in corresponding-sized holes made in the soil. These should be planted on 6- to 12-inch centers (Figure 4). Wider spacing prolongs the establishment phase. They must be tamped or rolled to minimize ending up with a tufted appearance. Plugs do not dry out as rapidly as sprigs, and therefore water is not as critical. However, rate of coverage is slower than if the grass was sprigged or stolonized. Mulching will help improve moisture retention and prevent erosion of the soil between the plugs.

Turfgrass	Spacing (inches)	Amount of sod (sq. ft.) per 1000 sq. ft.[1]
St. Augustinegrass		
2-in plugs	6 - 12	30 - 50
sprigs	6 - 12	10 - 15
Centipedegrass		
2-in plugs	6	100 - 150
sprigs	6	30 - 50
Zoysiagrass		
2-in plugs	6	100 - 150
sprigs	6	8 - 15
Bermudagrass[2]		
2-in plugs	12	30 - 50
sprigs	12	2 - 5

[1] Based on estimates of 1 sq ft of sod = linear ft of sprigs; 1 sq yd of sod = 1 bushel of sprigs; and 1 sq yd of sod yields 324 two-inch plugs. The numbers in the column refer to the square feet of solid sod from which either 2-inch plugs or sprigs can be obtained.

[2] Broadcast sprigging or stolonizing is used for planting large areas such as golf courses, football fields, etc. Usually 5 to 10 bushels of sprigs are required per 1000 ft² (approximately 200 to 400 bushels/acre) for best results.

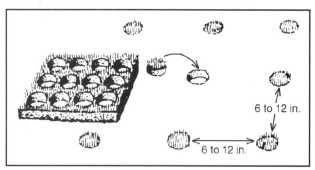

6 to 12 in.

6 to 12 in.

Figure 4. Plugs are normally spaced on 6- to 12-inch centers.

POST PLANTING CARE

As previously mentioned, proper water management the first several weeks after planting is crucial. For seeded areas, keep the seedbed continuously moist with light frequent sprinklings several times daily. Avoid too much water, as this can cause seed movement and soil erosion. As the seedlings or planting material take root and grow, decrease watering frequency and increase the amount applied each time.

Fertilize the new seedlings approximately 4 to 5 weeks after seeding or after the second mowing. Apply a complete (N-P-K) turf-type, slow-release nitrogen fertilizer (e.g., 16-4-8) so as to provide 1 pound of actual nitrogen per 1000 square feet.

Fertilize vegetatively established grasses with $^1/_2$ to 1 pound of nitrogen per 1000 square feet every 2 to 3 weeks

once the runners begin to spread. Continue this until a solid stand of grass is achieved. Once a solid stand results, follow the fertilizer programs listed in other sections for established turf.

Begin mowing as soon as the grass reaches 30% over the desired height. For example, mow bahiagrass back to 3 inches when it reaches 4 to $4^1/_2$ inches. Use a mower with a sharp blade. If a sharp blade is not used, seedlings may be torn from the ground or the grass will have a ragged appearance.

Do not mow when the grass is wet. If clippings are heavy enough to shade the grass, catch them or rake and remove them. Otherwise, leave the clippings as they may result in a reduction of fertilizer usage by 20 to 30%.

Newly planted areas often become infested with weeds. Proper mowing height and frequency are the best methods of controlling many weeds in newly established lawns. Remaining weeds may be controlled with herbicides or by hand removal. *Do not apply herbicides until the lawn has been mowed at least three times.*

TIPS FOR TURFGRASS

Follow these tips to reduce runoff and thus save fertilizer. Remember, your objective is to keep water and fertilizer in the root zone of the grass for as long as possible.

❑ Apply no more than $^3/_4$ inch of water per irrigation.

❑ Make sure your sprinkling system applies water uniformly. Do not mix sprinkler head types or let the reach of two sprinklers overlap excessively.

❑ Know how much water your system applies over a time period. Simply place coffee cans in a straight line from your sprinkler to the edge of the watering pattern. Turn the water on for 15 minutes and measure the average depth of water in each can with a ruler. Then multiply this number by four to determine the irrigation rate in inches per hour. Remember, no more than $^3/_4$ inch of water is needed per irrigation.

❑ Adjust irrigation to the season; in summer, watering several times a week may be required. In winter, you will normally be able to reduce irrigation substantially. Watch the grass for a bluish-gray color, slow recovery from foot or tire traffic, or the folding of grass blades. These symptoms indicate the grass is wilting and needs to be watered.

❑ Do not water when rain is forecasted for your particular area.

- Look for the words *slow-release* or *insoluble* on the fertilizer labels. Nitrogen in this type of fertilizer will not burn or wash away as readily as quick-release nitrogen sources.

- Don't be fooled by the word *organic*. Some organic fertilizers are soluble and can leach as quickly as inorganic.

- Lime your lawn only if your soil is highly acidic (has a low pH).

- Increase mowing height of lawns; this increased height allows the plant to develop a more extensive root system.

RENOVATION

To renovate an established turf several questions need to be asked. Included are:

- whether or not another turf species is to be planted;

- if over 50% of the present lawn is desirable turf or noxious weeds; and

- the available time and resources must also be considered.

If an area is to be completely reseeded, and if over 50% of plants currently present are weeds, or if the turf species is changed, the areas should be treated with a nonselective herbicide, such as glyphosate (Roundup). This area is then dethatched using a verticutter, power rake, or slicer/groover. Starter fertilizer is added, seeds sown and the area lightly raked to encourage the seed to come into contact with soil.

If the area is renovated by vegetative establishment such as sprigs or sod, the glyphosate-treated turf is removed with a sod cutter, surface regraded, soil amendments and starter fertilizer added and then grass planted. If the existing area does not need treatment with a nonselective herbicide, then the sprigs may be planted directly into the current turf.

Understanding Soil Analysis and Fertilization

J. B. Sartain and L. B. McCarty

SOIL ANALYSIS AND INFORMATION

One of the first steps in producing and maintaining beautiful turf is to obtain an analysis of a representative soil sample from the lawn area. The sample can be obtained by taking 15 to 20 small plugs at random over the entire lawn. Most plant roots are located in the top 6 inches of soil; therefore, limit sampling depth to 6 inches. Thoroughly mix the 15 to 20 soil plugs and send approximately 1 pint of the mixed sample to the University of Florida Extension Soil Testing Laboratory for chemical analysis (Figure 1). The county Cooperative Extension Service can also supply additional information on the proper technique of sampling and submitting a soil sample. Refer to the back of this book for these.

Figure 1. Soil sample bag.

A soil analysis supplies a wealth of information concerning the nutritional status of a soil and may aid in the detection of potential problems which could limit turfgrass growth. A typical soil analysis supplies information relative to soil acidity and the phosphorus, potassium, calcium, and magnesium status of the soil. Nitrogen is not determined because of its leaching nature.

SOIL ACIDITY

Turfgrasses differ in their adaptability to soil acidity. For example, centipede and bahia will grow in a more acid environment (pH 5.0 to 6.0) than St. Augustinegrass or zoysia, which grow best at near neutral (pH 6.0 to 7.0) soil reaction (Table 1).

Soil reaction or pH is important because it influences several soil factors that affect plant growth. Soil bacteria that transform and release nitrogen from organic matter function best in the pH range of 5.5 to 7.0; certain fertilizer materials also supply nutrients more efficiently in this range. Plant nutrients are generally more available to plants in the pH range 5.5 to 7.0.

Normally, liming materials are used to increase soil pH and supply the essential nutrients of calcium and magnesium. The two most commonly available liming materials are calcitic and dolomitic limes. In instances

Table 1. Desirable pH ranges for lawn grasses.

pH			
5.0 - 5.4	5.5 - 5.9	6.0 - 6.4	6.5 - 6.9
Bermuda Carpet Centipede Bahia	Bermuda Carpet Centipede Bahia Italian Rye	Bermuda Fescue Italian Rye St. Augustine Zoysia	Bermuda Fescue St. Augustine Zoysia

where the soil tests low in magnesium, dolomitic lime should be used. Generally, about 6 months' reaction time is required for calcitic and dolomitic lime to have their maximum effect on soil acidity. If more immediate results are desired, burned or hydrated lime can be used. In most cases, these materials are not recommended for home use because they can easily and severely damage the grass if improperly used. Basic slag is a slow-reacting product which also contains large amounts of phosphorus, but cost and availability limit its use.

The amount of lime necessary to properly adjust the soil pH depends on the soil type. The greater the amount of organic matter or clay in the soil, the more lime is required to change the pH.

SOIL BASICITY

If a soil is too alkaline, determine whether it is due to an inherent soil characteristic or previous excessive application of liming materials. It is quite difficult, if not impossible, to appreciably change the pH of naturally occurring alkaline soils such as those found in coastal areas or fill soil containing marl, shell, or limestone by use of sulfur, ammonium sulfate, or similar acid-forming materials. If a high pH is due to applied lime or other alkaline additive, then these acid-forming materials may be effective in reducing soil pH if applied at the proper rate and frequency.

Elemental sulfur may be used to decrease soil pH. Thoroughly water in sulfur after application, taking care to wash off all above ground plant parts. It takes approximately $1/3$ the amount of *sulfur* to *decrease* the soil pH 1 unit as it does *calcitic lime* to *increase* the soil pH 1 unit. Do not apply more than 5 to 10 pounds of sulfur per 1000 square feet per application. Repeat applications of sulfur should not be made more often than once every 2 to 3 months. Remember that sulfur oxidizes in the soil and mixes with water to form a strong acid (sulfuric acid) that can severely damage plant roots—use with caution.

SOIL FERTILIZATION

Essential Elements

All plants require certain chemical elements for proper growth and appearance. Of these nutrients at least 16 are known to be *essential elements*. Table 2 lists the 16 known elements and the sources from which plants obtain them. All essential elements except carbon, hydrogen, and oxygen are obtained from the soil and absorbed by plant roots. If limited nutrients are available in the soil, lawn growth and quality may be limited. However, essential elements can be added to the soil through fertilizer applications.

Lawns require the macronutrients nitrogen (N), phosphorus (P), and potassium (K) in greatest quantities. Calcium, magnesium, and sulfur are required less frequently and in smaller quantities. The micronutrients iron, manganese, zinc, copper, chlorine, molybdenum, and boron are required in very minute quantities and less often than the macronutrients. Micronutrients are as essential as the macronutrients but are required in micro amounts.

Table 2. Essential elements required by lawngrasses.

Macronutrients		Micronutrients
From Air/Water	From Soil	From Soil
Carbon Hydrogen Oxygen	Nitrogen Calcium Phosphorus Magnesium Potassium Sulfur	Iron Copper Manganese Molybdenum Zinc Boron Chlorine

Types of Fertilizers

Fertilizers are identified by analysis and/or brand name. Many common commercial fertilizers are known by their grade such as 16-4-8, 10-10-10 or 6-6-6. A complete fertilizer contains nitrogen, phosphorus and potassium. The numbers indicate the percentage of each of these nutrients. A 16-4-8 grade, for example, contains 16% nitrogen, 4% available phosphate, and 8% soluble potash. Thus, a 100-pound bag of 16-4-8 would contain 16 pounds of nitrogen, 4 pounds of phosphate, and 8 pounds of potash. These three constituents, nitrogen, phosphorus, and potassium, are called the primary plant nutrients; if all three are present, the fertilizer is a *complete fertilizer*. Complete fertilizers like 16-4-8, 12-4-8, 10-10-10, and 6-6-6 are commonly recommended for lawn fertilization.

Besides the primary elements (N, P, and K) the fertilizer may contain secondary plant nutrients. The secondaries may include calcium, magnesium, sulfur, manganese, zinc, copper, iron, and molybdenum.

Both primary and secondary elements, if present, are listed on the fertilizer label. The label also tells the materials from which the fertilizer has been made. This information appears beside the "derived from" statement. An example of a mixed fertilizer containing several different sources of nitrogen is shown in Text Box 1.

Text Box 1. Example of a fertilizer label.

Lawn (Turf-Type) Fertilizer 16-4-8 Guaranteed Analysis	

Total Nitrogen
   8.50% Ammoniacal Nitrogen
   2.00% Nitrate Nitrogen
   0.90% Water Soluble Organic Nitrogen
   4.60% Water Insoluble Nitrogen
	16%

Available Phosphoric Acid (P_2O_5)	4%
Soluble Potash (K_2O)	8%

In addition to complete fertilizers, some materials are used almost exclusively to supply nitrogen to the lawn for rapid growth and dark green color. These materials include ammonium nitrate (33% N), ammonium sulfate (20% N), IBDU (31% N), urea (45% N), calcium nitrate (15.5% N), and ureaforms (38% N). Nitrogen fertilizers are used as frequently or more frequently than complete fertilizers.

For Florida lawns, the best yearly fertilization program usually includes a combination of one or two applications of a complete fertilizer and several supplemental applications of a nitrogen fertilizer. The complete fertilizer supplies nitrogen, phosphorus, and potassium, while the nitrogen material supplies mainly nitrogen. While nitrogen fertilization is based on the desired growth rate and type of turfgrass being grown, the phosphorus and potassium fertilization rate should be based on the analysis of a lawn soil sample and the recommendations obtained from it.

FERTILIZER APPLICATION

Most fertilizers are applied at a rate determined by the type and amount of nitrogen present in the material. Nitrogen is the nutrient most used by the grass and often is the material that burns the lawn if applied at excessive rates. Injury from dog urine may also be mistaken for fertilizer burn (Plate 112).

An almost universal recommendation for turfgrasses is to apply *1 pound of actual nitrogen per 1000 square feet of lawn* if the nitrogen is from a water-soluble source. If most (greater than 50%) of the nitrogen in the fertilizer is water insoluble (organic nitrogen), then the rate may be 2 pounds of actual N per 1000 square feet. The pounds of actual N in every fertilizer can be determined by dividing the percent N listed on the label into 100. For example, in applying soluble nitrogen from ammonium sulfate, divide 20% (the N content of ammonium sulfate) into 100 to find out the number of pounds of fertilizer that will supply 1 pound of N. Since 100 divided by 20 equals five, apply 5 pounds of ammonium sulfate per 1000 square feet of lawn. If applying N in a 16-4-8 fertilizer and the nitrogen in the product is all slow-release organic nitrogen, one could apply 2 pounds of actual nitrogen. The calculation is the same as the first example. Divide 100 by 16 (16 is the percent N in the fertilizer). The answer is about six, so 12 pounds of the 16-4-8 would supply 2 pounds of nitrogen.

Several fertilizer materials are listed in Table 3, and the rate of application for 1 pound of N is already calculated. For example, if using ammonium nitrate on the lawn, note that the table lists the rate of application at 3 pounds of material per 1000 square feet.

When a soil test of the lawn soil is not available, Table 4 can be used a guide for lawn fertilization. Table 4 shows two lawn fertilization programs for each type of lawngrass for two regions of the state. Note that most programs use a combination of complete fertilizers and nitrogen fertilizers, applied during different months of the year.

One program is a minimum- or low-maintenance recommendation that will produce only a moderate quality lawn. The second program is a maximum or high-maintenance program that should produce a high-quality lawn. A program can also be chosen between these two extremes. The correct schedule is the one that produces the quality of lawn the individual desires.

To use Table 4, find the particular lawngrass and part of the state, then apply the fertilizer indicated during the month(s) recommended. For rates of various materials,

Table 3. A guide to rate of fertilizer material to use on Florida lawns.

Nitrogen Fertilizers	%N	Pounds needed to supply 1 pound actual nitrogen per 1000 sq ft
Rapid N Release (Inorganics)		
Nitrate of Soda	16.0	6
Nitrate of Soda-Potash	15.0	7
Nitrate of Potash	13.0	8
Calcium Nitrate	15.5	7
Ammonium Nitrate	33.5	3
Ammonium Nitrate + Lime	18.0	5
Ammonium Sulfate	20.5	5
Mono-ammonium Phosphate	11-48-0	9
Diammonium Phosphate	18-46-0	5.5
Rapid N Release (Organics)		
Urea	45 - 47	2
Cyanamid	21	5
Slow N Release (Natural Organics)		
Sewage Sludge	6.0	16
Castor Pomace	4 - 6	25 - 16
Cottonseed Meal	7.0	15
Processed Tankages	5 - 10	20 - 10
Garbage Tankage	2 - 3	40 - 30
Slow Release (Synthetics)		
Ureaform	38	2.5
Nitroform	38	2
IBDU	31	3
Sulfur coated urea	36	3
Polymer-/Plastic-/Resin-coasted urea	varies	varies

<u>Some common potassium and phosphorus fertilizers include:</u>

Muriate of Potash (60% K_2O)
Sulfate of Potash (50% K_2O)
Potassium Carbonate (64% K_2O)
Potassium Nitrate (44% K_2O)
Superphosphate (20% P_2O_5)
Conc. Superphosphate (46% P_2O_5)
Sulfate of Potash-Magnesia (22% K_2O)

CAUTION: Practically all inorganic fertilizers can burn grass foliage. These materials should be watered off the turf immediately after application. If using organic N sources (slow release), 2 pounds of N can be applied safely per 1000 square feet per application.

Table 4. Fertilization schedule for Florida lawns.

Lawngrass	Maintenance Level	J	F	M	A	M	J	J	A	S	O	N	D
North Florida[1]													
Bahia	High	–	–	C	Fe	N	–	N	–	C	Fe	–	–
	Low	–	–	C	Fe	–	–	–	–	C	Fe	–	–
Bermuda	High	–	–	C	–	C	–	N	–	C	N	–	N[2]
	Low	–	–	C	–	N	–	N	–	C	–	–	–
Carpet	High	–	–	C	–	–	–	–	C	–	–	–	–
	Low	–	–	C	–	–	–	–	–	–	–	–	–
Centipede	High	–	–	C	Fe	–	N	Fe	C	–	–	–	–
	Low	–	–	C	Fe	–	–	Fe	C	–	–	–	–
St. Augustine	High	–	–	C	–	N[3]	Fe	N[3]	–	C	–	–	–
	Low	–	–	C	–	–	Fe	–	–	C	–	–	–
Zoysia	High	–	–	C	–	N	–	N	–	C	–	N[2]	–
	Low	–	–	C	–	–	N	–	–	C	–	–	–
South Florida													
Bahia	High	–	C	Fe	–	N	–	–	–	C	N	–	N
	Low	–	C	Fe	–	–	–	–	C	–	N	–	–
Bermuda	High	–	C	–	N	N	C	–	C	–	N	–	N[2]
	Low	–	C	–	N	–	N	–	–	C	–	–	N[2]
Carpet	High	–	C	–	–	–	N	–	–	C	–	–	–
	Low	–	C	–	–	–	–	–	–	C	–	–	–
Centipede	High	–	C	Fe	–	N	–	Fe	–	C	–	–	–
	Low	–	C	Fe	–	–	–	Fe	–	C	–	–	–
St. Augustine	High	–	C	–	–	N[3]	Fe	N[3]	–	–	C	–	N
	Low	–	C	–	–	N[3]	Fe	–	–	–	C	–	–
Zoysia	High	–	C	–	N	–	N	–	N	–	C	–	N[2]
	Low	–	C	–	–	N	–	–	N	–	C	–	–

C = Complete fertilizer at 1.0 lb N/1000 sq ft.
N = Water-soluble inorganic nitrogen source applied at 1.0 lb N/1000 sq ft.
Fe = Apply iron to provide dark green color without stimulating excessive grass growth. Ferrous sulfate (2 oz in 3-5 gal water per 1000 sq ft) or a chelated iron source may be used.
[1] The arbitrary dividing line between north and south Florida is a straight east-west line from coast-to-coast through Orlando.
[2] Overseeded with ryegrass for winter color.
[3] To reduce chinch bug problems, use a slow-release N source during the summer.

refer to Table 3. For example, to obtain a desirable centipedegrass lawn in Gainesville (north Florida), apply a complete fertilizer (C) like 16-4-8, 10-10-10, or 6-6-6 in March and August, then apply a soluble nitrogen (N) material like ammonium sulfate in June. Rates for the nitrogen fertilizers are given in Table 3, and the rate for the complete fertilizer is shown at the bottom of the fertilization chart (Table 4).

ORGANIC vs INORGANIC FERTILIZERS

There is much confusion over whether to use organic or inorganic fertilizers on lawns. Both types have advan-

tages and disadvantages; however, the type of fertilizer makes no difference to the grass. Grasses absorb nitrogen as nitrate or ammoniacal-nitrogen. Organic nitrogen is not used directly by the plant but must first be converted to the chemical form by soil microorganisms.

The advantages and disadvantages of organic or chemical fertilizers relate to the consumer, not the lawngrass. Inorganic nitrogen fertilizers have advantages and disadvantages as listed in Text Box 2.

Organic nitrogen fertilizers also have advantages and disadvantages that are listed in Text Box 3.

Select a nitrogen source after considering the pros and cons of the various forms.

Text Box 2.

Inorganic Nitrogen Sources	
Advantages	Disadvantages
Readily available N	Leach readily
Low cost per unit N	Danger of fertilizer burn
Easily controlled N levels	High salinity potential
Little problem of residual N	Must be applied frequently at low rates
May have greater efficiency	Usually acid forming

Text Box 3.

Organic Nitrogen Sources	
Advantages	Disadvantages
Slow release of N	May be very expensive
Less subject to leaching	Not released in cold weather
Small danger of lawn burn	Slow response
Applied infrequently at high rates	May contain weed seeds (especially manure)

SUPPLEMENTAL IRON APPLICATION

Many times turfgrasses, such as centipedegrass, bahiagrass and St. Augustinegrass, turn yellow during the summer due to lack of nitrogen fertilizer. However, fertilization with nitrogen in summer is not always desirable since this often encourages disease and insect problems. Many times the addition of iron (Fe) to these grasses provides the desirable dark green color, but does not stimulate excessive grass growth which follows nitrogen fertilization. Usually iron sulfate (2 ounces per 3 to 5 gallons of water per 1000 square feet) or a chelated iron source are used to provide this greening effect. The effect from supplemental iron application is only temporary (approximately 2 to 4 weeks), therefore, repeat applications are necessary for summer-long color.

PRECAUTIONS

All fertilizers may burn if improperly applied. Never exceed the recommended rate, or the lawn may be damaged. Always apply fertilizers when the grass leaves are *dry* and water thoroughly after application.

CHAPTER THREE

Maintenance

Maintenance of Bahiagrass Lawns

L. B. McCarty and J. L. Cisar

ESTABLISHMENT

Bahiagrass is planted by seed or sod. Success with either is dependent on proper soil preparation.

Sodding

Planting bahiagrass by sod is initially more expensive than seeding but produces an "instant lawn." For best results, good quality, weed-free sod should be used.

Seeding

Establishment from seed is easier and cheaper, but slower than sod. The best time to seed is from April through June, since this permits a full growing season before cold weather and takes advantage of the rainy season. Seed may be planted as late as September or early October. However, establishment is much slower in later plantings because of cooler weather, and in most instances a good sod will not be formed until the following summer. Using scarified seed will hasten germination.

FERTILIZING

Proper fertilization of bahia is a very important part of a sound maintenance program. Improper fertilization practices may contribute to maintenance difficulties and increase insect, disease, and weed problems. An optimum fertilization program for bahiagrass is shown in Table 1. A minimum-maintenance program would be two applications per year (spring and late summer) of a complete fertilizer such as 10-10-10 or 16-4-8.

One of the disadvantages of bahiagrass is its susceptibility to yellowing due to iron deficiency. This problem can be overcome by using a complete fertilizer which contains iron or by addition of an iron material in the fertilization program whenever the yellowing occurs. Materials which can be used include ferrous ammonium sulfate, ferrous sulfate, and various iron chelates. Apply the ferrous sulfate at the rate of 2 ounces in 3 to 5 gallons of water per 1000 square feet. This can be applied evenly and easily with a hose-end applicator. Follow chelated iron label directions if using one of these materials.

MOWING

Proper mowing height and frequency are necessary to keep the lawn attractive. Bahiagrass fertilized once or twice per year should be mowed every 7 to 14 days depending upon seedhead production. Height of cut should be 3 to 4 inches. If the optimum fertilization program is followed, it may be necessary to mow bahia every week. A sharp, heavy duty rotary mower blade is necessary to cut bahiagrass. Bahia leaves are so tough that the mower blade will have to be sharpened frequently. Otherwise, the cut will be ragged and the lawn will take on a dull, gray color and have a very poor appearance.

WATERING

Irrigation on an as-needed basis is an efficient way to water any grass, providing the proper amount of water is applied when needed and not at a later or more conve-

Table 1. Suggested fertilization schedule for bahiagrass lawns.

Fertility level	Jan	Feb	Mar	Apr	May	June	July	Aug	Sept	Oct	Nov	Dec
North Florida[1]												
High	–	–	C[2]	Fe[3]	N[4]	–	N	–	C	Fe	–	–
Low	–	–	C	Fe	–	–	–	–	C	Fe	–	–
South Florida[1]												
High	–	C	Fe	–	N	–	–	–	C	N	–	N
Low	–	C	Fe	–	–	–	–	C	–	N	–	–

[1] The arbitrary dividing line between north and south Florida is a straight east-west line from coast to coast through Orlando.

[2] Complete fertilizer at 1.0 lb of nitrogen/1000 sq ft.

[3] Apply iron to provide dark green color without stimulating excessive grass growth. Ferrous sulfate (2 oz in 3 to 5 gal water per 1000 sq ft) or a chelated iron source may be used.

[4] Water soluble inorganic nitrogen sources such as ammonium nitrate or ammonium sulfate applied at 1.0 lb of nitrogen/1000 sq ft.

nient time. When using this approach, apply $3/4$ inch of water per application, which is equivalent to 465 gallons per 1000 square feet. During prolonged droughts, irrigation may be needed more often. Bahiagrass has the best drought tolerance of all lawngrasses grown in Florida and will usually recover from severe drought injury soon after rain or irrigation. Do not over-water bahiagrass lawns as this weakens the turf and encourages weeds. Refer to the section "Watering Your Florida Lawn" for additional information.

PEST PROBLEMS

Bahiagrass is troubled by fewer insects, diseases and nematodes than the other Florida lawngrasses, but it is not pest-free.

Insects

The most serious insect is the mole cricket. It burrows though the soil and damages the roots, causing rapid wilting of the grass. Several lawn caterpillars can also cause damage.

Diseases

The only serious disease of bahiagrass is dollar spot which is expressed as spots several inches in diameter scattered across the turf. A light application of nitrogen ($1/2$ pound nitrogen per 1000 square feet) should encourage the grass to outgrow these symptoms. If this treatment does not provide satisfactory results, refer to the chapter, "Disease Problems."

Nematodes

Bahiagrass can be parasitized by nematodes but the damage is much less than for other lawngrasses.

Refer to the chapter in the book on nematodes for additional information.

Yearly Calendar for Bahiagrass Care and Culture

L. B. McCarty and J. L. Cisar

Bahiagrass forms a coarse-textured, open turf with an upright growth habit which gives a lawn a sparse, open appearance. It is light green in color and grows best in full sun. Establishment is by sod or seed. Bahiagrass avoids drought damage by dropping its leaves, forming extensive rooting depth and undergoing dormancy (browning). When water is applied, new leaves appear quickly. Major pest problems in bahiagrasses include mole crickets, weeds and occasionally dollar spot disease. If the homeowner does not have an irrigation system or prefers a low-maintenance utility turf area, bahiagrass is a good choice for a lawn. Under most conditions, bahiagrass will not produce a turf comparable in quality to St. Augustinegrass. Those who desire a high quality lawn appearance should choose another lawngrass.

Bahiagrass should be fertilized annually with a total of 2 to 3 pounds nitrogen per 1000 square feet for low-maintenance lawns or 4 to 5 pounds nitrogen per 1000 square feet for high-maintenance lawns. Due to its tough leaves and stems, only a heavy duty rotary mower with sharp blades should be used. The following is a suggested guideline for those managing bahiagrass lawns (refer to Table 1). Local growing conditions and resources available may require you to slightly deviate from these guidelines.

February - May

Mowing

If bahiagrass is green and growing, mow it at 3 inches or as high as most home-type rotary mowers will allow. High mowing promotes a deeper, more extensive root system which enables the grass to better withstand drought and nematode stress. Remove no more than $1/3$ the height of the leaf blades with any mowing (e.g., for a lawn to be maintained at 3 inches in height, mow when the turf reaches 4 to $4^1/2$ inches). In many cases, mowing may be required more than once a week. Use only a sharpened, balanced mower blade; otherwise the cut will be ragged and the lawn will have a poor appearance. Resharpen and balance blades monthly. Leave clippings unless amounts are excessive (clumping occurs). If excessive clippings remain, allow them to dry in the sun and then scatter by removing, blowing, or raking.

Fertilization

Two weeks following spring regrowth, apply a complete fertilizer such as 16-4-8 at the rate of 1 pound nitrogen per 1000 square feet (6.25 pounds 16-4-8 = 1 pound nitrogen, 0.25 pound P_2O_5, 0.5 pound K_2O per 1000 square feet). The 16-4-8 refers to percent nitrogen, phosphorus, and potassium, respectively, in the bag. For example, a 50-pound 16-4-8 bag contains 16% nitrogen or 8 pounds total nitrogen. For a 1 pound nitrogen rate per 1000 square feet, this bag will cover 8000 square feet. For *highly* maintained lawns, apply 1 pound nitrogen per 1000 square feet (e.g., 3 pounds 33-0-0 = 1 pound nitrogen per 1000 square feet) again in late April or early May. Yellow appearance may be an indication of iron deficiency due to low soil temperatures, restricted rooting, and excessive soil phosphorus and/or pH (>7.0). Correct iron deficiency by spraying ferrous sulfate (2 ounces in 3 to 5 gallons of water per 1000 square feet) or a chelated iron source to enhance color as needed. Iron applications every 6 weeks will help maintain green color and, unlike nitrogen, will not promote excessive topgrowth. Lowering the soil pH to 6.0 would help reduce iron deficiency. Use ammonium nitrogen fertilizer sources (e.g., ammonium nitrate or sulfate) to help reduce pH. Elemental sulfur may be added to the soil *prior* to bahiagrass establishment at 15 pounds per 1000 square feet for short-term pH reduction. Once the grass is established, up to 5 pounds of elemental sulfur may be added per 1000 square feet if it is immediately irrigated in to prevent burn.

Irrigation

Irrigate on an as-needed basis to prevent drought symptoms. Determine this when the turf begins to wilt, turn blue-gray in color, or recovery from foot or tire tracks is slow. Apply water to rewet the entire root zone and then wait until the turf shows signs of wilting again before watering. For most Florida soils, this is usually no more than $3/4$ inch of water based on an eight-inch rootzone. A higher mowing height will help the grass stay greener during drought. Place several coffee cans throughout your irrigation system zone to determine when an average of $3/4$ inch of water has been applied to each zone.

Note: During extended drought periods, instead of the homeowner trying to maintain green, growing grass, bahiagrass may be allowed to go dormant (turn brown). Afterwards, once water is available, the grass will green back up without major damage to the grass. Refer to the sections on "Watering Your Florida Lawn" and "How to Calibrate your Sprinkler System" in this publication for further details on water requirements and irrigation system calibration.

Table 1. Suggested maintenance schedule for bahiagrass lawns.

		Month											
		J	F	M	A	M	J	J	A	S	O	N	D
Fertilization													
North Florida[1]	Low maintenance	–	–	C[2]	Fe[3]	–	–	–	–	C	Fe	–	–
	High maintenance	–	–	C	Fe	N[4]	–	N	–	C	Fe	–	–
South Florida	Low maintenance	–	C	Fe	–	–	–	–	C	–	N	–	–
	High maintenance	–	C	Fe	–	N	–	–	–	C	N	–	N
Weed control	North Florida	–	–	PE[5]	–	PO[5]	–	–	PO	–	–	PO	–
	South florida	–	PE	–	–	PO	–	–	PO	–	–	PO	–
Insect Control		–	–	mole crickets							–	–	–
Disease Control		–	dollar spot disease									–	–
Mowing (3- to 4-inch height)		Frequency changes with the season. Typically, bahiagrass must be mowed every 7 to 14 days except during rapid seedhead formation periods. This may require more frequent mowing. Do not scalp bahiagrass, and only mow with a sharpened, balanced blade.											
Seeding/Renovation (7 lbs per 1000 sq ft)		Use brown top millet (20 lb/A) as a cover crop to prevent soil erosion, help retain soil moisture, and reduce weed invasion. Seeding during cool, winter months will reduce bahiagrass seed germination and establishment. Best seeding time is April through August.											
Irrigation ($^3/_4$ inch water per irrigation)		Irrigate when leaves show signs of stress: blue-gray color, slow recovery from footprinting or folded leaf blades. Avoid light, frequent waterings (<$^3/_4$ inch) and overwatering (puddling). Best time to irrigate is in the early morning.											

[1] The arbitrary dividing line between north and south Florida is a straight east-west line from coast to coast through Orlando.

[2] Apply a complete (C) fertilizer at a rate of 1 lb of nitrogen per 1000 sq ft (e.g., 6.2 lb 16-4-8 per 1000 sq ft).

[3] Apply iron (Fe) to provide dark green color without stimulating excessive grass growth. Ferrous sulfate (2 oz in 3-5 gal water per 1000 sq ft) or a chelated iron source may be used.

[4] A straight nitrogen source (N) may be used at a rate of 1 lb nitrogen per 1000 sq ft (e.g., 3 lb 33-0-0 or 4.8 lb 21-0-0 per 1000 sq ft). A slow release source of nitrogen is preferred (e.g., IBDU, milorganite, urea formaldehyde, sulfur coated urea).

[5] Use a preemergence herbicide (PE) for control of summer annual grasses such as crabgrass or goosegrass. Repeat 8 to 12 weeks later for summer long control. Herbicides include benefin, bensulide, dithiopyr, oxadiazon, DPCA, pendimethalin, prodiamine and oryzalin. **Do not** use atrazine or simazine. Note: Currently, no postemergence herbicides for grassy weeds are labeled for use on bahiagrass lawns.

[6] Use postemergence broadleaf herbicides (PO) for control of broadleaf weeds such as dichondra, pennywort, Florida betony, clover, oxalis, matchweed, plus others. Herbicides include 2,4-D + dicamba and/or mecoprop. Do not use when air temperatures exceed 85°F or when the grass is under moisture stress. Repeat application two weeks apart may be necessary for complete control.

Refer to the text for more details.

Weed Control

The best method of weed control is a healthy, vigorous turf. Apply preemergence herbicide (e.g., benefin, bensulide, prodiamine, dithiopyr, pendimethalin, oryzalin, dacthal) if crabgrass or sandbur was present in previous years.

Timing of application is important for successful control. A general rule of thumb for application is Feb. 1 in south Florida, Feb. 15 in central Florida, and March 1 in north Florida. For season-long control, repeat application should be made 3 months after the initial application. *Note:* Preemergence herbicides do not control visible weeds.

Apply postemergence herbicides (e.g., 2,4-D, dicamba, and/or MCPP) in May as needed for control of annual and perennial broadleaf weeds such as knotweed, spurge, lespedeza, etc. Several formulations of these herbicides are available; therefore, check with your local county Cooperative Extension Service office for the latest recommendations.

Note: Many popular "weed-n-feed" type fertilizers for home lawns contain the herbicide atrazine. Atrazine will result in some damage to bahiagrass; therefore, it is not recommended for use on this grass.

Insect Control

Check for mole crickets by: 1) looking for their tunneling and mounds; or 2) applying 2 gallons of water with 1 to 2 ounces of detergent soap per 2 square feet of turf in suspected damaged areas. If present, the mole crickets will surface in several minutes. Recently, several bait-type insecticides have been introduced and show real promise as a control measure. However, insecticides available for mole crickets constantly change. Check with your county Cooperative Extension Service office for the latest control recommendations.

Renovation

Replant large bare areas in April through July, using scarified seed (7 pounds per 1000 square feet) or sod. Prepare a proper seedbed by rototilling or hand raking. Keep these areas moistened with daily irrigations until roots develop and peg down. Plan to fertilize with 0.5 pound nitrogen per 1000 square feet 4 to 5 weeks following planting. For further information, refer to the section "Establishing Your Florida Lawn" in this publication.

June - August

Mowing

Mow as previously described. Frequent mowings may be required to remove the tall, V-shaped seedheads which continuously emerge from late May through early fall. Use only a sharp, balanced-bladed mower.

Fertilization

Fertilize with 1 pound of nitrogen per 1000 square feet (e.g., 6.5 pounds 15-0-14 = 1 pound nitrogen per 1000 square feet) in July for *more highly* maintained areas. Due to naturally high levels of phosphorus in many Florida soils, fertilizers without phosphorus (i.e., 15-0-14, 8-0-24) may be used during all times, unless soil test results indicate low levels. For lower maintenance lawns, iron in the form of ferrous sulfate or as a chelated source may be applied as previously described for green color without excessive growth.

Irrigation

Irrigate to prevent drought stress on an as-needed basis. Normally, summer is a period of increased precipitation. Do not overwater, as this encourages shallow roots, disease, and weed invasion. Apply water at $3/4$ inch per application and then wait until the turf shows signs of wilting (blue-gray color, or footprinting occurs) before watering again. Watering may be discontinued during extended dry periods, if temporary brown dormant turf is not objectionable.

Weed Control

Selective control of emerged grass weeds such as goosegrass, crabgrass, or alexandergrass is only by hand pulling. Bahiagrass is severely damaged by postemergence grass herbicides such as DSMA, MSMA, or asulox. Following suggested management practices, such as proper mowing, fertilizing, irrigation, etc., will encourage bahiagrass to outcompete weeds. Control of broadleaf weeds such as pusley, matchweed, knotweed, spurge, and lespedeza is available with herbicides such as 2,4-D, dicamba, and/or MCPP. Check with the county Cooperative Extension Service office for positive identification of weeds and exact herbicide recommendations. Apply herbicides only when adequate soil moisture is present, air temperatures are between 60° and 85°F, and the turf is not suffering from water or mowing stress. Failure to follow these precautionary statements will result in damaged turf.

Insect Control

Check for mole crickets by methods previously described. Refer to your county Cooperative Extension Service office for control recommendations if insects are present.

Nematode Control

Due to bahiagrass's deep, extensive rooting, nematode damage seldom becomes noticeable. However, if grass becomes thin in density, less vigorous in growth, and develops a weak root system, nematode presence should be suspected. Take a representative soil sample to your county Cooperative Extension Service office to be assayed, and if nematodes are found, ask for control recommendations. Proper cultural factors to encourage bahiagrass root growth will lessen nematode stress. This includes applying less nitrogen, providing less frequent but deep watering, and ensuring ample soil potassium and phosphorus.

Disease Control

Bahiagrass damage by diseases is normally minimum. Dollar spot disease, if present, is expressed as brown color spots several inches in diameter, which appear scattered across the turf and on its seedhead stalks. A light application of nitrogen ($1/2$ pound nitrogen per 1000 square feet, which equals 3.3 pounds 15-0-14) should encourage the grass to outgrow these symptoms.

September - November

Mowing

Continue mowing at the specific height and frequency as previously described. Prolific seedhead production may require increased mowing frequency.

Fertilization

Apply 1 pound of nitrogen per 1000 square feet (e.g., 6.5 pounds 15-0-14 or 6.25 pounds 16-4-8 per 1000 square feet) in September and then discontinue nitrogen application for north and central Florida lawns. For south Florida lawns, apply this 1 pound of nitrogen in October. In order to promote rooting prior to winter, more highly maintained bahiagrass areas may have 1 pound of potash (K_2O) per 1000 square feet using 1.6 pounds muriate of potash (0-0-60) or 2 pounds of potassium sulfate (0-0-50) applied 1 month before first expected frost. Do not apply potash during hot periods or if the lawn is under moisture stress. Water-in the fertilizer to prevent burn.

Yellow appearance may be an indication of iron deficiency. Spray ferrous sulfate (2 ounces in 3 to 5 gallons of water per 1000 square feet) or a chelated iron source to enhance color as needed.

Irrigation

Continue irrigating as needed to prevent drought stress. Apply $3/4$ inch of water when turf turns blue-gray in color and/or footprinting occurs. Irrigation may be discontinued during extended dry periods, if temporary brown dormant turf is not objectionable. Irrigate during cold, windy periods to prevent winter soil dehydration.

Insect Control

Check for mole crickets and follow control recommendations as previously described.

Disease Control

Check for dollar spot and follow control recommendations as previously described.

December - January

Mowing

Remove lawn debris (rocks, sticks, and leaves) or any unsightly tall weeds or plants. In south Florida, mow if growth warrants it.

Fertilization

Do not fertilize at this time in north or central Florida. A light fertilization in December may be desired in south Florida. If so, apply $1/2$ pound nitrogen per 1000 square feet (e.g., $1/2$ pound nitrogen = 3.3 pounds 15-0-14 or 6.2 pounds 16-4-8 per 1000 square feet).

Submit soil samples for analysis every 3 years to determine pH and nutrient requirements. Contact your county Cooperative Extension Service office for details. Apply lime or sulfur, if suggested based on soil tests, to raise or reduce soil pH, respectively.

Irrigation

Normally, this is the driest period of the year; however, due to cooler weather, grass growth is not vigorous. Apply water in south Florida to avoid drought if brown, dormant turf is objectionable. Turf dormant due to frost will require warm spring weather to resume growth, thus do not irrigate except for overseeded grass.

Weed Control

Apply broadleaf herbicides (i.e., 2,4-D) as necessary for control of winter broadleaf weeds such as betony, beggarstick, chickweed, henbit, clover, dandelion, or wild garlic/onion. Follow label directions for rates and use with caution.

Miscellaneous

Make plans and arrangements for any lawn renovations to be made in spring. Purchase preemergence herbicides, seeds, and other supplies. Service your lawn mower and sharpen and balance the blade. Check irrigation system for leaky lines, joints, or damaged heads.

Maintenance of Bermudagrass Lawns

L. B. McCarty

ESTABLISHMENT

Hybrid bermudagrasses are established vegetatively by planting sprigs, sod, or plugs. Each of these methods can be equally successful if the site is properly prepared before planting and proper establishment practices are followed. For detailed information on lawn establishment, refer to the section entitled "Establishing Your Florida Lawn" in this publication.

The planting sites should be fumigated because of the high cost of installation and the subsequent value of the bermudagrass planting. Fumigation reduces potential problems caused by weed seeds, nematodes, and other pests.

The best time to plant bermudagrass is when plants are actively growing, normally April through September. Other times may be suitable if sufficient care is given to prevent desiccation and cold damage.

Sprigging

The most common method of planting bermudagrass is by sprigging. This is done mechanically over large areas and can be done by hand in small areas. Fresh sprigs are rhizomes and stolons that have at least two nodes or joints. Sprigs are usually broadcast over an area at a rate of 200 to 400 bushels per acre, or 5 to 10 bushels per 1000 square feet, then pressed into the soil. An alternative method of establishment is to plant the sprigs end-to-end in furrows 6 to 12 inches apart.

Sodding

Establishment of bermudagrass by sodding produces an instant turf surface. Sod should only be laid over bare moist soil with pieces laid in a staggered brick-like pattern and the edges fitted tightly together to avoid any open cracks. Rolling and watering thoroughly will ensure good contact with the soil for fast rooting. Sodded areas should be watered at least twice per day at 10:00 a.m. and 2:00 p.m. with $1/4$ inch of water until the sod is held fast (usually 2 to 3 weeks) to the soil by roots; then watering should be reduced to an as-needed basis.

Plugging

Sod can be cut into round plugs with a golf green cup-cutter or into small squares with a machete. Spacing of plugs varies from 12 to 24 inches, with the closer spacing covering in 3 to 6 months and the farther spacing covering in 6 to 9 months.

Seeding

Only common type bermudagrasses can be established from seed. Bermudagrass seed should be planted at a rate of 1 to 2 pounds of hulled seed per 1000 square feet.

MOWING

Proper mowing practices are important in maintaining an attractive bermudagrass area. Both height and frequency of cut need to be adjusted for the level of turf management and season of the year. Under low to moderate levels of management, bermudagrass should be cut at a height of $3/4$ to $1^{1}/2$ inches, one to three times per week. The higher level should be used when mowing common bermudagrass. This will help the grass develop a deep root system and give a better appearance to the turf. Under high levels of management, bermudagrass can be maintained at a height of $1/2$ inch if the turf is mowed daily during the growing season. Mowing at this height and frequency requires more fertilizer and water to maintain an attractive and durable turf. It should be noted that low cutting heights and high maintenance levels can predispose the turf to many weed and pest problems. Mowing frequency under low to moderate management practices should be adjusted to the amount of growth. Remove no more than one-third the height of the leaf blades with any mowing.

A reel mower is preferred to mow bermudagrass because the machine can be adjusted accurately for mowing heights below 1 inch, and a reel mower will give a cleaner cut than a rotary mower. Bermudagrass grown at a high cutting height can be successfully mowed with a rotary mower if the blades are sharp and well adjusted to get a clean smooth cut. Dull blades on either mower will shred the leaf blades and give the lawn a brownish cast.

Grass clippings can be left on the turf maintained with low to moderate fertility levels if it is mowed at the proper height and frequency. In this way, clippings do not contribute to the thatch layer and help to recycle nutrients. Remove the clippings only if the amount is excessive so as clumps form, or if appearance is important.

WATERING

An established bermudagrass turf should be watered as needed. Grass blades will begin to wilt as moisture is depleted from the soil. If 30 to 50% of the lawn shows signs of slight wilting, it is time to water with $3/4$ inch of water. The turf will fully recover within 24 hours. The turf should show signs of wilting again before it is watered. This method of irrigation scheduling works for any soil type and environmental condition. Refer to the section "Watering Your Florida Lawn" for more information.

FERTILIZING

Maintaining a good quality bermudagrass lawn requires a properly planned fertilization program. Fertilizer timing and amounts for bermudagrass are based largely on the turf use. Generally, bermudagrasses require higher levels of fertilizer than other Florida turfgrasses for acceptable growth, durability, and appearance. A suggested fertilization program for bermudagrass is shown in Table 1.

Bermudagrasses can be maintained at moderate maintenance levels in areas such as lawns, athletic fields, or golf course fairways. These areas should be fertilized six times per year or approximately every other month. Apply a complete fertilizer such as 16-4-8 with micronutrients or similar high analysis fertilizer at the rate of 1.0 pound of nitrogen per 1000 square feet per application. Never apply more than 1 pound of nitrogen per 1000 square feet at any one time unless a slow-release nitrogen source is used. A complete fertilizer can be used at every fertilization, although two applications per year is a minimum. Other applications can be a straight nitrogen fertilizer unless the grass is grown on sandy soil. When grown on sandy soil, bermudagrass requires as much potassium as nitrogen. Use equal ratio fertilizers with nitrogen and potassium under these circumstances. It is best on these areas to leave the clippings to recycle nutrients.

On high-maintenance bermudagrass areas such as putting greens, bowling greens, or tennis courts, fertilizer should be applied at least monthly. Slow release fertilizers or "fertigation" is useful in providing uniform nitrogen distribution. A total of 1 pound of nitrogen as a slow release, complete fertilizer should be applied per 1000 square feet per growing month.

Since bermudagrasses are used primarily for sports activities, fertilization programs are often arranged to provide the optimum turf quality during the season. Heavier rates of fertilizers can be used during the season to keep the turf healthy and vigorous. This practice is especially important if the turf is used extensively in the winter. During off-season periods, low levels of fertilizer can be applied to maintain adequate turf quality.

High fertilization rates will produce a faster buildup of thatch than low rates, and can also increase the amount of insect damage to the turf. Additionally, the amount of mowing and watering increases with the amount of fertilizer. Careful planning is necessary to grow the type of turf desired.

PEST PROBLEMS

Several severe pest problems can affect bermudagrass. Diagnosis and recommended treatment of pest problems are available from your county Cooperative Extension Service office. Refer to the pest chapters for additional information.

Nematodes

The most serious pests of bermudagrasses in Florida are nematodes. Nematodes cause a yellowing and general thinning of older turf especially during hot, dry periods. These pests cause extensive turf damage, particularly on sandy soils and turf under high maintenance levels. Although some cultivars tolerate nematodes better than others, no cultivar is resistant to nematode infestation. Chemical nematode control is extremely limited for home lawns and usually requires commercial applicators.

Insects

Mole crickets are a major insect pest of bermudagrass. Other insects which can cause damage in bermudagrass

Table 1. Suggested fertilization schedule for bermudagrass lawns.

Fertility level	Jan	Feb	Mar	Apr	May	June	July	Aug	Sept	Oct	Nov	Dec
North Florida[1]												
High	–	–	C[2]	–	C	–	N	–	C	N	–	N[4]
Low	–	–	C	–	N[3]	–	N	–	C	–	–	–
South Florida[1]												
High	–	C	–	N	N	C	–	C	–	N	–	N[4]
Low	–	C	–	N	–	N	–	–	C	–	–	N[4]

[1] The arbitrary dividing line between north and south Florida is a straight east-west line from coast-to-coast through Orlando.

[2] Complete fertilizer at 1.0 lb of nitrogen and potassium/1000 sq ft.

[3] Water soluble inorganic nitrogen source applied at 1.0 lb of nitrogen/1000 sq ft.

[4] Fertilize only those areas overseeded with ryegrass for winter color.

are sod webworms, armyworms, cutworms, grass loopers, and bermudagrass mites. High levels of nitrogen fertilizer encourage insect problems. Several means of chemical control are available for insect pests.

Diseases

Several diseases can infest bermudagrasses; dollar spot, brown patch, and *Helminthosporium* leaf spot are the most common. A sound cultural program can minimize most disease problems, and fungicides can be used to cure major disease outbreaks.

Weeds

Bermudagrass turf with weed problems is a sign that the turf has become weakened by improper management practices or damage from pests. Refer to the chapter entitled "Weed Control" in this publication for more information.

Proper management practices can eliminate most weed problems. If weeds are a persistent problem, herbicides labeled specifically for bermudagrass can be used for preemergent or postemergent weed control.

Other Problems

A number of other things can damage turf quality. Among these are excessive thatch layering, shade, and the improper use of rotary mowers. To ensure a good bermudagrass lawn, refer to other chapters of this publication for recommended management practices, and follow label directions when applying fertilizers and pesticides.

Maintenance of Carpetgrass Lawns

L. B. McCarty

ESTABLISHMENT

Carpetgrass may be seeded or sprigged. However, carpetgrass sod is not commonly available. Success with either propagation method is highly dependent on proper soil preparation. Refer to the section titled "Preparing to Plant a Florida Lawn" for information on seedbed preparation.

Seeding

Seeding is easier and less expensive than sprigging. Use fresh, weed-free seed. Broadcast at the rate of 5 pounds per 1000 square feet. Planting dates are April to July. It is advisable to kill any existing weeds with a non-selective herbicide such as glyphosate before planting.

Sprigging

Planting carpetgrass by sprigs is as effective as seeding but more laborious. Fresh vigorous stolons (runners) having at least two nodes or joints should be planted in rows 12 inches apart, spacing the sprigs end-to-end or 6 to 12 inches apart in the row. Cover sprigs about 1 to 2 inches deep, leaving a portion of the sprig exposed to light. Rolling will press sprigs into close contact with the soil. Soil must be kept continually moist until the plants initiate new growth.

FERTILIZING

Proper fertilization of carpetgrass is an important practice in a good maintenance program. Carpetgrass is a low-maintenance lawngrass and does not tolerate excessive use of fertilizer, especially nitrogen. A complete fertilizer such as 16-4-8, 10-10-10, or 6-6-6 can be applied once a year, in the spring, for a minimum-maintenance program. To produce a high-quality lawn, follow the fertilization program shown in Table 1.

MOWING

If fertilized as recommended, carpetgrass will require mowing every 10 to 14 days at a height of 1 to 2 inches. Weekly mowing with a rotary mower may be necessary during the summer to remove the unsightly seedheads.

WATERING

Due to the ability to thrive in wet soil, carpetgrass requires a lot of water if grown on well-drained soils. Irrigation on an as-needed basis is an excellent way to water any grass, provided the proper amount of water is applied when needed and not at a later or more convenient time. When using this approach, water at the first sign of wilt and apply $3/4$ inch of water (465 gallons per 1000 square feet) per application. During prolonged droughts, it may be necessary to water carpetgrass every other day. If carpetgrass is grown on naturally wet soils where it is best adapted, irrigation may not be necessary.

PEST PROBLEMS

Carpetgrass is damaged by nematodes and several insects and diseases. Refer to pest chapters for control measures.

Table 1. Suggested fertilization schedule for carpetgrass lawns.

Fertility level	Jan	Feb	Mar	Apr	May	June	July	Aug	Sept	Oct	Nov	Dec
North Florida[1]												
High	–	–	C[2]	–	–	–	–	C	–	–	–	–
Low	–	–	C	–	–	–	–	–	–	–	–	–
South Florida[1]												
High	–	C	–	–	–	O[3]	–	C	–	–	–	–
Low	–	C	–	–	–	–	–	C	–	–	–	–
[1] The arbitrary dividing line between north and south Florida is a straight east-west line from coast to coast through Orlando.												
[2] Complete fertilizer at 1.0 lb of nitrogen/1000 sq ft. A slow- or control-release nitrogen source is preferred.												
[3] Organic nitrogen such as sewage sludge, ureaform or others.												

Insects

Lawn caterpillars, mole crickets and spittlebugs cause damage. Worms are especially damaging on well-fertilized carpetgrass.

Diseases

The principal disease affecting carpetgrass is brown patch.

Nematodes

If carpetgrass is grown on poorly drained, wet soils, nematodes should not be a major problem. But on well-drained soils, nematodes can be very serious on carpetgrass. These soilborne, microscopic worms attack the grass roots and if not controlled, can weaken or ultimately kill the entire lawn.

Maintenance of Centipedegrass Lawns

L. B. McCarty

ESTABLISHMENT

Centipedegrass can be established by seed, plugs, sprigs (runners), or sod. Proper preparation of the area before planting is critical to ensure successful establishment. Refer to the section on "Preparing to Plant a Florida Lawn" for complete information.

Centipedegrass is best adapted to a soil pH of 5.0 to 5.5. Severe iron chlorosis may occur if pH is above 6.5 to 7.0. *Preplant* application of wettable sulfur at the rate of 430 pounds per acre (10 pounds per 1000 square feet) can be used to lower the pH of some Florida soils 1 pH unit. Do not apply more than 10 pounds per 1000 square feet of wettable sulfur per application. Where more is required, allow 60 days between applications. Irrigate with 1 inch after each application to activate the sulfur. Lime is seldom required for centipedegrass.

Sodding

Planting centipedegrass by sod is more expensive initially than seeding, but this produces an "instant lawn." For best results, good quality, weed-free sod should be used. Lay the sod in a well-prepared seedbed, fitting the pieces tightly together to avoid cracks in the turf. Wet the soil surface thoroughly prior to laying the sod. After the sod is in place, water thoroughly and roll with a lightweight roller to ensure firm contact between the sod and soil. The entire area should be watered daily applying $1/2$ inch of water per application. Once the sod has rooted into the soil, irrigation frequency can be reduced to an as-needed basis. Sodding is best done in the spring and summer months. If the area is suspected of producing a severe weed problem, a pre-emergence herbicide may be used after the sod is laid.

Seeding

Seed of centipedegrass is expensive, but the seeding rate is low and this method of establishment is probably cheaper than vegetative planting if time and labor are considered. The suggested seeding rate is 4 ounces per 1000 square feet. The best time to seed is during the period from April to July, since this permits a full growing season before winter weather. Fall seeding is undesirable because the young seedlings may not become sufficiently established to withstand cold injury during the winter. *Centipedegrass seed is naturally slow to germinate;* 2 to 3 weeks should be expected before this occurs. Soil washing due to heavy rain or excessive irrigations should be minimized by lightly mulching the planted area.

Seed quality should be considered when purchasing seed for planting. Cheap seed does not pay, it costs. Insist on seed with a purity of 90% or better and a minimum of 85% germination.

Sprigging and Plugging

Planting centipedegrass by sprigs and plugs is as effective as seeding but more laborious. See section "Establishing Your Florida Lawn."

FERTILIZING

Proper fertilization of centipedegrass is very important to its survival. Centipedegrass is a low-maintenance turfgrass and does not respond well to excessive use of fertilizer, especially nitrogen. *Do not overfertilize centipedegrass with nitrogen to equal St. Augustinegrass color.*

Apply all fertilizers at recommended rates, and water the soil immediately after application (Table 1). Thatch accumulation and the incidence of pests are more severe when the grass is overfertilized. To minimize these problems, choose a low-maintenance fertilization program.

As mentioned previously, one of the common problems of centipedegrass is a mottled yellowing called chlorosis, which is usually caused by iron deficiency. This condition is most severe where soil pH is high (above 6.5) or where calcium or phosphorus is excessive in the soil.

Normally this yellowing is most severe in early spring. This corresponds to when daytime temperatures are warm but nighttime temperatures are still cool. Warm daytime air temperatures promote leaf and stolon growth but due to the cool nighttime temperatures, root growth is limited. As a result, roots cannot assimilate enough nutrients such as iron or manganese to supply the growing leaves. The leaves, therefore, turn yellow. As the soils become warmer, this temporary nutrient deficiency disappears.

Avoid using excessive phosphorus fertilizers unless soil test results indicate to do so. Iron chlorosis can be controlled by several methods. Correcting (lowering) the soil pH can make more iron available for plant use. Regular use of acid-forming fertilizers such as ammonium nitrate or ammonium sulfate is suggested. If control of pH is not feasible, or if the soil is naturally iron deficient, iron fertilization is necessary. Centipedegrass usually responds well to supplemental applications of iron. Chelated or ferrous sulfate iron can be applied evenly and easily with a

Table 1. Suggested fertilization schedule for centipedegrass lawns.

Fertility level	Jan	Feb	Mar	Apr	May	June	July	Aug	Sept	Oct	Nov	Dec
North Florida[1]												
High	–	–	C[2]	Fe[3]	–	N[4]	Fe	C	–	–	–	–
Low	–	–	–	C	Fe	–	–	Fe	C	–	–	–
South Florida[1]												
High	–	C	Fe	–	N	–	Fe	–	C	–	–	–
Low	–	C	Fe	–	–	–	Fe	–	C	–	–	–

[1] The arbitrary dividing line between north and south Florida is a straight east-west line from coast to coast through Orlando.

[2] Complete fertilizer at 1.0 lb of nitrogen/1000 sq ft.

[3] Iron (Fe) may be applied to provide dark green color without stimulating excessive grass growth. Ferrous sulfate (2 oz in 3 to 5 gal water per 1000 sq ft) or a chelated iron source may be used.

[4] Water soluble inorganic nitrogen sources such as ammonium nitrate or ammonium sulfate applied at 1.0 lb of nitrogen/1000 sq ft.

hose-end applicator. Apply the ferrous sulfate at the rate of 2 ounces in 3 to 5 gallons of water per 1000 square feet. Consult the label for chelated iron rates.

Fertilizers containing iron and a combination material of ammonium sulfate and ferrous sulfate are also available.

MOWING

Correct mowing, which includes both height and frequency of cut, is necessary to keep an attractive lawn. Centipedegrass should be mowed at 1½ to 2 inches.

Frequency should be adjusted so that no more than 30% of the leaf blades are removed at any one mowing. During periods of moisture stress, or if the grass is growing in shade, increase the mowing height to 2 to 2½ inches. A sharp and well-adjusted rotary or reel mower should be used. Mowing closer than 1½ inches repeatedly will reduce the density and thin the turf, and should be avoided.

Mowing too high and too infrequently will also be detrimental by allowing an excessive buildup of thatch. Heavy thatch can lead to winter injury and drought stress.

WATERING

Irrigation on an as-needed basis is an excellent way to water any grass, provided the amount of water is applied when needed and not at a later or more convenient time.

PEST PROBLEMS

Centipedegrass is damaged by nematodes, insects, and diseases. Help in identification of pest problems and current control recommendations can be obtained from your county Cooperative Extension Service office.

Insects

Several insects may damage centipedegrass, but the hardest to control are scale insects called ground pearls. At the present time, there are no effective chemicals to control these pests. Lawn caterpillars, grubs, mole crickets, spittlebugs and sod webworms also damage centipedegrass. Refer to the chapter on Insect Problems.

Diseases

The principle disease affecting centipedegrass is brown patch, but dollar spot can be a problem. Both can be controlled with fungicides. Refer to the chapter on "Disease Problems."

Nematodes

Nematodes can be a most serious problem on centipedegrass. These are microscopic worms that attack the grass roots and cause the lawn to thin and eventually die. Areas of heavy infestation will show symptoms of severe wilt, even when well watered. The Extension Service nematode lab in Gainesville can diagnose whether nematodes are a problem by looking at a soil sample taken from the margin of the affected area.

Refer to the section entitled "Diagnosis: When Nematodes Should be Suspected as Pests" or contact your county Cooperative Extension Service for instructions on sampling your lawn for nematode analysis. A fee is charged for this service.

Weeds

Weeds easily invade newly established or poorly maintained lawns. Grass weeds include crabgrass, goosegrass, dallisgrass, annual bluegrass and torpedograss. Broadleaf weeds include dandelions, clover, pennywort, betony, oxalis, henbit and others. Refer to the chapter entitled "Weed Control" for more information.

Centipedegrass Decline

Established centipedegrass (after a few years) may develop yellowing (chlorosis) and/or dead spots as spring growth resumes (Plate 106). Numerous conditions may contribute to the problem and include:

❑ High pH (>6.5)

❑ Excessive nitrogen fertilization the previous year

❑ Uneven soil surface from stolons being suspended above the soil and over a mat of thatch. (Such stolons never sufficiently develop roots and are killed by freezing weather. Alternating freezing or cool temperatures and thawing conditions accentuate this.)

❑ Nematodes and/or other disease organisms such as *Gaeumannomyces*, *Rhizoctonia* or *Pythium* species weaken the grass making it susceptible to injury from otherwise normal conditions.

Some remedies for this condition are:

❑ Check soil pH and adjust it if it's too high.

❑ **Do not overfertilize with nitrogen or phosphorus.**

❑ Follow recommended mowing heights and frequencies to avoid scalping or excessive thatch buildup.

❑ Spray with 2 oz ferrous sulfate per 1000 sq ft or use chelated iron as directed if excessive yellowing occurs.

❑ Check with your Cooperative Extension Agent to send samples for identification.

Maintenance of St. Augustinegrass Lawns

L. B. McCarty and J. L. Cisar

ESTABLISHMENT

St. Augustinegrass is established by vegetative propagation because its seeds have poor germination and do not remain true to type. St. Augustinegrass is a stoloniferous grass (with above ground stems) and can be planted by sod, sprigs, or plugs (Table 1). Each of these methods can be equally successful if the site is properly prepared and maintained before and after planting.

New home or building sites should be rough graded. Rocks, roots, and other debris need to be removed. On existing sites, unwanted vegetation should be removed by a nonselective herbicide such as glyphosate (Roundup). A soil test should be taken in the area to determine the pH and the need for plant nutrients. These nutrients need to be applied before planting, and tilled in if the soil is bare. The next step is the installation of a new irrigation system, or repairs to an existing system. Before any grass is planted, the area should be final graded and thoroughly moistened to help the establishment process.

The best time to plant St. Augustinegrass is during active growth, normally April through July. Other times may be suitable, with sufficient care to prevent desiccation and cold damage. The sections entitled "Preparing to Plant a Florida Lawn" and "Establishing Your Florida Lawn" in this publication give additional details on turf establishment.

Sodding

Establishment of St. Augustinegrass by sodding produces an instant lawn. Sod should only be laid over bare, moist soil, with pieces laid in a staggered, brick-like pattern and the edges fitted tightly together to avoid cracks. Often, sod is placed over existing turf. This generally produces a lower quality turf and should be avoided. Fill any cracks between strips with soil to avoid open spaces for weed encroachment. Rolling and thorough watering will ensure good contact with the soil for fast rooting. Newly sodded areas should be watered at least twice daily with $^1/_4$ inch of water until the sod is held fast to the soil by roots, then watering ($^3/_4$ inch) should be reduced to an as-needed basis (e.g. when the turf wilts).

Sprigging

Planting St. Augustinegrass by sprigging is an effective way to patch small areas of turf but is too labor-intensive for large areas unless it is performed mechanically. Fresh sprigs are stolons (runners) that have at least two nodes or joints. These are planted end to end in rows 6-12 inches apart. The runner should be covered with soil, leaving the leaves exposed. Tamping the soil and a thorough watering help establish the plants. The soil should be kept moist until new stolons are produced.

Plugging

A number of the new varieties of St. Augustinegrasses are available commercially as plugs. Sod also can be made into plugs by cutting it into small squares. Spacing of plugs varies from 6 to 24 inches. The closer spacing provides full coverage in 3-6 months and farther spacing covers in 6 to 12 months. Plugs are placed in holes of the same size or in open furrows and tamped into place. A thorough watering completes the installation. The turf should then be cared for like a sprigged lawn.

Table 1. Relative growth characteristics for St. Augustinegrass cultivars.

Characteristics	Normal Growth Habit Cultivars							Semi-dwarf Growth Habit Cultivars		
	Common/ Roselawn	Bitterblue	Raleigh	Floratine	Floratam	Floralawn	FX-10	Delmar	Jade	Seville
Mowing Ht. (in)	3 - 4	3 - 4	3 - 4	2 - 3	3 - 4	3 - 4	3 - 4	1.5 - 2	1.5 - 2	2 - 2.5
Cold Tolerance	poor	good	very good	fair	poor	poor	poor	very good	good	good
Shade Tolerance	poor	very good	good	fair	poor	poor	poor	good	good	very good
Chinch Bug Resistance	poor	light	poor	slight	good*	good*	good	poor	poor	slight
Green Color	light	dark	medium	dark	dark	dark	medium	dark	dark	dark
Texture	coarse	coarse	coarse	coarse	v. coarse	v. coarse	coarse	fine	v. fine	fine
Density	poor	good	good	good	good	good	good	good	good	good

* Isolated evidence of a new chinch bug which can feed on these cultivars has been reported.

MOWING

Proper mowing practices are important in maintaining an attractive lawn. Both height and frequency of cut need to be adjusted for the level of turf management (Table 1). Under high levels of management, St. Augustinegrass can be maintained at 2 inches if the lawn is mowed at least weekly during the growing season. Mowing at this height and frequency requires more fertilizer and water to maintain an attractive lawn. Also, low cutting heights and high maintenance levels can predispose the turf to many pest problems. Under moderate or low levels of management, St. Augustinegrass should be cut at a height of 3 to 4 inches. To obtain this height with most home rotary lawn mowers, the highest wheel height setting should be used. This height will help the grass develop a deep root system and give a better appearance to the turf. Mowing frequency under moderate or low management should be adjusted to the amount of growth. No more than one-third the height of the leaf blades should be removed with any mowing. During periods of moisture stress, or if the grass is growing in shade, increase the mowing height to 4 inches. Newer semi-dwarf varieties have a lower growth habit, and should be mowed at 1½ to 2 inches for optimum quality.

Mowing too infrequently and improper watering can cause a thatch buildup. The secret to mowing St. Augustinegrass at 3 inches is to water the lawn only when there are signs of moisture stress. This will keep growth to a minimum and reduce the rate of thatch accumulation. The section entitled "Thatch and its Control in Florida Lawns" in this publication has more information on thatch.

Mowing too low can also cause problems in turf quality. Constant low mowing reduces the density and vigor of St. Augustinegrass. Weed problems in St. Augustinegrass lawns can usually be attributed to a low height of cut and improper watering.

Either a rotary or reel mower can be used on St. Augustinegrass. It is important to keep the blades sharp and well-adjusted to get a clean cut. Dull blades will give the lawn a brownish cast, because a ragged cut shreds the leaf blades rather than cutting them. During the growing season blades should be sharpened on a monthly basis.

Grass clippings can be left on a lawn that is mowed at the proper height and frequency. Under these conditions, clippings do not contribute to the thatch layer. Clippings should be left on lawns maintained with low to moderate fertility levels to help recycle nutrients. Remove clippings if the amount is excessive (e.g., clumping occurs).

WATERING

The best way to irrigate an established lawn is on an as-needed basis. Grass blades will begin to wilt (e.g., fold, turn bluish-green in color and not recover from traffic or footprinting) as the moisture begins to be depleted in the soil. If 30 to 50% of the lawn shows signs of slight wilting, it is time to irrigate with ¾ inch of water. The turf will fully recover within 24 hours. The turf should not be watered again until it shows signs of wilting. This irrigation schedule works for any soil type and environmental condition. For further information on recommended watering practices see the section in this publication entitled "Watering Your Florida Lawn."

Proper watering practices will help maintain a lawn that requires less mowing and has little thatch buildup. Proper watering will also help develop a deep root system and encourage plants which are less susceptible to damage by pest and environmental stresses. If the diseases brown patch or gray leaf spot are a continuous problem, overwatering and excessive nitrogen fertilization may be responsible. Certain weeds (like pennywort and nutsedge) also thrive in soils which are continuously wet. Regulate these management practices closely to reduce disease and weed severity.

FERTILIZING

Maintaining a good quality lawn requires a properly planned fertility program. An acceptable quality St. Augustinegrass lawn can be grown with a low to a high level of fertility, depending on what the homeowner wants. First, decide how much time and effort can be spent on lawn maintenance. A low fertility lawn is best for those with little time to spend on lawn care. A high fertility lawn may be better suited to those who find a low fertility St. Augustinegrass lawn unattractive, and have more time for lawn care.

A low-maintenance St. Augustinegrass lawn should be fertilized twice a year, once in the spring and again in the late summer while the grass is actively growing (Table 2). Apply a complete fertilizer such as 16-4-8, 10-10-10, or 6-6-6 with micronutrients at the rate of 1 pound of actual nitrogen per 1000 square feet per application. It is best to leave the clippings on these lawns to recycle nutrients.

At the optimum maintenance level, a St. Augustinegrass lawn should receive 4 pounds of nitrogen per 1000 square feet per year. Apply fertilizer four times per year, in March, May, July, and September, at the rate of 1 pound of actual nitrogen per 1000 square feet. Never apply more than 1 pound of actual nitrogen per 1000 square feet at any one time. A complete fertilizer can be used at every fertilization, although two applications per year is sufficient. A slow-release, nitrogen-only fertilizer may be applied in between complete fertilizer applications. This fertility level, combined with the proper watering practices, will result in a good quality lawn with minimal thatch buildup.

Table 2. Suggested fertilization schedule for St. Augustinegrass lawns.

Fertility level	Jan	Feb	Mar	Apr	May	June	July	Aug	Sept	Oct	Nov	Dec
North Florida[1]												
High	–	–	C[2]	–	N[3]	Fe[4]	N	–	C	–	–	–
Low	–	–	C	–	–	Fe	–	–	C	–	–	–
South Florida[1]												
High	–	C	–	–	N[3]	Fe	N	–	–	C	–	N
Low	–	C	–	–	N[3]	Fe	–	–	–	C	–	–

[1] The arbitrary dividing line between north and south Florida is a straight east-west line from coast to coast through Orlando.

[2] Complete fertilizer at 1.0 lb of nitrogen/1000 sq ft.

[3] Slow release nitrogen fertilizer sources should be used to prevent an excess of succulent growth during chinch bug season. Apply 1.0 lb of nitrogen/1000 sq ft as activated sewage sludge, urea formaldehyde, sulfur-coated urea, IBDU, resin-coated material or other slow-release source.

[4] Iron (Fe) may be applied in summer to provide dark green color without stimulating excessive grass growth. Ferrous sulfate (2 oz in 3 to 5 gal. water per 1000 sq ft) or a chelated iron source may be used.

Heavy fertilization rates will produce a faster buildup of thatch than lower rates. High rates of fertilizing can also encourage insect damage to the turf. Additionally, the necessary amount of mowing and watering increases with the amount of fertilizer. Careful planning is necessary to grow the desired type of lawn. The section entitled "Understanding Soil Analysis and Fertilization" provides details on fertilizing turfgrasses in north and south Florida.

PEST PROBLEMS

Several pest problems can affect St. Augustinegrass. Diagnosis and recommendations for treatment of pest problems are available from your county Cooperative Extension Service.

Insects

The major pest of St. Augustinegrass is chinch bugs. Large populations of this insect have become resistant to organophosphate insecticides. Alternative chemicals are available, but the best solution is to plant Floratam or Floralawn, since these cultivars are resistant to chinch bugs. Other insect pests, including webworms, armyworms, grass loopers and mole crickets, can cause damage on St. Augustinegrass. High levels of nitrogen fertilizer encourage insect problems. Refer to the sections on specific insect pests for descriptions and information about their control.

Diseases

Brown patch and gray leaf spot are the two major disease problems of St. Augustinegrass. Brown patch occurs in warm, humid weather and is encouraged by excessive nitrogen. Brown patch is generally most noticeable during spring and fall months. Gray leaf spot occurs during the summer rainy season and is primarily a problem on new growth. Both diseases can be controlled with fungicides. Refer to the chapter on disease problems for additional information.

Nematodes

Several types of nematodes infest St. Augustinegrass lawns. Nematodes cause yellowing and general thinning of older lawns. Refer to the chapter on nematodes or contact your county Cooperative Extension Service for additional information.

Weeds

Weed problems in a lawn indicate that the turf has been weakened by improper management practices or damage from pests. Proper management practices can eliminate most weed problems. If weeds are a persistent problem, herbicides labelled specifically for St. Augustinegrass should be used. Many commercial weed and feed formulations will provide control, but they should not be used every time the lawn is fertilized. Read and follow any pesticide label before use. The section entitled "Weed Control Guide for Florida Lawns" gives specific weed control recommendations.

Other Problems

Many other factors can decrease the quality of a lawn. To ensure a good St. Augustinegrass lawn, refer to other sections of this publication for recommended management practices, and follow label directions when applying fertilizers and pesticides.

Yearly Calendar for St. Augustinegrass Care and Culture

L. B. McCarty and J. L. Cisar

St. Augustinegrass is a fast-growing, warm-season turfgrass used extensively in Florida. It grows well on most well drained soils. For optimum quality, adequate irrigation and fertilization are required. St. Augustinegrass is tolerant to saline irrigation and brackish water, and is the best shade tolerant grass suitable for Florida. Since most St. Augustinegrass cultivars are quite sensitive to freezing temperatures, other turfgrasses may be more appropriate in the northern and panhandle areas of Florida. Also, St. Augustinegrass is coarse (wide) in leaf texture and has poor wear tolerance, which may be undesirable for some purposes.

Cultivars of St. Augustinegrass differ in their resistance to plant pests. Only the cultivars Floralawn and Floratam are tolerant to the southern chinch bug, a common turfgrass insect. Another insect, sod webworm, and the fungal diseases brown patch and gray leaf spot can also cause damage.

As discussed in this section, proper lawn management practices are the best means of avoiding plant pest problems and obtaining high quality turfgrass. If problems continue, contact your local Cooperative Extension Service office for assistance. For further information on available cultivars and establishment practices, refer to lawn establishment and maintenance sections. Local growing conditions and resources available may require growers to slightly deviate from these guidelines.

GENERAL MAINTENANCE

The level of lawn maintenance is dependent on turfgrass quality desired, time, and money available (Table 1). These factors will regulate the amount of fertilizer and pesticides applied each year. Persons requiring minimal maintenance for their lawns should have a low fertility program and apply pesticides on a curative basis only. This consists of two fertilizer applications per year at the rate of 1 pound of nitrogen per 1000 square feet per application (e.g., $6^1/_4$ pounds 16-4-8 = 1 pound nitrogen, $^1/_4$ pound P_2O_5, and $^1/_2$ pound K_2O per 1000 square feet). The first application should follow the onset of spring green-up, and the last should be timed for late summer in north Florida and early fall in south Florida. A high-maintenance lawn in Florida would receive 4 pounds of nitrogen per 1000 square feet per year applied in 1-pound increments during March, May, July, and September. In south Florida, an additional application of fertilizer may be

required in early winter due to the extended growing season and sandy soils. Although nitrogen is the element most commonly applied to turfgrass, other essential elements, plus micronutrients, should be part of a fertilizer maintenance program. For all maintenance levels, a minimum of two treatments of a complete fertilizer such as 16-4-8 or 12-4-8 should be made per year in order to supply the other essential elements of phosphorus and potassium. Complete fertilizers (N-P-K) containing nutrients such as manganese (Mn), iron (Fe), sulfur (S), magnesium (Mg) and boron (B) should also be considered, especially if nutrient deficiencies are expected for the lawn site. Other applications can be just a nitrogen fertilizer source or fertilizer with nitrogen and potassium (e.g., 15-0-14). Additional applications may be required to encourage turf recovery from environmental stress or pest damage or to encourage rapid coverage for a newly sprigged or plugged lawn.

February - May

Mowing

Proper mowing practices are essential for maintaining a quality lawn. Mow the lawn at 3 inches as needed on low-maintenance lawns or $2^1/_2$ inches on higher-maintenance lawns. Mowing at a lower height will encourage shallow rooting, which is less tolerant to drought and nematode pressure. Remove no more than $^1/_3$ the height of the leaf blade with any mowing (e.g., for a lawn to be maintained at 3 inches in height, mow when the turf reaches 4 to $4^1/_2$ inches). Rotary mowers are typically used to maintain home lawns. Over time, impact of the rotary blade with St. Augustinegrass will dull the mower blades. Mowing with dull blades will shred leaf blades, extend the recovery period of the grass, and lower the aesthetic quality of the lawn. Use only a sharp, balanced mower blade and return clippings on the lawn unless the amount is excessive (e.g., clumping occurs). If clippings are excessive, allow them to dry in the sun and then scatter them by removing, blowing, or raking.

Fertilization

Two weeks following spring regrowth (approximately March in north Florida, February in south Florida), apply a complete fertilizer such as 16-4-8 at the rate of 1 pound nitrogen per 1000 square feet (e.g., 6.25 pounds 16-4-8 per 1000 square feet). The numbers refer to percent nitrogen,

Table 1. Suggested yearly maintenance schedule for St. Augustinegrass.

		Month											
		J	F	M	A	M	J	J	A	S	O	N	D
Fertilization													
North Florida[1]	low maintenance	–	–	C[2]	–	–	Fe[3]	–	–	C	–	–	–
	high maintenance	–	–	C	–	N[4]	Fe	N	–	C	–	–	–
South Florida	low maintenance	–	C	Fe	–	N[4]	Fe	–	–	–	C	–	–
	high maintenance	–	C	Fe	–	N[4]	Fe	N	–	C	–	–	N
Weed control	North Florida	–	–	PE[5]	–	PO[6]	–	–	PO	–	–	–	B[7]
	South Florida	–	PE	–	–	PO	–	–	PO	–	–	–	B

Mowing (3-inch height)	Frequency is approximately every 5-14 days for a height of 2-3 inches, depending on season and management practices. Best mower: rotary. Remove no more than ⅓ of the leaf blade height per mowing. Leave clippings unless clumping occurs.
Irrigation (¾ inch water per irrigation)	Irrigate when leaves show signs of drought: blue-gray color, slow footprinting recovery, folded leaf blades. A simple irrigation schedule is to apply ¾ inch of water 2 to 3 times per week in the summer and once every 7-14 days in the winter. Reduce this frequency following rain. Avoid light, frequent (daily) watering and overwatering (point of runoff). Best time of day to water is in early morning.
Disease Control	Primary diseases are brown patch and gray-leaf spot. Brown patch tends to be more troublesome in spring and fall when the soil remains continuously wet and the turf is overfertilized. Gray-leaf spot tends to occur in the summer when the turf is overfertilized and overwatered. Continually check for symptoms and submit suspected disease samples to your local county agent's office.
Insect Control	Greatest damage usually results from chinch bugs and mole crickets. Chinch bug damage is greatest during hot, dry periods when the grass in not actively growing. Check for these by inserting a coffee can into the soil and filling with water. If present, chinch bugs will float to the surface. Check for mole crickets by observing tunnels or by applying 1-2 oz of soap in 2 gallons of water over suspected damaged areas. Mole crickets, if present, will surface within 5 minutes.
Vertical mowing/ dethatching	Using a 3-inch blade spacing, begin in May in north Florida and April in south Florida. Discontinue by August. When completed, remove the debris, mow the lawn, apply 1 lb of nitrogen per 1000 sq ft and irrigate to prevent drying out and fertilizer burn.

[1] The arbitrary dividing line between north and south Florida is a straight east-west line from coast to coast through Orlando.

[2] Apply a complete (C) fertilizer source (e.g., 16-4-8) at a rate of 1 lb of nitrogen per 1000 sq ft (e.g., 6.2 lb 16-4-8 per 1000 sq ft).

[3] Iron (Fe) may be supplied with ferrous sulfate (2 oz in 3-5 gal water per 1000 sq ft) or a chelated iron source.

[4] Apply the equivalent of 1 lb of nitrogen (N) per 1000 sq ft as a slow release form (e.g., IBDU, SCU, urea formaldehyde, milorganite, etc.) to help prevent succulent growth which is more susceptible to chinch bug damage.

[5] Use a preemergence herbicide (PE) such as atrazine, bensulide, oxadiazon, benefin, or pendimethalin for crabgrass, and goosegrass control. Plan to reapply herbicides approximately 2 months later for season-long control.

[6] Use postemergence broadleaf herbicides (PO) such as asulox for crabgrass control or one-half the label rate of 2,4-D, dicamba and/or mecoprop mixtures for broadleaf weed control. Note: **Do not apply** postemergence herbicides when air temperatures exceed 85°F or the grass is under any moisture stress. Objectionable turf injury may result.

[7] If Broadleaf (B) weeds are present, apply atrazine or one-half the label rate of 2,4-D, dicamba and/or mecoprop. (Some degree of turf injury may occur.)

phosphorus (P_2O_5), and potassium (K_2O), respectively, in the bag. A complete fertilizer contains all three major nutrients. For example, a 50-pound bag of 16-4-8 contains 16% nitrogen or 8 pounds total nitrogen. For a 1-pound nitrogen per 1000 square foot rate, this bag will cover 8000 square feet. For higher-maintained lawns, apply 1 pound nitrogen per 1000 square feet again in May. On high pH (>7.0) soils or where high pH water is applied, yellow appearance may be an indication of iron or manganese deficiency. For iron deficiency, spray ferrous sulfate (2 ounces in 3 to 5 gallons of water per 1000 square feet) or a chelated iron source (refer to the label for rates), to temporarily enhance color. Iron applications every 6 weeks will help maintain green color and, unlike nitrogen, will not promote excessive top growth. On high pH soils (>7.0) or where high pH (>7.0) water is applied, manganese deficiency may also become evident. Lower the soil pH by applying 15 pounds elemental sulfur per 1000 square feet prior to grass establishment. Once the grass is established, up to 5 pounds of elemental sulfur may be added per 1000 square feet, if it is immediately irrigated in to prevent burn. Using ammonium nitrate or sulfate as a fertilizer source will also help to temporarily reduce soil pH. Apply manganese as a fertilizer with micronutrients or as straight manganese sulfate ($MnSO_4$) bimonthly at 0.41 pound per 1000 square feet (18 pounds per acre) to relieve deficiency symptoms if present. Submit a soil sample yearly to your local county Cooperative Extension Service office to determine the soil pH, nutrient levels present, and if any deficiencies exist.

Irrigation

Normally, fall through spring is the driest period of the year. Therefore, irrigation is required to replace water lost via evapotranspiration. For water conservation, irrigate to prevent drought stress on an as-needed basis. Irrigate when the turf begins to wilt, turns blue-gray in color, and/or recovery from foot or tire tracks is slow. Apply enough water to rewet the soil rootzone and then wait until the turf shows signs of drought (e.g., wilting) again before the next irrigation (usually every 7 to 14 days in winter, 3 to 4 days in April-May, depending on soil type and maintenance practices). For most Florida soils, no more than $3/4$ inch of water is necessary for each irrigation period to rewet the top 8 to 12 inches of the root zone. To determine the amount of water being applied, place several coffee cans around your irrigation system. Turn on the system for a specific time period. Measure the depth of water in each can, and take an average. The time required to achieve an average of $3/4$ inch depth of water is the time period one should use for each irrigation period. The length of the irrigation period to apply this $3/4$ inch can stay constant year round; only the *frequency* between irrigations should change. Therefore, irrigation programs set by automatic timers do not need to operate on a daily schedule. They need only to operate after the turf begins to show signs of drought and then be programmed to apply an average of $3/4$ inch of water. Overwatering encourages nutrient leaching, increased pest problems, shallow rooting, and, of course, water waste. For further information refer to the section on "How to Calibrate Your Sprinkler System" in this publication.

Weed Control

The best approach to weed control is a healthy, vigorous turf. Proper mowing height, fertilization, and watering must be followed to encourage a competitive lawn grass. If a herbicide is needed, apply preemergence herbicides (i.e., pendimethalin, benefin, bensulide, atrazine, or others) to control crabgrass if it was present in previous years. Timing is critical for successful control. A general rule of thumb for application is Feb. 1 in south Florida, Feb. 15 in central Florida, and March 1 in north Florida. *Note: Preemergence herbicides will not control weeds which are actively growing.* Apply postemergence herbicides (e.g., atrazine) in May as needed for control of summer annual and perennial broadleaf weeds such as knotweed, spurge, lespedeza, etc. To control emerged

summer annual grass weeds such as crabgrass and goosegrass, the herbicide asulam may be used. Do not apply these materials if the turf is under moisture stress or if air temperatures exceed 85°F. Check with your local County Cooperative Extension Office for positive weed identification and latest recommendations.

Insect Control

Chinch bugs are foliar feeding insects which suck plant juices through a needle-like beak, resulting in yellowish to brownish patches in turf. Injured areas are usually first noticed, as the weather begins to warm, along sidewalks adjacent to buildings and in other water stressed areas where the grass is in full sun. Check for chinch bugs by removing the ends of a coffee can, inserting one end through the soil at the margin of suspected damaged areas and fill with water. Chinch bugs will float to the water surface within 5 minutes. In areas where chinch bugs are a serious problem, a single thorough insecticide treatment may offer only temporary control ($1^1/_2$ to 2 months). Therefore, repeat applications may be required. Mole crickets damage turfgrass areas primarily by the tunnels or soft mounds they leave while searching for food. Additional damage may result from small animals digging through the soil profile in search of the mole crickets as food. Check for mole crickets by: 1) examining an area for the tunnels, or 2) applying 2 gallons of water with $1^1/_2$ ounces of detergent soap per 2 square feet in suspected damaged areas. Mole crickets will surface in several minutes.

Check with your local county Cooperative Extension Service office for positive mole cricket identification and latest control recommendations. When applying any pesticide, read and follow all label instructions.

Nematode Control

Population peaks of nematodes typically occur in late April to early May and again in late August to early September. Damage symptoms include thin stand density, less vigorous growth, a weakened root system, slow recovery following rain or irrigation application, and certain weed invasion (e.g., prostrate spurge and Florida pusley). Soil nematode levels can only be positively identified through laboratory procedures. Inquire with your local county Cooperative Extension Service office on proper sample submission to the University of Florida Nematode Assay Laboratory. Encourage deep turfgrass rooting by raising the mowing height, irrigating less frequently but deeper, and providing ample soil potassium and phosphorus.

Thatch Removal

Thatch is the layer of undecomposed leaf blades, stolons, roots and crowns intermingled with soil. Contrary to popular belief, return of mowing clippings do not cause thatch. Excessive thatch develops when the grass is overfertilized, overwatered, and improperly mowed. If thatch layer exceeds 1 inch, remove by vertical mowing in early-spring (e.g., April) south of Orlando and late-spring (e.g., May) north of Orlando. A 3-inch spacing between the dethatching blades is best. *Caution: Vertical mowing may result in damaged turf which will require a period of recuperation. Do not attempt vertical mowing unless the grass is actively growing (April to May). A professional landscaping maintenance service or the local county Cooperative Extension Service office should be consulted before attempting lawn renovation.* Remove the debris by raking, sweeping or vacuuming and follow with a conventional mowing to improve turf appearance. Immediately irrigate to prevent rootzone dehydration. One week following vertical mowing apply 1 pound soluble nitrogen per 1000 square feet (e.g., 3 pounds ammonium nitrate or 5 pounds ammonium sulfate per 1000 square feet) to encourage recovery. This material must be watered in immediately following application to prevent plant burn. Periodic topdressing (adding a uniform layer of soil on top of the grass) with $1/8$ to $1/4$ inch of soil similar to that underlying the turf is the best method to alleviate thatch accumulation; however, the physical labor required limits its practicality for most homeowners. If this is performed, use soil free of weed seeds and nematodes. Do not exceed recommended topdressing rates as this encourages brown patch disease.

Renovation

Replant large bare areas in April-May by broadcasting sprigs (1 bushel per 1000 square feet), planting 2-inch plugs every 12 inches, or by sodding. Keep these areas continuously moist with light, frequent irrigations several times daily until runners develop or when sod is well rooted. Over time, gradually reduce irrigation frequency, but increase irrigation duration to apply $3/4$ inch in order to wet the top 8 to 12 inches of the rootzone. Refer to the section "Establishing Your Florida Lawn".

June - August

Mowing

Mow at 3 inches (as high as possible with a home rotary mower) on low-maintenance lawns or $2^1/_2$ inches on higher-maintained ones. Use only a sharp, balanced mower blade and return clippings on the lawn unless the amount is excessive and clumping occurs. If clippings are excessive, allow them to dry in the sun and scatter them by removing, blowing, or raking.

Fertilization

Fertilize with 1 pound of nitrogen per 1000 square feet (e.g., 1 pound nitrogen = 6.5 pounds 15-0-14 or 6.25 pounds 16-4-8 per 1000 square feet) in early July for higher-maintained areas. A slow release nitrogen source

(e.g., IBDU, milorganite, SCU, urea formaldehyde, poly-coating sources) will extend nitrogen response and discourage rapid flushes of growth or nitrogen loss due to excessive rainfall. Using an iron source during summer is an alternate recommendation to nitrogen to provide desirable dark color without undesirable flush of growth. Using a quick-release nitrogen or water soluble nitrogen source at this time may encourage chinch bugs or disease development. Fertilizers without phosphorus (e.g., 15-0-14, 8-0-24) are acceptable during this time if soil tests indicate moderate to high levels of soil phosphorus. If excessive yellowing occurs, supplemental iron applications may be required.

Refer to the fertilization for February through May section for information on iron application. Check for manganese deficiency as mentioned previously.

Irrigation

Frequent, intense rainfall normally occurs during this period. Therefore, irrigate to prevent drought stress only on an as-needed basis. Apply water ($3/4$ inch) as previously noted, and then wait until the turf shows signs of wilting (blue-gray color or footprinting occurs) before irrigating again.

Weed Control

The best method to control weeds is through a healthy, vigorous turf. Applying any postemergence herbicides during summer may result in objectionable turf injury.

St. Augustinegrass is damaged by certain herbicides (e.g., MSMA, DSMA). Follow label directions and use with caution. Do not apply herbicides unless grass and weeds are actively growing and not suffering from drought stress and air temperatures are below 85°F. See the chapter on weed control for specific recommendations.

Insect Control

Check for chinch bugs by the previously described method. If the turf turns yellow in spots or responds poorly to watering and fertilization, suspect root damage from white grubs. Check for white grubs (root feeders) by cutting three sides of a 1-foot square piece of sod about 2 inches deep with a spade/shovel at the edge of one of the yellow areas in the lawn. Lay back the sod and check for white C-shaped grubs. Apply an insecticide if two or three grubs are found per square foot. Check for additional insects such as armyworms, sod webworms, and mole crickets by mixing 1 to 2 ounces of dishwashing soap in a 2-gallon sprinkling can full of water. Drench a 2 square foot area with this solution. If insects are present, they will surface in several minutes. (Refer to your local County Cooperative Extension Office for the latest control recommendations.) Read and follow all pesticide labels.

Disease Control

Important disease symptoms are usually expressed as circular brown patches one to several feet in diameter or by spots (lesions) yellow, brown or purplish in color on individual leaves (gray leaf spot disease). Many times these result from overirrigation or excessive nitrogen fertilization. Therefore, reduce the amounts of these applied. If damage is extensive, a fungicide application may be necessary. Refer to your local county Cooperative Extension Service office for disease sample submission and the latest fungicide recommendations.

September - November

Mowing

Continue mowing at the specific height and frequency for the desired maintenance level as previously described.

Fertilization

Apply 1 pound of slow release nitrogen per 1000 square feet as a complete fertilizer (e.g., 6.25 pounds 16-4-8 per 1000 square feet) in September for north Florida or in October for south Florida and then discontinue nitrogen application. One month before expected first frost, 1 pound of potassium per 1000 square feet using 1.6 pounds muriate of potash (0-0-60) or 2 pounds of potassium sulfate (0-0-50) may be applied to increase winter hardiness of the grass. Do not apply potassium during hot periods or if the lawn is under moisture stress. Irrigate after application to prevent burn.

Irrigation

Continue irrigating (as needed) to prevent drought stress. Apply amounts previously noted (³/₄ inch) when turf turns blue-gray in color and/or footprinting occurs.

Irrigate following onset of frost (browning of foliage) if needed to prevent winter dehydration in cooler portions of Florida.

Insect Control

Check for white grubs, armyworms, sod webworms, and mole crickets as previously discussed. Contact your local county Cooperative Extension Service office for recommended control measures.

Disease Control

Do not overirrigate, as this encourages disease growth (especially in heavy or poorly drained soils). If disease is suspected, consult your local county Cooperative Extension Service office concerning identification and control recommendations.

December - February

Mowing

Remove lawn debris (rocks, sticks, and leaves) or any unsightly tall weeds or plants. Mow as required in south Florida.

Fertilization

Do not fertilize at this time in north or central Florida. A light fertilization may be desired in south Florida in November or December. If so, apply ¹/₂ pound nitrogen per 1000 square feet (e.g., ¹/₂ pound nitrogen = 3.3 pounds 15-0-4 or 3.1 pounds 16-4-8 per 1000 square feet). Submit soil samples for analysis at least every other year to determine nutrient requirements (contact your local county Cooperative Extension Service office for details). Apply lime or sulfur if suggested, based on soil test, to raise or reduce soil pH, respectively.

Irrigation

In south Florida, irrigate as described previously to avoid moisture stress.

Weed Control

Apply broadleaf herbicides (e.g., atrazine) as necessary for control of chickweed, henbit, clover, pennywort, dandelion or wild garlic/onion. Selected herbicides (e.g., atrazine or simazine) can be applied for control of annual bluegrass (*Poa annua*) and several winter annual broadleaf weeds. A repeat application 3 to 4 weeks after the first may be necessary to achieve satisfactory control. Follow label directions for rates and use with caution.

Miscellaneous

Make plans and arrangements for lawn renovation to be made in spring, if needed. Service your lawn mower and sharpen the blade. Check irrigation system for leaking lines, joints, or damaged heads.

Maintenance of Zoysiagrass Lawns

L. B. McCarty

ESTABLISHMENT

With one exception, zoysiagrasses must be planted vegetatively: sod, plugs, and sprigs. *Zoysia japonica* is the only species for which seed is commercially available. Success with any propagation method is highly dependent on proper soil preparation. All construction debris, large brush, and other undesired vegetation should be removed prior to grading the lawn site. If necessary, lower tree limbs should be removed to allow better sunlight penetration and make soil preparation and mowing easier. Slope the lawn away from the house for drainage purposes. Refer to chapter entitled "Establishment" in this publication for detailed establishment procedures.

Sodding

Planting of zoysiagrasses by sod is a common establishment method and produces an "instant lawn." For best results, good quality, weed-free sod should be used.

Plugging

Plugging is the planting of small square or circular pieces of sod. The plugs are cut from sod and placed into holes of the same size. Because of slow growth, zoysiagrass plugs are usually planted on 6- to 8-inch centers. This means that plugs are planted every 6 inches in a row and rows are spaced 6 inches apart. Even with 6-inch spacing, at least one full season will be required for complete coverage. Plugs should be tamped firmly into the soil. The soil should be kept moist until the grass is well rooted.

Sprigging

Planting zoysiagrasses by sprigs is a laborious, but effective method of establishment. Fresh, vigorous sprigs (runners) having at least two or four nodes (joints) should be planted in rows which are 6 inches apart. Plant the sprigs end-to-end or no more than 6 inches apart in the row, and cover them about 1 to 2 inches deep, leaving a portion of each sprig exposed to light. A roller can be used to press sprigs into the soil. Soil must be kept moist until plants initiate new growth and the lawn is completely covered.

FERTILIZING

To look their best, zoysiagrasses require frequent fertilization. In deep sands, equal to one-half amounts of potassium to nitrogen should be supplied with each fertilization. For minimum maintenance, a complete fertilizer like 16-4-8, 10-10-10 or 6-6-6 can be applied in the spring and fall with one or two additional applications of nitrogen and potassium in the summer. To produce a high-quality, deep green zoysia lawn, follow the fertilization program shown in Table 1.

MOWING

If fertilized as recommended, zoysiagrasses will require frequent mowing (e.g., weekly) during the summer to look their best. *Zoysia japonica* should be mowed every 7 to 10 days at a height of 2 to 3 inches using a rotary mower. Meyer zoysiagrass looks best when cut at 1 to 2 inches

Table 1. Suggested fertilization schedule for zoysiagrass lawns.

Fertility level	Jan	Feb	Mar	Apr	May	June	July	Aug	Sept	Oct	Nov	Dec
North Florida[1]												
High	–	–	C[2]	–	N[3]	–	N	–	C	–	N[4]	–
Low	–	–	C	–	–	N	–	–	C	–	–	–
South Florida[1]												
High	–	C	–	N	–	N	–	N	–	C	–	N[4]
Low	–	C	–	–	N	–	–	N	–	C	–	–

[1] The arbitrary dividing line between north and south Florida is a straight east-west line from coast to coast through Orlando.

[2] Complete fertilizer (C) at 1.0 lb of nitrogen/1000 sq ft.

[3] Water soluble inorganic nitrogen (N) sources such as ammonium nitrate or ammonium suflate applied at 1.0 lb of nitrogen/1000 sq ft. Equal rates of potassium are suggested.

[4] Fertilize only if lawn is overseeded with ryegrass for winter color.

every 10 to 14 days using a reel mower. Emerald and Manilagrass should be cut at ¹/₂ to 1 inch every 10 to 14 days with a reel mower for excellent appearance.

WATERING

Zoysiagrasses require watering especially if parasitized by nematodes, which greatly restrict the root system. During prolonged droughts, it may be necessary to water zoysia every other day.

Irrigation on an as-needed basis is an excellent way to water any grass, provided the proper amount of water is applied when needed; not at a later or more convenient time. When using this approach, water at the first sign of wilt and apply ³/₄ inch water (465 gallons per 1000 square feet) per application.

THATCH CONTROL

Zoysiagrasses typically develop a thick thatch layer several years after establishment. This thatch must be controlled or removed mechanically to maintain a uniform grass appearance. Refer to the section "Thatch and its Control in Florida Lawns" for complete information.

PEST PROBLEMS

Zoysiagrasses are troubled by several insects, diseases and nematodes. Periodic control of one or more of these problems will be necessary to grow a high quality lawn.

Insects

The most serious insect is the hunting billbug. Billbugs destroy and feed on roots and the grass dies in irregular patches. Billbugs may require periodic chemical control. Lawn caterpillars may also damage zoysias.

Nematodes

Probably the most serious pests on zoysiagrasses are nematodes. These soilborne, microscopic worms attack the grass roots, and if not controlled, can ultimately kill the entire lawn.

Diseases

Disease problems of zoysiagrass include dollar spot, brown patch and rust. These are generally suppressed in properly fertilized and watered lawns.

Information on identification and control of pests of zoysiagrasses is located in the chapters of this publication entitled "Weed Control," "Insect Problems," "Disease Problems" and "Nematodes."

Overseeding Florida Lawns for Winter Color

L. B. McCarty

In many parts of Florida, it is not possible to have an attractive, green lawn throughout the winter months due to low temperature exposure. Permanent lawngrasses in upstate Florida (bahiagrass, bermudagrass, centipedegrass, St. Augustinegrass, and zoysiagrass) go dormant in the late fall and winter. These grasses grow very slowly, lose color in the fall, then turn completely brown with the first frost. Brown lawns throughout the winter are unattractive and weeds are easily seen, so a practice called "overseeding" is often used to provide a green winter lawn. Overseeding is the practice of using a temporary grass which is seeded into the permanent lawn to provide winter color (Plate 21). Overseeding is easy to achieve provided the proper steps are followed. They include:

❑ selection of a good grass,

❑ establishment, and

❑ maintenance.

WHICH GRASS TO USE

Several cool season grasses can be used for overseeding, including ryegrass, bluegrass, bentgrass and tall fescue. Bentgrass, bluegrass and fescue are beautiful and because of their fine texture are very compatible with bermudagrass and zoysiagrass. However, due to their maintenance difficulties and costs, they are not generally recommended for the average homeowner. By far the most common temporary grass is ryegrass. Annual, intermediate, and improved (perennial) ryegrasses are popular because of rapid seed germination, fast growth, adaptability, and reasonably low cost. Ryegrass is widely adapted, does well in either sun or shade and tolerates close, frequent mowing. If seeded heavily and mowed closely, ryegrass can provide a very dense and beautiful lawn throughout the winter. By the time the ryegrass dies, the permanent lawngrass should be actively growing again, and will provide color and cover the rest of the growing season. Of course, the ryegrass will have to be reseeded each fall to provide a green wintertime lawn.

RYEGRASS FOR WINTER LAWNS

Timing

Establishment of winter ryegrass is a fairly simple procedure. Seeding time varies from October to early November in north Florida to mid-November and early December in central Florida. It is best to wait until the daytime temperatures are consistently in the low- to mid-70°F range. If the seeds are planted during warmer periods, water stress and diseases will reduce the chance of seedling survival. In frost-free areas of south Florida, it is usually warm enough so the lawn does not go dormant. In this case, overseeding is probably not needed for winter color.

Seedbed Preparation

The two most important steps in overseeding are proper seedbed preparation and proper watering. A seedbed where the overseeded grass contacts the soil is necessary for optimum performance. To prepare the lawn for overseeding, the grass should first be raked thoroughly to remove all debris. Next, mow the lawn closely, catching all clippings, or rake the grass afterwards. The lawn may need to be cut more than once to reduce it to the desired height. If the lawn has excessive thatch, dethatching with a power vertical mower or power rake (these can be rented) is advisable. A heavily thatched lawn tends to result in irregular overseeding patches. Vertical mower blade spacing should be 3 inches for St. Augustine and bahiagrass, 1 to 2 inches for centipedegrass, and 1 inch for bermuda and zoysiagrass. A final raking will remove additional material and loosen the soil somewhat so that the seed can come in contact with the soil.

The next step is seeding. There are no "magic" seeding rates. Rates listed in Table 1 will produce reasonably good color and density. If a heavy thatch layer exists, increase seeding rates 25 to 50%. If available, buy fungicide-treated seed. For best coverage, use a mechanical seeder and sow half the seed as you walk in one direction, and the remaining by walking at right angles to the first. A very uniform stand can be established this way. After seeding, rake the ground with a stiff broom to

Table 1. Overseeding rates for homelawns.

Grass Type	Seeding Rate (lbs/1000 sq ft)
Bentgrass	1
Bluegrass	3
Fescue	7
Ryegrass (annual or common or Italian)	10
Ryegrass (intermediate)	10
Ryegrass (perennial or improved)	10 - 20

ensure the seed gets through the grass and is in contact with the soil.

Watering

Watering is the last, but most important step in establishing the winter lawn. Water should be applied lightly and carefully to the seeded lawn once or twice a day until the seeds have germinated. Watering should continue until seedlings are well established. *Do not overwater* as this will wash seed away and encourage disease development. Once the plants are well established (e.g., mowed several times), water on an as-needed basis to prevent wilting.

MAINTENANCE OF WINTER LAWN

Once the winter lawn is established, it will require the same maintenance as the permanent lawn. This includes mowing, watering, fertilizing, and controlling pests.

Begin mowing when the grass is tall enough to be cut (around 1 to 2 inches). Properly fertilized ryegrass grows very fast, so weekly mowing will probably be required. Do not mow with a dull blade or the seedlings may be torn from the ground or will have a ragged appearance. Water as needed to keep the grass from wilting.

Fertilization is needed to keep the ryegrass growing vigorously and to maintain a deep green color. To help prevent root burn, the first application should follow the second mowing. For the first application, apply $1/2$ pound nitrogen per 1000 square feet using a complete fertilizer such as 16-4-8, 6-6-6 or others. Thereafter, use a nitrogen fertilizer such as ammonium nitrate, ammonium sulfate, IBDU, or others monthly at 0.5 pound nitrogen per 1000 square feet.

Ryegrass is very susceptible to a disease called *Pythium* (damping off, cottony blight). The disease appears to be most severe on overwatered, overfertilized ryegrass, especially during warm, humid (foggy) weather. Using fungicide-treated seed, along with cultural practices such as seeding during the coolest months, proper watering and fertilizing and appropriate fungicide applications, may be necessary to prevent disease. If *Pythium* occurs, a fungicide should be applied immediately because this disease can kill the entire winter lawn in 24 to 48 hours. For chemical disease control recommendations, refer to the chapter on disease problems.

REESTABLISHING PERMANENT GRASS

To maintain good vigor in the permanent lawngrass, do not encourage the winter grass after temperatures warm up in the spring. The permanent lawngrass can be weakened by the highly competitive ryegrass during this overlapping (transition) season of growth.

Ryegrass will normally die out in late spring, but if the weather is cool, and the lawn is watered frequently, it can be very persistent. To discourage the ryegrass, discontinue fertilization in February (south Florida) and March (north Florida). Water as infrequently as possible, but make sure the permanent lawngrass does not suffer excessively. Continue to mow the ryegrass as close as possible each week. These practices tend to weaken the winter grass and facilitate a faster transition back to the permanent lawngrass. Once the permanent lawngrass has resumed growth, begin your regular lawn maintenance program.

How to Calibrate Your Fertilizer Spreader

L. B. McCarty and J. B. Sartain

Fertilizer application is only effective if you ensure uniform coverage (Plate 22). Dry fertilizers can be applied with either a drop (gravity) spreader (Figure 1) or a rotary (centrifugal) spreader (Figure 2).

A drop spreader has the advantage of applying a fairly exact pattern since this is limited to the distance between the wheels. This also allows a "tight" pattern (line) to be cut but requires that each pass meets exactly with the previous one or skips will be noticeable. Wide (> 6 feet) drop spreaders can become cumbersome in the landscape by limiting access around trees and shrubs and getting through gates. The agitator in the bottom of the drop spreader's hopper also may break the coating of some slow-release fertilizers.

The cyclone (also known as rotary or centrifugal) spreader (Plate 23) generally has a wider pattern of distribution compared to a drop spreader and thus can cover a larger area in a short time. The application pattern of the cyclone spreader also gradually diminishes away from the machine, reducing the probability of an application skip. The uneven, wide pattern of the cyclone spreader is initially harder to calibrate and heavier fertilizer particles tend to sling farther away from the machine. However, proper calibration and experience minimize these.

A recent improvement in fertilizer spreader technology is the use of air to apply the material to the turf. This produces a fairly wide pattern (like the cyclone spreader) that is somewhat exact (like the drop spreader) without damaging the granules or slinging heavier particles farther. Wind and rain effects also are reduced using the technology but initial equipment expense and application expertise are higher.

Spreader calibration involves measurement of the fertilizer output as the spreader is operated over a known area. One way to ensure uniform application of material is to divide the material into two equal portions. Use a spreader calibration which will deliver one-half the correct amount of material. Make an application over the entire area, turn the spreader direction ninety degrees (90°) from the initial application, and make a second application. This eliminates skips in the coverage. Accordingly, calibration of the spreader should be based on one-half desired application rates. A flat surface, a method of collecting the material, and a scale for weighing the material is needed for calibration. The following sequence of steps will aid in calibrating a fertilizer spreader.

CALIBRATING A DROP-TYPE (GRAVITY) SPREADER

Follow these steps, in order, to calibrate your drop-type (gravity) spreader (Figure 1).

1. Check the spreader to make certain all the parts are functioning properly.

2. Mark off an area which when multiplied by the width of the spreader will give 100 square feet of area. For example, the length required for a $1\frac{1}{2}$-, 2-, and 3-foot spreader is $66\frac{2}{3}$, 50, and $33\frac{1}{3}$ feet respectively.

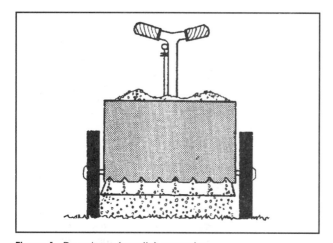

Figure 1. Drop-type (gravity) spreader.

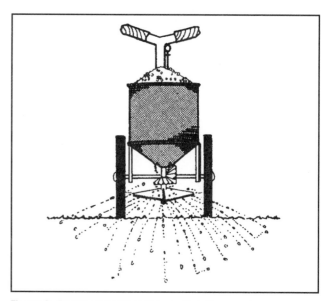

Figure 2. Rotary (centrifugal or cyclone) spreader.

3. Fill the spreader with the material you wish to apply (fertilizer, seed, herbicide, lime, other). Fill the hopper only to the level you will have when the material will actually be applied.

4. Make several trial runs over the area and practice opening the spreader as you cross the starting line and closing it at the finish line. Opening the spreader before it is in motion will result in nonuniform distribution. Walk at a pace which will be used when actually applying the material. Open and close the spreader gradually, not in a fast, jerky motion.

5. The weight of the material applied by the spreader must be determined. It can be swept up from a hard surface or caught on a large piece of paper or plastic. The easiest method is to attach a catch pan (cardboard works nicely) under the spreader openings and catch the material in the catch pan during the test run to determine how much was applied.

6. Begin calibration at the lowest setting and proceed at progressively higher settings (larger openings). The more trials at a given setting, the better will be the average rate of application. Usually three trials at a given setting are enough to obtain a reliable application rate. Weigh the material and record the information on each trial run for future use.

7. One of the calibrated settings will approximate the correct rate of material. *Example:* You want to calibrate a spreader to apply 1 pound of nitrogen per 1000 square feet using a 10-10-10 fertilizer. This calculates to 10 pounds of fertilizer per 1000 square feet since the material is 10% nitrogen (10% x 10 pounds = 1 pound nitrogen). Since the area for calibration trials is only 100 square feet, apply one-tenth of 10 pounds or one pound of fertilizer per 100 square feet. The spreader setting should be 11 for this example if you obtain the following results shown in Table 1 from your calibration trials with your spreader. If the desired application rate was $1/2$ pound of nitrogen (5 pounds of material per 1000 square feet or $1/2$ pound per 100 square feet) a setting of 7 should be used. Careful calibration is suggested for the complete spreader range. Settings are not necessarily linear, therefore, half of a particular application rate

may not necessarily be obtained by using a setting number half the original.

8. The same calibration procedure is used for any material you want to apply. Since the quantity applied depends upon the physical properties of the material, the same settings cannot be used for different materials, even if the ratios are the same. Once the spreader is calibrated and set for the proper rate, any size area can be treated accurately.

CALIBRATING A ROTARY (CENTRIFUGAL) SPREADER

It is important that the "effective" width of application be determined first. Follow these steps, in order, to calibrate your rotary (centrifugal) spreader.

1. Check the spreader to make certain all parts are operating properly.

2. Fill the hopper about half full with the material you plan to apply and run it with the spreader setting about half open (medium setting). Make the application on bare ground or hard surface where the width of surface covered by the material can be measured.

3. Rotary spreaders (Figure 2) do not apply a constant amount of material across the entire width of application. More material is applied toward the center and less at the edges. For this reason, the width of application is accurate for a constant application rate only at about $2/3$ (60 to 70%) of the actual width measured. *Example:* If the application width is 12 feet, only about 8 feet or 4 feet across both sides of the spreader, within the band of application, is receiving approximately the same application rate. The other 2 feet on each edge respectively receive much less material than the center area. Once this "effective" width is determined, calibration is fairly simple.

4. Mark off a test distance which when multiplied by the effective width will give you a 1000 square foot area. For this example, assume that the "effective" width is 10 feet. Then the test strip will be 100 feet long since width times length is 10 x 100 or 1000 square feet. *Note:* This calculation is based on "effective" width of application and not the total width.

5. Determine the amount of material to be applied. *Example:* To apply 1 pound of nitrogen per 1000 square feet using a 16-4-8 fertilizer, 6.25 pounds of material should be applied per 1000 square feet.

6. Fill the hopper with a known weight of fertilizer and adjust the spreader to the lowest setting which will allow the material to flow. Push the spreader down the center of the test area, opening the hopper at the starting line and closing it at the finish. Weigh the

Table 1. Example of calibration trial results from No. 7.

Setting	Output
1	2 ounces
3	3 ounces
5	6 ounces
7	8 ounces
9	10 ounces
11	16 ounces

material left in the spreader and subtract that amount from the starting weight to determine the amount used per 1000 square feet. The beginning weight minus the ending weight tells how much material was applied per 1000 square feet.

7. Repeat the preceeding step at successively greater settings (openings) and record the material applied at each setting.

8. Select the spreader setting which most closely applies the desired rate of material, set the spreader accord-ingly, and use it on any size area. To obtain uniform spread of material, remember to set the spreader at half the desired rate of application and make two passes at 90° to each other. Strive for proper spread overlap during application. *Example:* If the "effec-tive" width is 10 feet, after each pass, move the spreader over 10 feet from the center of the tire tracks. This will give a fairly constant rate of application over the entire area.

Watering Your Florida Lawn

J. L. Cisar, L. B. McCarty and R. J. Black

Water is an essential element in all living plants:

❑ It combines with carbon dioxide and sunlight for photosynthesis.

❑ Food manufactured by photosynthesis and nutrients absorbed by the roots are transported by water to all parts of the plant.

❑ Plant temperatures are maintained by transpiration of water.

❑ Seeds need water to germinate.

❑ Turfgrasses that have been fully watered can withstand more stress and wear.

Lawn irrigation is often necessary in Florida's hot climate. Daily temperatures can be over 90°F (32.2°C) 6 months per year which causes large water losses from soils and plants. Rainfall averages 60 inches per year, but half the amount falls from June through September, often in sporadic large rainstorms. Less rainfall occurs during the winter and spring. Another reason for lawn irrigation is the fact that Florida's sandy soils do not hold much water.

An efficient watering program must include three basic steps:

1. determining when water is needed,

2. determining how much should be applied, and

3. deciding how water is to be applied.

DETERMINING WHEN TO WATER

The most efficient way to water a lawn is to apply water when it begins to show signs of stress from lack of water. The following signs are indications of water need:

❑ bluish-gray areas in the lawn,

❑ footprints or tire tracks that remain in the grass long after being made (Plate 24),

❑ many leaf blades folded in half (Plate 25 and Figure 1), and

❑ soil sample from the rootzone feels dry.

Prolonged dry periods of high temperatures, strong winds, and low relative humidity cause these symptoms. During such times, plants wilt even though water may be in the soil, because they are losing water faster than it is absorbed through root systems. However, watering may be needed.

Watering immediately when the lawn first shows signs of stress is the most economical way to water; delay can cause permanent damage. Add-on devices are available for some sprinkler systems to automatically determine when to water. Electronic moisture sensing units or tensiometers (Figure 2) allow automatic sprinkler systems to operate only when soil water is getting low. These devices eliminate overwatering and have potential for water savings.

AMOUNT OF WATER TO APPLY

The amount of water to apply at any one time varies with the amount of water present in the soil, the water-holding capacity of the soil, and drainage characteristics. *An efficient watering wets only the turfgrass rootzone, does not saturate the soil, and does not allow water to run off.*

Florida soils are typically sandy and hold 1 inch of water in the top 12 inches of soil. If the roots are in the top 12 inches of soil and the soil is dry, then 3/4 to 1 inch of water is required to wet the area thoroughly. This is equivalent to 465 to 620 gallons of water for each 1000 square feet of lawn.

Generally, turfgrasses require no more than 0.3 inches of water per day. Under extreme summer conditions, water use can be as high as 0.4 inches of water per day.

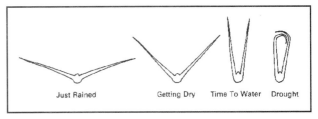

Figure 1. Cross sections of grass leaves showing varying degrees of wilting. Left: leaf fully expanded. Center: leaves wilting and folded. Right: leaf rolled up under drought conditions.

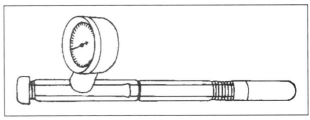

Figure 2. Tensiometer.

During the winter when grasses are not actively growing, water use can be as little as 0.05 inches of water per day.

A simple watering schedule would be to apply 3/4 inch of water when the turfgrasses show water deficiency symptoms as discussed earlier. Once this 3/4 inch of water is applied, do not apply any more until water stress symptoms are again noticeable. Typically, two to three waterings per week in the summer and once every 10 to 14 days in the winter are required. If rainfall occurs, irrigation should be suspended according to the rainfall amount.

MANNER OF APPLYING WATER

Water should never be applied at a rate faster than it can be absorbed by the soil. If the sprinkler applies too much water, it runs off, and is wasted. This seldom happens with small sprinklers unless the lawn is thick or the soil compacted.

Avoid extremes in watering frequency and amount. **Light, frequent watering is inefficient and encourages shallow root systems. Excessive irrigation, which keeps the root system saturated with water, is harmful to the lawn.** Roots need a balance of water and air to function and grow properly.

The time of watering is important. The best time for lawn irrigation is in the early morning hours. Watering during the day can waste water by excessive evaporation and during very hot periods can scald the lawn. Watering in late afternoon or late morning may be detrimental if it extends the time the lawn is naturally wet from dew. Lawn irrigation should be scheduled to avoid peak residential water demand if using municipal water.

LAWN WATERING ECOLOGY

To ensure quality turf, bermudagrass (*Cynodon* spp.) and St. Augustinegrass (*Stenotaphrum secundatum* [Walt.] Kuntze) need supplemental irrigation. Lack of properly timed irrigation can weaken the turfs and predispose them to weed invasion and other pest problems. Centipedegrass (*Eremochloa ophiuroides* [Munro.] Hack.) often needs no supplemental irrigation under shaded conditions where natural rainfall and runoff is often sufficient. However, in sunny open areas, centipedegrass may need supplemental irrigation. Bahiagrass (*Paspalum notatum* Flugge.) is the southern turfgrass that when properly established and maintained requires less irrigation than the others. Improper watering of bahiagrass lawns is detrimental to turf quality and leads to weed problems.

Underwatering of turf is obvious by wilting of the leaves, but overwatering is not so obvious and may show up in numerous ways. Excessive thatch buildup and constantly wet turf are signs of overwatering. The presence of pennywort (*Hydrocotyle umbellata*) and sedges (*Cyperus* spp.) indicate too much water is being applied and turf disease and other pests may invade the lawn under this situation.

An efficient watering program combined with a moderate level of fertilizing and proper mowing height will produce a superior lawn. Not only will your lawn look good, but it will also be able to withstand the stresses it encounters.

INSPECT SPRINKLER SYSTEM FREQUENTLY

❑ Check sprinkler heads for an even spray pattern and direction of spray.

❑ Check for damaged sprinkler heads, replace these if leaking.

❑ Check that valves open and close properly.

❑ Check for proper time on controller if your system has one.

TIPS FOR TURFGRASS

Follow these tips to reduce leaching, thus saving fertilizer. Remember, your objective is to keep water and fertilizer in the root zone of the grass for as long as possible.

❑ Know how much water your system applies over a time period. Simply place coffee cans in a straight line from your sprinkler to the edge of the watering pattern (Plate 26). Turn the water on for 15 minutes and calculate the average depth of water. Multiply this number by four to determine the irrigation rate in inches per hour.

❑ Make sure your sprinkling system applies water uniformly. Don't mix head types or let the reach of two sprinklers overlap excessively.

❑ Apply no more than 3/4 to 1 inch of water per irrigation.

❑ Wait until turf stress symptoms are noticeable before applying 3/4 inch of water. Watch the grass for a bluish-gray color, folded leaf blades, and/or inability to recover from foot or vehicular traffic.

❑ Don't water when rain is forecasted for your area.

❑ Don't be fooled by the word "organic." Some organic fertilizers leach as quickly as inorganic.

❑ Look for the words "slow release" and "insoluble" on the fertilizer labels. Nitrogen in this type of fertilizer will not wash away as quickly.

- ❏ Include potassium (K) in your fertilizer as this element is necessary to increase the turf's drought tolerance.

- ❏ Lime your lawn if your soil is highly acidic (a low pH) to reduce phosphorus solubility.

- ❏ Increase mowing height of lawns; this increased height allows the plant to develop a deep root system.

How to Calibrate Your Sprinkler System

J. L. Cisar and L. B. McCarty

Knowing the amount of water your sprinkler system applies to your lawn is an important step in using water efficiently. Most people irrigate their turf for a given number of minutes without knowing how much water they are really applying. This leads either to giving too little water or to wasted water which runs down sidewalks and streets, or through the rootzone and deep into the ground where turfgrass roots cannot reach it.

Calibrating or determining the rate of water your sprinkler system applies is an easy job. You can use the following steps, in order, if you have an in-ground system or a sprinkler at the end of a hose.

1. Obtain several (5 to 10) coffee cans, tuna fish cans, or other straight-sided containers to catch the irrigation water. Containers which are 3 to 6 inches in diameter work the best.

2. If you have an in-the-ground system, place the containers in one zone at a time. Scatter the cans at random within the zone (Plate 26). Repeat the entire procedure in every zone because there may be differences in the irrigation rates.

- OR -

If you use a hose-end sprinkler to water your turf, place the containers in a straight line from the sprinkler to the edge of the watering pattern. Space the containers evenly.

3. Turn the water on for 15 minutes.

4. Use a ruler to measure the depth of water in each container. *Note:* The more precise the measurement, the better your calibration will be. For most cases, measurements to the nearest $1/8$ inch are adequate.

5. Find the average depth of water collected in the containers (add up the depths and then divide by the number of containers).

6. To determine the irrigation rate in inches per hour, multiply the average depth of water times four.

Now that you know your sprinkler system irrigation rate, you can more efficiently apply water to your turf.

Use Table 1 as a guide for sprinkler times. For example, if the sprinkler system applies water at the rate of 2 inches per hour and you wish to apply $3/4$ inches of water, then you would need to run your sprinklers for about 23 minutes.

Table 1. Time required to apply water for a given irrigation rate.

	Irrigation Rate (Amount of water per hour)			
	0.5 in	1 in	1.5 in	2 in
Amount water to be applied	Minutes to run each zone			
0.25 in	30	15	10	8
0.50 in	60	30	20	15
0.75 in	90	45	30	23
1.00 in	120	60	40	30

To calculate the time of irrigating for rates not listed in Table 1, use Equation 1.

$$\text{Minutes required to run each zone} = \frac{\text{Amount of water to be applied} \times 60}{\text{Your calibrated irrigation rate}} \quad (1)$$

CALIBRATION POINTERS

❑ Try to calibrate the sprinkler system during the same time the system is normally run, so that water pressures are similar.

❑ Low water pressure can significantly reduce the amount and coverage of water applied by a sprinkler system.

❑ Application rates normally should not exceed $3/4$ inch of water per irrigation.

❑ Most time clocks can be adjusted for accurate time settings. Consult your local sprinkler company for details.

❑ If you use a hose-end sprinkler, a mechanical timer and shut-off switch that attaches to the faucet will help make watering more efficient.

❑ Avoid mixing sprinkler head types. Mist heads apply more water than impact heads. Match sprinkler heads for uniform coverage.

❑ For more specific information on turf irrigation, see the section "Watering Your Florida Lawn."

❑ Check the sprinkler system frequently. Replace broken sprinkler heads, clear clogged nozzles, and adjust the direction of spray.

❑ Use water efficiently; do not waste it.

Preparing Your Lawn for Drought

L. B. McCarty and J. L. Cisar

Turfgrasses, like all green plants, require water for growth. It is well known that supplementing inadequate rainfall with irrigation water produces a better-quality lawn. Irrigation also allows the introduction of new grasses that are not adapted to the rainfall pattern of our climate. The quest for better lawns has produced management practices that have intensified to the point that today many lawns will not thrive without supplemental irrigation. In order for a lawn to survive with little or no water, it is necessary to condition the lawn before a drought occurs.

Droughts are periods of no rain during which the growth of plants is affected. Although droughts are usually thought of as long periods of time, such as months or years, Florida can experience drought conditions after only a few days without rain on sandy soils. Normally, supplemental irrigation provides adequate water for lawns between rainfalls.

The impact of drought conditions on lawns could be more severe if the water management districts restrict or eliminate supplemental landscape irrigation. Many lawns would not be able to survive a sudden restriction or elimination of irrigation. That is why it is important to prepare lawns for drought ahead of time.

OBJECTIVE OF DROUGHT CONDITIONING

To condition a lawn successfully, the objective of the program must be clearly understood. The primary objective is to grow a good quality lawn that will survive on little or no supplemental irrigation. A prepared lawn can withstand more stress than a lawn that is not conditioned. A properly prepared lawn will have a deep and extensive root system and leaves that are toughened through proper management practices.

IRRIGATION PRACTICES

Proper irrigation is the first step in conditioning a lawn for drought. Frequent (e.g., daily), light waterings cause shallow root systems that are not good for healthy turf. To develop a deep root system, lawns should only be watered when the first signs of wilt occur. Spots in the lawn that turn bluish-gray, footprints that remain in the grass long after being made, and many leaf blades folded

in half length-wise are all indications that the lawn needs water. Apply only enough water to wet the soil in the rootzone. For Florida's sandy soils, $3/4$ inch of water is sufficient. The next irrigation should be withheld until signs of wilt occur again. This technique works regardless of turfgrass species, soil type, season, or other environmental conditions.

It may take up to 6 weeks to condition a turf to survive several days or more without wilting between irrigations or rainfalls. During this time the root system is developing and growing deeper into the soil. Stolons (above ground stems) that are not rooted will tend to die and be mowed off. In time, the lawn will establish a more uniform appearance with less thatch and better rooted plants.

MOWING PRACTICES

Proper mowing practices are essential for good quality and drought-prepared turf. Every time a lawn is mowed, there is stress on the metabolism of the grass plant, which reduces root growth. Mowing frequency and cutting height need to be carefully considered for a healthy lawn.

Use the highest setting on the mower for conditioning the turf, because a low cutting height will needlessly stress the turf. By increasing the grass leaf area, more photosynthesis can occur. This results in more carbohydrates for plant growth, especially root growth. The higher the cut of a lawn, the deeper and more extensive the root system will be. Although transpiration (water loss through leaves) will be slightly greater with higher mown turf, the expanded root system proves more advantageous.

Mowing should be done often enough to minimize the shock of cutting. Never mow off more than one-third the height of the lawn at any one time. If the lawn is allowed to grow to 4 inches, do not mow it lower than 3 inches. Adjust the frequency of mowing to the growth of the turf. In the summer, it may be necessary to mow several times a week, but in the winter, once a month may be enough.

Keeping the mower blades sharp and properly balanced is also an important part of the mowing practices. A leaf cut by a sharp blade will recover quicker and lose less water than a leaf blade shredded by a dull mower blade.

FERTILIZATION PRACTICES

Fertilization practices can enhance drought tolerance of turfgrasses if properly done. Understanding plant responses to nitrogen and potassium fertilization is helpful in developing a beneficial program as well as providing a well-balanced nutritional program.

All of the drought conditioning accomplished by proper irrigation and mowing practices can be eliminated by excessive nitrogen fertilization. Shoot growth is enhanced and root growth reduced by excessive nitrogen. Leaf blades become more lush as nitrogen fertilization increases.

Drought conditioning can only be accomplished by applying just enough nitrogen to obtain a small but continuous amount of growth. Lawns should never be fertilized to deepen the green color, since southern turfgrasses, except bermudagrass, are often more yellow-green.

Potassium fertilization can help turfgrasses increase their tolerance to stress. Potassium promotes increased root growth and thicker cell walls. Drought tolerance is improved by applying potassium. Turfgrasses require potassium in nearly the same amount as nitrogen, especially in sandy soils where both can readily leach out.

Other macro and micronutrients, as well as the soil pH, should be kept at recommended levels for optimal growth. Supplemental iron application often provides desirable green turf without succulent growth. Iron applications also have been shown to increase the rooting of turfgrass. An occasional soil test is helpful in monitoring nutrient levels.

PEST CONTROL

Pest control on lawns should be done with a great deal of care because pesticides can add the extra stress of phytotoxicity (chemical damage to plants). Once a pest problem has been diagnosed, it should be promptly treated following recommendations from your Cooperative Extension office. Spot treatment of a pest problem is usually as effective as treating the whole lawn. Be particularly watchful for insects and diseases that attack turfgrass root systems.

TURFGRASS SPECIES

Drought tolerance varies greatly with turfgrass species and cultivars. Bermudagrass, zoysiagrass and bahiagrass have the best drought tolerance of the southern turfgrasses, followed (in descending order) by St. Augustinegrass, centipedegrass and carpetgrass. Under severe drought conditions with no supplemental irrigation, turfgrasses go dormant, growth ceases, and leaves die. After the soil moisture becomes adequate, new growth will start from buds on rhizomes (underground stems) or stolons. Bermudagrass, zoysiagrass, and bahiagrass can usually recover from drought-induced dormancy because they have rhizomes that are protected from desiccation (drying out) in the soil. St. Augustinegrass, centipedegrass and carpetgrass do not survive droughts as well because they have stolons which lie exposed on top of the soil.

Choosing a grass to plant in Florida for drought tolerance is difficult, because each species has particular pest problems. Bermudagrass and zoysiagrass tend to have trouble with nematodes, although both make an exceptional turf when nematodes are controlled. Bahiagrass has mole cricket problems, but they are easier to control than nematodes. If a person can accept an open growth habit and not overmanage the turf, then bahiagrass is the best selection. Bahiagrass is adapted to a wide range of soils and can survive under minimum management.

ALTERNATIVES TO TURFGRASS

People often attempt to grow turf where it will not survive without extraordinary care. High-quality turf cannot be achieved without supplemental irrigation, although a lower-quality turf may persist. In landscapes where poor-quality turf may detract from the design, alternatives to turf should be considered. Mulched beds or groundcovers may be more suitable. Plant materials that do not require supplemental irrigation should be chosen. Consult your county Cooperative Extension office for the plants that grow best in your area.

Mowing Your Florida Lawn

L. B. McCarty and J. L. Cisar

Mowing is one of the primary maintenance practices essential for a good quality lawn. Mowing is the process which creates a lawn rather than a pasture or a meadow. A smooth, dense turf surface is attained from frequent and regular cutting of grass leaf blades at a constant height.

The metabolism and appearance of grass are changed by mowing. Immediately after mowing, plant respiration increases and root growth temporarily ceases.

The two main components of mowing are cutting height and frequency. Both of these factors are dependent on the turfgrass species and level of lawn maintenance. Several other practices involving the use of mowers are also important in creating a quality lawn.

HEIGHT OF MOWING

The optimum cutting height is determined by the turfgrass growth habit and leaf width. A grass that spreads horizontally can usually be mowed shorter than an upright-growing, bunch-type grass. Grasses with narrow blades can generally be mowed closer than grasses with wide blades. Bermudagrass is mowed the shortest of the Florida turfgrasses because of its numerous narrow leaf blades and low growth habit. On the other hand, bahiagrass needs to be mowed the highest of the Florida turfgrasses to produce a good quality lawn because of its open, upright growth habit.

Proper mowing height is important in creating a good quality lawn because it encourages a dense stand of grass plants (Plate 27). A dense turf keeps out weeds through competition for sunlight and nutrients. A weak thin turf allows weed seeds to germinate and grow.

Turfgrasses can be mowed at heights other than their optimum if the management practices are properly altered. Cutting turf below the optimum height requires production of enough leaf blades to keep a dense green lawn. To accomplish this, more fertilizer and water need to be applied to stimulate growth. The disadvantages of low mowing heights are increased pest problems and faster than normal thatch accumulation. Cutting heights can get too low, and turf quality will be reduced because of severe defoliation. *Mowing turf too low probably ruins more lawns than any other turf management practice.*

Cutting turf at the high end of the recommended height range requires a reduction in the level of management (Table 1). Less water and fertilizer are required since

Table 1. Suggested mowing practices for Florida lawns.

Turfgrass Species Name	Optimal Height (inches)	Frequency (days)	Best Mower Type
Bahiagrass	3.0 - 4.0	7 - 17	Rotary/flail
Bermudagrass	0.5 - 1.5	3 - 5	Reel
Carpetgrass	1.5 - 2.0	10 - 14	Rotary
Centipedegrass	1.5 - 2.0	10 - 14	Rotary
St. Augustinegrass	2.5 - 4.0	7 - 14	Rotary
Zoysiagrass	1.0 - 2.0	10 - 14	Reel

there are more than enough grass blades to give a good appearance. Also, by reducing the amount of water applied, plants will develop more extensive root systems and thatch accumulation will be reduced. Other advantages of a high cutting height include better pest tolerance and better survival from environmental stress, such as drought.

FREQUENCY OF MOWING

The growth rate of the lawn determines how frequently it needs to be mowed. The growth rate is influenced by weather conditions, level of management, and grass species. The slowest growth rates occur in the winter or under low fertility and irrigation, while the fastest growth rates occur in the summer or under high fertility and watering practices. Bermudagrass is a rapidly growing grass compared to zoysiagrass. Low-maintenance grasses like bahiagrass and centipedegrass are frequently mowed just to remove seedheads rather than to cut leaf blades.

The best recommendation on mowing frequency is to determine the need for mowing based on growth of the turf. Mow often enough so that no more than one-third the blade height is removed per mowing. For example, if your St. Augustinegrass lawn is mowed at a height of 3 inches it should be mowed when it grows to a height of 4 to $4^1/_2$ inches. The grass plant metabolism is stressed every time the lawn is mowed, but the stress can be minimized by removing only one-third of the leaf blade at each mowing. It is important to always leave as much leaf surface as possible for photosynthesis to provide food for regrowth.

CLIPPINGS REMOVAL

Leaf clippings result from mowing and a common problem is what to do with them. Contrary to popular belief, clippings do not contribute to the thatch layer; stems, rhizomes and stolons produce thatch. On most lawns, clippings should be returned to help recycle nutrients to our sandy soils. If the lawn is mowed frequently enough, clippings cause few problems. Problems arise when turf is mowed infrequently and excess clippings (e.g., clumping) result (Plate 28).

MOWING EQUIPMENT

Lawn mowers are available in a wide variety of sizes and styles with numerous features. The two basic types are the reel mower and the rotary mower. More recently, mulching, flail, and string mowers have been introduced. Most mowers can be obtained as push or self-propelled models. Front, side, and rear clipping discharge models are available. The choice of mower often depends on personal preference. Points to consider when purchasing a mower are the size of the lawn, turfgrass species, and level of lawn maintenance.

Rotary mowers are the most popular because of their low cost, easy maneuverability, and simple maintenance (Plate 29). A large motor is required to horizontally turn the blade. The grass blade is cut on impact with the mower blade. Rotary mowers can pose a safety problem if improperly used. Most rotary mowers cannot mow lower than 1 inch and are best used for higher mowing heights. The blade needs to be frequently sharpened and balanced for the best possible cut.

A modification of rotary mowers is mulching mowers. These are designed to cut leaf blades into very small pieces which are able to fall into the turf rather than remain on top of the grass. Being so small, these pieces can decompose quicker than blades cut to traditional size. The mower blades are designed to create a mild vacuum in the mower deck until the leaf blades are cut into these small pieces. Mulching mowers do not have the traditional discharge chute as do most rotary mowers (Plate 32). Advantages and disadvantages of mulching mowers are listed in Table 2.

Reel mowers are for highly maintained turf where appearance is important (Plate 30). Reel mowers cut with a scissor-like action to produce a very clean, even cut.

They are used at cutting heights of 2 inches or less. The number of blades needed to produce a smooth, uniform cut will depend on the mowing height. Generally, as the height is lowered, the greater number of blades needed on the reel (Table 3). Sharpening reel mowers is difficult and is best left to a professional mower repair service.

Table 2. Advantages and disadvantages of mulching mowers.

Advantages
1. Clippings are returned to the turf; reduces yard waste and recycles nutrients to the turf.
2. Mulching avoids contributing to land-fill overuse and eliminates clipping collection and disposal costs.

Disadvantages
1. Becomes ineffective on wet or tall turf.
2. Blades must be kept sharp.
3. Current models are small and require higher horsepower.

Table 3. The number of blades needed on a reel mower for various cutting heights.

Cutting height	Number of blades
> 1 in	5
$1/2$ - 1 in	6
$1/4$ - $1/2$ in	7 - 9
< $1/4$ in	11 - 13

Flail mowers have numerous, loose-hanging small knives which are held out by centrifugal force as the shaft rotates at high speeds. The blades sever grass by impact. Flail mowers are used for low maintenance, utility sites that are cut infrequently. Mowing quality is inferior compared to a reel or rotary mower and the time it takes to sharpen the many small blades limits flail mower use.

String mowers are similar to rotary mowers, but the blade has been replaced with a monofilament line. This is a definite safety feature when operating the mower in some locations. A high-speed motor is needed in these mowers to spin the line fast enough for a clean cut. String mowers are most often used for trimming and hard-to-mow areas.

GOOD MOWING PRACTICES

Follow these procedures and precautions for safe, good mowing:

❑ Pick up all stones, sticks and other debris before mowing to avoid damaging the mower or injuring someone with flying objects.

❑ Never mow wet turf with a rotary mower because clippings can clog the machine. Mow only when the turf is dry.

❑ Sharpen the mower blade frequently enough to prevent a ragged appearance to the turf (Plate 31a and b).

❑ Mow in a different direction every time the lawn is cut. This helps prevent wear patterns, reduces the grain (grass laying over in the same direction), and reduces the possibility of scalping (Plate 33).

❑ Do not remove clippings. If clumping occurs, distribute these by remowing or by lightly raking.

❑ Check your mower every time it is used.

❑ Follow manufacturer's recommendations for service and adjustments.

❑ Adjust cutting height by setting the mower on a driveway or sidewalk and using a ruler to measure the distance between the ground and the blade.

❑ Never fill a hot mower with gasoline.

❑ Always wear heavy leather shoes when mowing the lawn.

❑ Wash mower decks after use to reduce rusting and weed seed movement.

Thatch and Its Control in Florida Lawns

L. B. McCarty and J. L. Cisar

Thatch is defined as an intermingled layer of dead and living shoots, stems, and roots that develops between the zone of green vegetation and the soil surface (Plate 34). Thatch consists of a loosely interwoven collection of plant matter that imparts a sponginess to the turf (Figure 1). There is a gradual decrease in organic matter size from the top of the thatch layer to the bottom of the mat. Mat is very fine, dense, peat-like, and not very compressible. When excessive (1 inch or more), thatch causes serious problems in Florida lawns.

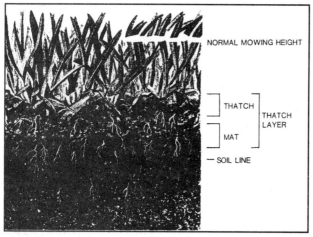

Figure 1. Cross section of St. Augustinegrass showing thatch layer.

WHY IS THATCH A PROBLEM?

Thatch accumulations are undesirable for a variety of reasons.

❑ *Thatch can restrict water and air movement into the soil.* Dry thatch tends to repel water rather than allow infiltration, and wet thatch enhances disease problems. If your lawn has dry spots that are difficult to rewet (unless you almost flood the areas), these are probably dry thatch spots.

❑ *Thick thatch makes mowing very difficult.* As thatch builds up, mowing height actually increases above the soil line, and the turf becomes very spongy, allowing the mower to sink into the turf and scalp the lawn. This results in an uneven appearance and often a mottled brown and green surface.

❑ *Thatch provides an ideal habitat for insects and disease.* Thatch accumulation is associated with an increased incidence of brown patch, dollar spot, and leaf spot diseases as well as sod webworm insects.

❑ *A thatchy condition elevates the growing points (crowns), runners (rhizomes and stolons) and roots above the soil surface.* As a result, the lawn is prone to winter injury because elevated plant parts are exposed to greater extremes in temperature. Winter kill of lawns is often associated with thick thatch layers. Centipedegrass is especially sensitive to winter kill from their stolons being elevated and more prone to cold temperatures in thatchy lawns. Heavily thatched lawns also brown-off quickly (go dormant) following the first exposure to cold weather, and green-up more slowly in spring.

❑ *Thatch can interrupt and restrict the downward movement of pesticides and fertilizers into soil.* This reduces the effectiveness of these materials, making pest control difficult and producing a nonuniform, erratic response to fertilization.

CAUSES OF THATCH BUILDUP

Thatch is basically a residue problem that occurs in most turfgrasses. Thatch buildup has been attributed to numerous factors. Excessive plant growth (when vegetative production exceeds decay) results in the accumulation of thatch. Grasses depend upon constant regeneration for survival, and new growth of creeping grasses covers the old, causing residue accumulation.

St. Augustinegrass, hybrid bermudagrass and zoysiagrass may have excessive thatch accumulation; centipedegrass and bahiagrass also form thatch, but at a slower rate.

Improper management practices can also result in thatch accumulation. Overfertilizing, overwatering and infrequent mowing are the biggest contributors to a thatch problem.

In addition, failure to keep the soil environment favorable for bacterial and fungal growth by pH control, adequate irrigation, and aeration decreases the rate of decomposition of thatch residues, because these organisms are responsible for decay of organic matter.

Failure to remove clippings after mowing has been cited as a cause of thatch buildup, but research findings do not support this concept. If properly mowed, leaf clippings decompose readily and *do not* cause thatch.

THATCH CONTROL

Effective control of thatch requires a combination of several management practices. These include reducing the buildup rate by reducing plant growth and increasing microbial decomposition, and by periodic physical removal by vertical mowing.

Cultural Practices

Fertilizer should be applied as necessary to maintain reasonable growth and density. This will minimize weed invasion. Excessive succulent growth not only increases thatch, but also often makes the lawn more susceptible to pests.

A soil pH of 7.0 is ideal for maximum microbial activity and decomposition. Liming of acid soils may help increase decomposition of thatch residues and thus retard buildup. Proper watering can also aid thatch decomposition. Maximum decomposition occurs if the soil is at optimum moisture, not too wet or too dry.

Mowing practices can help control thatch buildup. Lawns should always be mowed at the recommended height and frequency. Thatch seldom increases if no more than $1/4$ to $1/3$ of the leaf blade is removed at each mowing.

Cultivation and Soil Topdressing

Periodic cultivation by coring (aerification) and soil topdressing (application of soil to the turf surface) are standard maintenance procedures for control of thatch on highly managed turf areas. Mechanical cultivation removes small plugs of thatch and soil, thus leaving small holes in the soil that allow penetration by air, water, fertilizers, and pesticides (Plate 35). It also hastens decomposition by providing a more favorable environment for microbial activity. *Coring does not remove substantial amounts of thatch but does provide a more favorable environment for microbial activity.*

Topdressing increases decomposition by bringing soil microbes and moisture into contact with the thatch (Plate 36). Frequent, light soil topdressings have been repeatedly shown to be the most effective and consistent method to reduce thatch. Thick applications of topdressing or sand are not recommended and will only compound the problem by causing a layering effect and possibly increasing disease incidence. This results in restricted water and air movement, and encourages shallow root systems. Topdressing materials should be weed and nematode free soil (sterilized is ideal) of the same type on which the turf is growing.

Topdressing should begin in early spring when temperatures are conducive for turf growth. Light, frequent topdressing provide quicker results compared to infrequent, heavier ones. Topdressing rates (Table 1) should not exceed $1/2$-inch per application with lighter rates (e.g., $1/8$ to $1/4$ inch) more desirable. Topdressing should be repeated until the thatch layer is reduced or cool temperatures slow or stop turf growth.

Table 1. Approximate soil volumes needed to topdress 5000 square feet to various depths.

Depth (inches)	Soil Volume (cu yds/5000 sq ft)
$1/32$ (0.03)	$1/2$
$1/6$ (0.06)	1
$1/8$ (0.13)	2
$1/4$ (0.25)	4
$1/2$ (0.50)	8

MECHANICAL THATCH REMOVAL

Scalping

Close mowing or scalping is a procedure where the turf is mowed to a much shorter height than normal in a non-recommended attempt to remove thatch (Plate 37). However, scalping *is not a substitute for vertical mowing.*

Depending upon which turfgrass you have, scalping height will vary. Rhizomatous grasses like bermudagrass and zoysiagrass may be scalped to the point of removing most of the green vegetation without killing the turf. Centipedegrass and St. Augustinegrass spread by means of above-ground runners called stolons. Removing these may kill the turf by removing all of the stem tissue. Scalping is not recommended for bahiagrass, centipedegrass or St. Augustinegrass due to the potential of turf damage.

Vertical Mowing

The most common method of mechanical thatch removal is the use of a heavy-duty vertical mower. This specialized piece of equipment has evenly spaced, knife-like blades, revolving perpendicularly to the turf, that slice into the thatch to mechanically remove it (Figure 2). This removes both thatch and mat, and simultaneously cultivates the soil and topdresses the turf (Plate 38).

It is very important to use proper blade spacing when vertically mowing different turfgrasses. Use a blade spacing of 1 to 2 inches for bermudagrass and zoysiagrass, 2 to 3 inches for centipedegrass, and 3 inches for bahiagrass and St. Augustinegrass. Because of their underground rhizomes, zoysiagrass, bermudagrass, and bahiagrass may be vertically mowed down to soil level in several directions without killing the lawn (Plate 39). If all of the

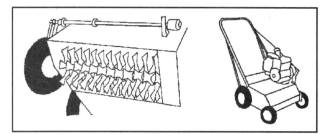

Figure 2. Vertical mower.

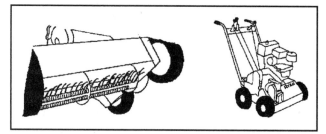

Figure 3. Power rake.

aboveground stolons are removed from centipedegrass and St. Augustinegrass, these turfgrasses may die. If thatch accumulation exceeds 2 to 3 inches, lawns should be vertically mowed carefully more than once, but the lawns should be allowed to fully recover between mowings.

Vertical mowing is an effective means of removing thatch, but if not done properly the grass can be so severely damaged that it may not survive. Experience with the method and equipment, and knowledge of the type of grass being renovated are essential. In many cases it may be advantageous to have a reputable commercial lawn maintenance company remove thatch.

Thatch removal should be considered necessary when thatch thickness exceeds 1 inch. Frequency of that removal will vary, depending on intensity of management.

The best time to vertically mow grasses south of Orlando is March through August; for grasses north of Orlando, the best time is April through July. Vertical mowing at these times ensures quick recovery since warm-season grasses grow rapidly during these periods.

After dethatching, cleanup is necessary. Thatch removed from an average sized lawn may fill several pickup trucks. This debris must be raked, swept or vacuumed, and removed from the lawn. Following cleanup, the lawn should be conventionally mowed closely to remove further debris. The lawn should then be thoroughly watered (e.g., $^3/_4$ inch of water) to prevent drying of exposed roots. Approximately one week following dethatching, nitrogen fertilizer should be applied to encourage turf recovery. Apply 1 pound of actual nitrogen per 1000 square feet in a quick-release soluble form (e.g., ammonium nitrate or ammonium sulfate). Be sure to irrigate after nitrogen application to minimize turf burn.

If the preceding steps are followed, excessive thatch can be physically removed. Such renovation greatly stresses the lawn. Special care will be needed until the grass completely recovers.

Power Raking

This specialized machine uses evenly spaced, flexible, spring steel tines that revolve at high speed to strip through turf and loosen debris for subsequent removal (Figure 3). The machine and procedures are often confused with vertical mowing. Power raking does not involve a cutting action, as does vertical mowing. Therefore, it is not a substitute for vertical mowing and thatch removal, but is used most often to remove a mat layer.

SUMMARY

The following steps should be followed to control thatch formation.

❑ Mow at recommended height and frequency.

❑ Avoid indiscriminate use of fertilizer. Use minimal amounts of nitrogen, and soil test for phosphorus and potassium levels.

❑ Maintain a soil environment conducive to rapid decomposition. This includes adequate aeration, irrigation, and soil pH control.

❑ Core cultivation (aerification) can help control thatch formation and soil layering.

❑ Topdressing with sand provides the best biological control of thatch. Proper timing and rates are necessary to provide the best thatch control with least chance of disease occurence.

❑ Use vertical mowers if mechanical removal of thatch becomes necessary. Follow this with irrigation.

Selecting a Lawn Maintenance Service

L. B. McCarty

Maintaining an attractive lawn requires attention to every aspect of turfgrass culture. Maintaining a lawn in Florida is a constant chore. Many people forego turf maintenance themselves and hire a lawn maintenance service. Selecting a lawn maintenance service best suited for individual needs is not an easy task, but this publication should provide some suggestions to help in making a good choice.

TYPES OF SERVICES

There are three types of basic services available; partial lawn care, total lawn care, and total landscape maintenance. The cost of a service and ability of the client to perform a portion of the landscape care are determining factors in the selection of a company. Naturally, the more services a company provides the more it will cost, but there are some common denominators that can be used in making the selection.

Partial Lawn Care

This is the type of lawn care used by many homeowners. Generally, these firms apply only chemicals to the lawn, mainly insecticides and fertilizers. The homeowner is responsible for mowing, irrigating and other cultural practices. The success of having a partial lawn care service typically depends on the homeowner performing proper routine turf maintenance.

The best way to judge the service is by how much and how often fertilizers are applied. Fertilizer should be applied at rates similar to the IFAS turf recommendations. Most good quality lawns can be maintained by three to four fertilizations per year. Low-maintenance lawns should have at least a spring and a fall fertilizer application.

Instead of routine pesticide application, lawn service companies should monitor lawns and apply pesticides only when pests are present. Many areas of Florida have chinch bugs that have developed resistance to organophosphate insecticides and using these materials will not control chinch bugs, no matter how often they are sprayed. Firms should be able to identify the target pest they are spraying.

Selecting a partial lawn care company is largely a matter of checking with friends and neighbors to find out the performance of lawn care companies in your area. The firm should give some guarantee of results and provide liability for its actions. Check to make sure the firm has both a business license and a pesticide business license (Florida Statute 482).

Total Lawn Care

Companies that provide total lawn care are often hired by condominiums, businesses, and some homeowners to manage turf. Usually these firms mow, fertilize, trim, and apply pesticides. Irrigation system operations and maintenance may be part of their service. The extent of the services a company provides is based on a written contract. The quality of turf produced is totally the firm's responsibility.

Selection of a total lawn care company should be made on the basis of bids on maintenance specifications provided by the client. Turf management practices should closely follow those recommended by IFAS. Information on writing specifications is contained further in the next section. Firms should provide a reference list of past and current jobs and the client should investigate the performance of the company under consideration.

Total Landscape Maintenance

Complete care of all the landscape is provided by some companies. Clients who utilize these services are interested in more complete care than is provided by total lawn care companies. Usually these clients have no provisions within their organizations to provide any portion of the landscape management. A landscape maintenance company's services include lawn care, maintenance of trees, shrubs, annual flowers, and other landscape plantings. These firms are totally responsible for the appearance and upkeep of the landscape. Selection of a landscape maintenance service company should be made similarly to selecting a total lawn care company, with bids and written contracts.

SELECTION CONSIDERATIONS

When selecting a turf maintenance company, consider the following:

❑ *Ask for consultation which will include a survey of the landscape by the lawn applicator, agronomist or horticulturist. A description of services and treatments should be included and the pricing structure determined.*

❑ *Make certain the program will meet local needs for fertility, mowing and pest control.* IFAS recommendations should be closely followed for maintenance practices. Ask your county Cooperative Extension Service agent or refer to the other sections in this handbook for specific maintenance recommendations.

❑ *Lawn maintenance firms should have capable personnel that can promptly and courteously answer your questions.* Ask the contact person how much training and experience they have with Florida turfgrasses. Some companies have been known to initiate business and hire people with no previous experience or educational background in lawn care, pesticide application, agronomy or horticulture. Many people that have relocated from cool-season turfgrass areas are not familiar with Florida's warm-season turfgrasses and their maintenance and pest problems. It takes years of training for an individual to correctly identify turfgrass and weed species, insect and disease problems, and to thoroughly understand turfgrass cultural practices.

❑ *Ask if all personnel are licensed for pesticide application.* This is a critical point since many of these materials can be hazardous to humans, pets, and nontarget landscape plants, if improperly applied. The correct pesticide applied at the correct rate and for a specific pest problem is essential for proper maintenance practices.

❑ *As with all commercial businesses, some lawn service companies are better than others.* Find out the reputations of specific companies within your community. Some have better maintenance programs than others, and more satisfied customers than others. Ask them for references you may contact to verify results.

CONTRACTS AND COSTS

Contracts may be written or verbal, on a yearly or monthly basis, very detailed or very sketchy. Try to be aware of the pricing system and included services. Look at the cost of the total program and compare pricing for fertilization, pest control, and cultural practices like mowing (if included) or cultivation (vertical mowing and aerification for dethatching).

Have the salesman or applicator explain pesticide application to you. More is not always best. For example, increasing the number of insecticide applications and increasing the insecticide rate may not give better insect control.

Be wary of those companies whose service provides preventative controls for all pests on a year-round basis. Heavy pesticide applications may only kill predators which help keep disease organisms and damaging insects in check.

Finally, be careful of oversale. Weed-free, trouble-free lawns can be maintained, but not as easily as is sometimes portrayed. Florida's climate and soil conditions require keen attention to cultural details. Find out if you can expect service within a reasonable time if problems arise once the contract begins.

SUMMARY

Lawn maintenance companies help to provide a high quality turf. But keep in mind, that a partial lawn maintenance program is no better than the care given outside the maintenance contract. If not mowed and irrigated correctly, proper fertilization and pest control will not produce optimum turf quality.

Considerations for Developing a Lawn and Landscape Maintenance Contract

S. P. Brown and M. J. Holsinger

The following sample contract includes landscape maintenance practices which are in accordance with University of Florida recommendations. These recommendations are based on research and objective-based information specific to Florida and reflect the philosophy of Environmental Landscape Management (ELM). The ELM concept integrates environmental concerns into landscape maintenance. Water and energy conservation, fertilizer, and pesticide management and the reduction and reuse of plant clippings are important components.

The sample contract suggests additional topics which should be considered when creating a contract or reviewing one. This sample was developed as an educational resource for lawn and landscape professionals and users of their services. *However, final decisions on what to incorporate in a lawn and landscape contract must be made by individual professionals and their clients.*

This publication is distributed with the understanding that the authors are not engaged in rendering legal advice or opinion, and that the information contained herein is not to be regarded or relied upon, as a substitute for professional legal service. If legal advice or opinion is required, the services of an attorney should be sought.

ADDITIONAL INFORMATION

Table 1 lists mowing height recommendations and Table 2 lists fertilizer recommendations for various types of grasses and are provided for informational purposes. These are recommendations of the Cooperative Extension Service, University of Florida, Institute of Food and Agricultural Sciences as of 1997.

Table 1. Mowing Height Recommendations: The heights listed are the suggested lengths of the grass blade after mowing. The depth of thatch (if it exists) should not be included in this measurement.

Type turfgrass	Mowing Height
Bahiagrass and St. Augustinegrass varieties (Raleigh, Floratam, Floralawn, Bitterblue, Floratine, FX 10)	3.0 - 4.0"
Semi-dwarf St. Augustine varieties (Seville, Del Mar, Jade)	1.5 - 2.0"
Bermudagrass (Hybrids)	.75 - 1.5"
Bermudagrass (Common)	1.5"
Centipedegrass	1.5 - 2.0"
Zoysiagrass	1.0 - 2.0"

Table 2. Fertilizing Schedules for Various Turfgrasses Grown Under Low Maintenance: Fertilizers will be applied at a rate of 1 lb of nitrogen per 1000 sq ft. This is calculated by dividing the percent nitrogen into 100. (Example: If a 16-4-8 fertilizer is used, then 16 is divided into 100 = 6+ pounds of 16-4-8 will be spread over 1000 sq ft of lawn area).
Option: Consider splitting applications of nitrogen fertilizers into two applications 4 to 6 weeks apart. This approach can reduce the amount of nutrients lost to leaching.

	Jan	Feb	Mar	Apr	May	June	July	Aug	Sept	Oct	Nov	Dec
Bahiagrass												
North FL	–	–	C[1]	Fe[2]	–	–	–	–	C[1]	Fe[2]	–	–
South FL	–	C[1]	Fe[2]	–	–	–	–	C[1]	–	N[3]	–	–
Bermudagrass												
North FL	–	–	C[1]	–	N[3]	–	N[3]	–	C[1]	–	–	–
South FL	–	C[1]	–	N[3]	–	N[3]	–	–	C[1]	–	–	N[4]
Centipedegrass												
North FL	–	–	C[1]	Fe[2]	–	–	Fe[2]	C[1]	–	–	–	–
South FL	–	C[1]	Fe[2]	–	–	–	Fe[2]	–	C[1]	–	–	–
St. Augustinegrass												
North FL	–	–	C[1]	–	–	Fe[2]	–	–	C[1]	–	–	–
South FL	–	C[1]	–	–	N[3]	Fe[2]	–	–	–	C[1]	–	–
Zoysiagrass												
North FL	–	–	C[1]	–	–	N[3]	–	–	C[1]	–	–	–
South FL	–	C[1]	–	–	N[3]	–	–	N[3]	–	C[1]	–	–

[1] Complete fertilizer at 1.0 lb of nitrogen/1000 sq ft. See Option above for half-rate applications.

[2] Apply iron to provide dark green color without stimulating excessive grass growth. Ferrous sulfate (2 oz in 3-5 gal water per 1000 sq ft) or a chelated iron source may be used.

[3] Water soluble inorganic nitrogen sources such as ammonium nitrate or ammonium sulfate applied at 1.0 lb of nitrogen/1000 sq ft.

[4] Fertilize only those areas overseeded with ryegrass for winter color.

NOTE: If a supplemental application of nitrogen is desired, slow release nitrogen fertilizer sources should be used to prevent an excess of succulent growth during chinch bug season. Apply 1.0 lb of nitrogen/1000 sq ft as activated sewage sludge, urea formaldehyde, sulfur-coated urea, or IBDU.

SAMPLE LAWN AND LANDSCAPE MAINTENANCE CONTRACT

Part I—Lawn Maintenance Considerations

A. *Mowing, Edging and Trimming:* All turf areas shall be mowed as needed so that no more than 1/3 of the leaf blades are removed per mowing. Mowing shall be with a (reel/rotary/or mulching) mower. Mower blades will be sharp at all times to provide a quality cut. Mowing height will be according to grass type and variety. (See attached recommendations for mowing heights.) Clippings will be left on the lawn as long as no readily visible clumps remain on the grass surface 36 hours after mowing. Otherwise, large clumps of clippings will be distributed by mechanical blowing or collected and removed by the contractor. In the case of fungal disease outbreaks, clippings will be collected until the disease is undetectable.

Tree rings and plant beds and all buildings, sidewalks, fences, driveways, parking lots, and other surfaced areas bordered by grass will be edged every other mowing. Turf around sprinkler heads will be trimmed or treated with a non-selective herbicide so as to not interfere with or intercept water output. Isolated trees and shrubs growing in lawn areas will require mulched areas around them (minimum 2-foot diameter) to avoid bark injury from mowers and filament line trimmers and to reduce root competition from grass. Such mulched areas will be charged to the customer. Contractor will clean all clippings from sidewalks, curbs, and roadways immediately after mowing and/or edging. Clippings will not be swept, blown or otherwise disposed of in sewer drains.

B. *Fertilization:* All turf areas shall be fertilized as per the maintenance specifications attached (see the University of Florida recommendations provided as an example at the end of this document). Complete fertilizers shall be granular in composition and contain 30% to 50% of the nitrogen in a slow or controlled release form. The ratio of nitrogen to potash will be 1:1 or 2:1 for complete fertilizer formulations. Phosphorus shall be no more than $\frac{1}{4}$ of the nitrogen level. They shall also contain magnesium and micronutrients (i.e., manganese, iron, zinc, copper, etc.). Fertilizer will be swept off of walks and drives onto lawns or beds. After fertilization, a minimum of $\frac{1}{4}$ inch of water will be applied by the client.

C. *Pest Control:* The contractor will inspect lawn areas each visit for indications of pest problems and advise the client or representative of such problems.

Upon confirmation of a specific problem requiring treatment, pesticides will be applied as needed on a spot treatment basis, whenever possible, using the least toxic, effective pesticide. All spraying of pesticides and fertilizer applications will be performed when temperatures are below 90°F and wind drift negligible. No pesticide will be applied to turf areas without the express approval of the client. This includes weed and feed formulations. Records will be kept on pests identified and treatment(s) rendered for control.

All pest control service is *in addition* to the basic contract charges. The amount charged will be on a per job basis based on materials cost plus labor. The cost will be agreed on by client and contractor before such service is rendered.

Pesticide applications will be made in accordance with the rules and regulations governing use of pesticides in Florida. Posting and notification of pesticide sensitive persons will be done. The pest control applicator will be operating under License #_____. Expiration Date _____.

D. *Thatch Control:* (See Optional Services)

Part II—Landscape Plant Maintenance Considerations:
Trees, Palms, Shrubs, Ground Covers

A. Fertilization: Ornamental shrubs, trees and ground covers planted less than three (3) years shall be fertilized four (4) times per year. Applications shall be made during the months of February, April, June, and October. Shrubs, trees and ground covers more than three (3) years old in the landscape shall be fertilized two (2) times a year in March and September. Rate will be one (1) pound of nitrogen per 1,000 square feet per application.

Mature palms in the landscape shall be fertilized four times per year at a rate of $1/2$ pound per 2 feet of height, up to 15 lbs. Palms under 8 feet tall will receive 2-5 pounds per application 4 times per year.

All fertilizers should contain equal amounts of nitrogen and potassium and at least 30% of both elements should be available in slow release form. The fertilizer should also contain magnesium and a complete micronutrient amendment. The fertilizer analysis shall be similar to 8-2-8, 10-5-10, and 12-4-12.

Established shrubs and trees in lawn areas exposed to lawn fertilizations will not be fertilized supplementally. Fertilizer applied to shrubs and trees planted in beds shall be broadcasted over the entire plant bed. Fertilizer may be punched into the soil on berms and slopes where runoff is likely.

Nutrient deficiencies shall be treated with supplemental applications of the specific lacking nutrient according to University of Florida Cooperative Extension recommendations.

B. Pest Control: Contractor shall practice Integrated Pest Management (IPM) to control insects, diseases, and weeds on and around perennials, ground covers, shrubs, vines, and trees. This will include frequent monitoring and spot treatment as necessary using least toxic methods. All spraying will be performed when temperatures are below 90°F and when wind drift is negligible. First choice will be insecticidal soaps, horticultural oils and biological controls such as *Bacillus thuringiensis (Bt)* formulations. Weeds in beds or mulched areas will usually be removed mechanically or by hand. Upon client approval, herbicides may be employed for heavy weed infestations.

C. Pruning: Shrubs will be pruned with hand shears as needed to provide an informal shape, fullness and bloom. Tree and palm pruning will be done once (1) per year and is limited to branches and/or brown fronds and seed heads below 20 feet in height. No green palm fronds shall be removed. All litter will be removed by the contractor. No trees under utility lines will be pruned and no pruning will be done during or immediately following growth flushes. Branches will be pruned just outside the branch collar. Pruning paint will not be applied. Sucker growth will be removed by hand from the base of trees. No herbicides will be used for this purpose.

D. Mulching: All mulched areas will be replenished <u>once</u> a year during the winter months (Nov. - Feb.). "Alternative" mulches (pine bark, pine needles, melaleuca, recycled, etc.) should be considered. Mulch should be maintained at a depth of three (3) inches. All curb, roadway and bed line edges will be trenched to help contain the applied mulch. Additional mulch will be billed at $_____/yard. Mulch will not be placed against the trunks of plants.

Part III—Considerations for Optional Services

A. Annual Flowers: Replacement of existing annuals will be done _____ times per year. Major renovation of annual beds shall be accomplished once per year in _____ (month).

Replacement of dead or injured plants due to pests or contractor negligence will be done without cost to client. Replacement of stolen, vandalized or damaged flowers will be charged based on _____ /plant.

Annuals and perennial bedding plants shall be fertilized monthly, at a rate of $1/2$ pound of nitrogen per 1,000 square feet of area every 3-4 weeks. An optional fertilizer schedule would use a slow-release fertilizer such as Osmocote or Nutricote (3-4 month release) incorporated in the bed at planting. Contractor will be responsible for weed control. Pest control will follow IPM principles.

B. Irrigation Systems: The contractor shall inspect and test all components and zones in the irrigation system monthly and shall reset zone times according to seasonal evapotranspiration changes. Minor adjustments and repairs such as head/emitter cleaning or replacement, filter cleaning, small leaks, and minor timer adjustments shall be made by the contractor, with the client paying for parts. Once a year the contractor will recalibrate each zone following Cooperative Extension Service recommendations. During weekly maintenance the contractor will note and report to client any symptoms of inadequate or excessive irrigation, drainage problems, etc.

Repairs or system service beyond the above scope will be charged to the client at an hourly rate per person plus parts. The contractor will notify the client or client's agent, of the nature of the problem before repairs are made.

C. Thatch Removal/Scalping: Removal of thatch (a spongy, build-up of dead and living grass shoots, stems, and roots) should be considered when thatch thickness exceeds one inch. The best time for thatch removal is March through August when the turfgrass is rapidly growing. Thatch removal is in addition to the basic contract charges.

Verticutting, using a vertical mower, is the recommended method of mechanically removing thatch from Bermuda, St. Augustine and Centipede lawns. Blade spacing shall be 3" for St. Augustine and Bahiagrass, 2-3" for centipedegrass, and 1-2" for Bermudagrass and Zoysiagrass.

Bahiagrass lawns can be power-raked rather than verticut. Resulting debris will be removed. Remaining turf will be mowed and irrigated with at least $1/2$ inch of water. Fertilization with a soluble nitrogen source at 1 pound nitrogen per 1000 square feet will be applied one week after dethatching. *Scalping (close mowing) is not a substitute for vertical mowing and is not recommended for this purpose.*

D. Other Services Available: (Priced by contractor on a per job basis):

❑ Installation of a rain shut-off device.

❑ Landscape additions/renovations/transplanting. Transplanting of existing trees will be accomplished during January/February for dormant species, and April - August for palms.

❑ Plant or turf replacement (not attributed to contractor negligence).

❑ Maintenance of aquatic sites.

❑ General hauling.

❑ Major irrigation system modifications.

❑ Interior plant maintenance.

❑ Topdressing turf with sand to smooth uneven surfaces or control thatch.

Part IV—Considerations for Insurance, Licenses, Permits and Liability

The contractor will carry liability amounts and workmen's compensation coverage required by law on his operators and employees and require same of any sub-contractors and provide proof of same to the client. The contractor is also responsible for obtaining any licenses and/or permits required by law for activities on client's property.

Situations which the Contractor may deem are his/her responsibility:

1. Any damage due to operation of his equipment in performing the contract.
2. Complying with all laws pertaining to protected plant species such as the mangrove.
3. Damage to plant material due to improper horticultural practices.
4. Improper replacement or retrofitting of irrigation system components.
5. Injury to non-target organisms in application of pesticides.

Situations which the Contractor may deem are *not* his/her responsibility:

1. Death or decline of plant materials due to improper selection, placement, planting or maintenance done before the time of this contract.
2. Damage due to improper irrigation components existing at the time of contract execution.
3. Exposed cables/wires or sprinkler components/lines normally found below the lawn's surface.
4. Flooding, storm, wind, or cold damages.
5. Disease or damage to lawns or landscape plants caused by excessive irrigation or lack of water due to inoperative irrigation components provided these were reported to client, or irrigation restrictions imposed by the Water Management District or civil authorities.
6. Damage caused by or to any item hidden in the landscape and not clearly guarded or marked.
7. Damage due to vandalism.

Part V—Property Description, Services Provided, Terms, Conditions and Charges (for possible inclusion)

1. Contracts are normally for maintenance of property at an identified location and specifically described:

   _____

   _____

2. The term of the contract. A contract can be for a single year or multiple years with a beginning and ending date. A cancellation provision should be included.
3. The charge for monthly, specified services should be specified. A deadline date should be included and late payment charges should also be considered. Any additional or unscheduled services agreed on by client and contractor could be billed separately.
4. Contract renewal provisions may also be included.

The contract is signed by both parties, dated and can be witnessed or notarized.

Renovation of Turf Areas

L. B. McCarty

Renovation is the improvement of a turfgrass stand without complete reestablishment. Reestablishment refers to complete destruction of the old stand, thorough site preparation, and replanting. The decision on whether to renovate or reestablish is usually based on the turfgrass species and how much desirable turf cover is present. If there is less than 60% desirable cover, reestablishment should be considered.

Factors which can cause deterioration of a turfgrass include one or more of the following:

❑ Poor management by improper cultural practices which result in thin and weakened turf. Among these practices are using unadapted species or cultivars; using improper cutting height or frequency; and not following IFAS recommendations for proper fertilization, irrigation, and pest controls.

❑ Excessive thatch accumulation.

❑ Predominance of unadapted or undesirable species.

❑ Undesirable physical soil conditions like compaction, rock layers, buried foreign matter, the presence of a severe layering problem, or poor drainage.

❑ Chemical soil conditions such as acidity, alkalinity, or salinity.

❑ Excessive shade plus tree or shrub root invasion.

❑ Severe damage by diseases, insects, nematodes, or the toxic effect of chemicals.

The causes for deterioration of the turf must be determined. No renovation procedure will be effective and 100% successful without correction of these factors.

Interest in commercial turf renovation has been erratic in the past. The 1960s brought new equipment which was designed for specific cultural purposes, predominantly specialized vertical mowers designed to thin thatch. Many individuals entered the business, only to have poor results because thatch removal alone often did not solve the problem.

Renovation failures were usually due to several factors:

❑ There was a lack of available information on the quantity of green vegetation which could be removed by vertical mowing and permit full recovery of the turf.

❑ Attempts to renovate excessively thatched and/or shallow-rooted turf in a single operation rather than permitting full recovery between several, less severe vertical mowings. Consumer resistance to the cost of several procedures versus just one also probably motivated commercial concerns to try accomplishing too much at one time.

❑ Failure by consumers to irrigate and fertilize properly following renovation caused additional damage or death of remaining turf. Unfortunately, most commercial firms had to rely on customers for proper postrenovation care.

❑ Undesirable soil conditions such as layers or compaction which affected plant growth were not corrected during renovation.

Consumer awareness of the benefits of professional lawn care has resulted in a resurgence in the interest for commercial turf renovation. This document provides information on cultural practices for renovation of turf areas.

TURFGRASS RENOVATION

A careful examination of the turf to be renovated is the single most important step in deciding if renovation or reestablishment is required. Items to check include turf type; turf quality in terms of density, color, and weed infestation; thatch thickness; depth and density of the root system; and soil conditions. Careful examination of these factors does not take long and provides the basis for recommendations and of permissible renovation.

Grass type. Bahiagrass, bermudagrass, and zoysiagrass if vertically mowed in two directions will require approximately 30 days for full recovery during the growing season, whereas St. Augustinegrass and centipedegrass may require 30 to 90 days.

Turf quality. The turf quality aspect of evaluation is important in determining the degree of renovation to attempt. Overall turf appearance also is indicative of customer interest and the type of care the turf will receive following renovation. Turf that is excessively spongy but has fairly good color and density and minimal weed contamination is healthier and can be more successfully renovated than turf that has deteriorated to the point where it has become thin and weed-infested.

Thatch thickness and root quality. These factors are usually evaluated jointly since thatch thickness indicates the quantity of organic matter which should be removed, while root system quality usually dictates the extent of permissible renovation.

The first step in root system evaluation is to grab a handful of turf and vigorously attempt to pull it out of the soil, much like a piece of carpeting. Poorly rooted turf may be due to one or more of the following:

❑ poor management practices (watering, mowing, etc.),

❑ excessive thatch,

❑ poor soil topdressing practices,

❑ improper herbicide use, and/or

❑ insect and nematode damage.

Vertical mowing poorly-rooted turf in a weakened condition is not advised. The mechanical slicing action may loosen and strip the turf from the soil in patches. This will further weaken it, causing death following renovation. Options for such a situation include:

❑ *Reestablishment.* Virtually any turf can be reno-vated regardless of its condition, provided time, effort, and expense are no object. Economic practicality takes precedence when cost for proper renovation exceeds that for reestablishment. Reestablishment should be recommended when careful evaluation indicates it to be less expensive than renovation.

❑ *Scalping.* Poorly rooted bermudagrass, and zoysiagrass may have much of the above ground vegetation and thatch removed by mowing at a low height of cut or scalping. This is not as effective in removing thatch as is vertical mowing, but may precede vertical mowing in the renovation process.

One method for examining thatch thickness and root quality is to use a straight bladed garden spade to remove an intact, 4 x 8 inch cross section of turf with approxi-mately 6 inches of attached soil. Overall thatch thickness should be carefully examined, especially on St. Augustinegrass and centipedegrass, to determine the quantity or thickness of thatch and mat. Once the thatch layer exceeds 1 inch, it becomes excessive and needs to be removed. The preceding thatch profile examination should provide a rough estimate of how much thatch can be scalped off prior to vertical mowing and still ensure adequate green vegetation for reestablishment afterward.

Thatch profile examination can also reveal, to a certain degree, past cultural practices which can have a modifying effect on the best or most practical method for renovation. For example, very little dead and decomposed thatch in relation to a relatively thick layer of green thatch indicates rapid buildup over a short time span, probably from excessive fertilization and watering. Scalping combined with reduced fertilization and watering may be all that is required to effectively renovate the turf at this time.

Rooting depth and density. Depending upon original thickness, previous applications of soil topdressing may

occur in sample cross sections as alternating layers of soil and buried organic matter. One should gently attempt to pull the sample apart while grasping the lowermost soil portion in one hand and pulling on the thatch layer with the other hand. A reasonably clean separation at any of the layers indicates the effective rooting depth. Carefully shake or wash soil and/or organic matter from the sample to expose roots and their density. If the sample does not separate at any of the layers, then carefully shake and/or wash the entire sample to expose root systems.

There are no quantitative guidelines for root system evaluation relative to vertical mowing, but successful renovation becomes more difficult as root system depth and density decreases. A majority of the root system should extend a minimum of 6 or more inches into the underlying native soil. A healthy root system will include a large number of fibrous white roots in the sample. Roots which are yellowish-brown, stubby, and when pulled slough away from the core are indicative of nematode infestation. If you suspect a nematode problem, have an analysis made to determine if control is necessary.

STEPS IN TURFGRASS RENOVATION

The first step should be an evaluation of the site to determine if substantial weed populations are present. If undesirable weeds or grass species are a problem, a decision must be made on whether to use a selective or nonselective herbicide for weed control. The presence of a large population of weedy perennial grasses usually dictates spot treatment with a nonselective herbicide such as glyphosate (Roundup, Kleenup) or glufosinate (Finale). Advance planning is necessary for this procedure since the choice will determine if delays between steps are neces-sary. Removing the weeds will reduce competition within the turf stand and allow for faster recovery from the renovation procedure. For selective weed control, check current IFAS recommendations.

REMOVAL OF THATCH AND DEAD VEGETATION

Procedure

Flagging. Locate and mark irrigation heads, ground-level rocks, concrete slabs, or electrical outlets, and other obstructions that may damage or be damaged by equip-ment during renovation. Standard irrigation marker flags are excellent for this purpose. Remove concrete dough-nuts or rings used to protect irrigation heads during regular mowing. Inform the maintenance company where all irrigation and electrical lines are deeply buried to avoid damage to or by equipment, or injury to personnel during renovation.

Scalp. For bermudagrass and zoysiagrass, scalping can be performed to remove topgrowth. Adjust mower cutting height as low as compatible for the mower, or for the turf being renovated. A grass catcher, a vacuum, or a trailing brush-type sweeper should be used to remove the majority of clippings prior to vertical mowing.

Vertical mow. Consult Table 1 for recommended blade spacing. Changing blade spacings and/or reels is a difficult operation and is usually performed prior to the delivery of equipment to job sites. Blade spacings listed in Table 1 are adequate for most situations, but experience may dictate changes for optimal performance.

Table 1. Recommended vertical mower blade spacings.

Grass Type	Inches	Centimeters
Bahiagrass	3.0	7.5
Bermudagrass	1.0 - 2.0	2.5 - 5.0
Centipedegrass	2.0 - 3.0	5.0 - 7.5
St. Augustinegrass	3.0	7.5
Zoysiagrass	1.0 - 2.0	2.5 - 5.0

The most practical method for determining proper vertical mower blade depth is to make a series of downward adjustments interspersed with short test runs to determine the degree of thatch removal. Ideally, soil penetration of $1/4$ inch will cultivate and topdress while removing thatch. Usually three to four adjustments, each followed by a 5 to 10 foot test run, are sufficient to determine the best depth setting. The equipment operator should keep in mind that additional green vegetation will be removed when the area is vertically mowed a second time at right angles to the first mowing. A heavy duty vertical mower usually is best for areas reasonably free from obstructions, thus permitting straight line mowing. A lightweight, highly maneuverable unit is more suitable for restricted areas.

Thatch or debris brought to the surface as a result of vertical mowing should be removed each time the area is vertically mowed to reduce equipment flotation and drag on subsequent cuts. Failure to remove debris increases mower power requirements necessitated by having to recut debris left on the surface. Refer to other sections in this book for more information on thatch removal by vertical mowing.

Vacuum Sweep. The final step in thatch removal is to vacuum sweep the entire area to remove remaining debris and as much fine or powdery thatch as possible. Final scalp and vacuum sweep operations often are reversed since vacuum sweeping has a tendency to produce a slightly irregular surface.

Final Scalp. To smooth the turf surface.

Topdressing

The application of a thin layer of soil to the entire turf surface (topdressing) to level renovated areas or fill small depressions may be needed. In addition, proper topdressing has been documented by research to be the best overall method of controlling thatch. Topdressing provides an ideal habitat for soil microorganisms, that decompose thatch naturally. Topdress with soil similar to the native soil on which the turf is growing and use as little as possible to minimize layering. Never bury turf with topsoil when leveling or filling depressions since this will kill it. Do not topdress St. Augustinegrass heavily or conditions favorable for brown patch disease may develop. Sterilized topsoil should be used to prevent weed seed introduction and should be screened to remove foreign material such as small twigs and rocks. Table 2 contains volumes of topsoil required for varying thicknesses of topdressing.

Table 2. Volumes of topsoil required for topdressing 1000 square feet of turf area.

Normal Rate for Topdressing		
Topdressing Thickness (Inches)	Cubic Volume	
	Feet	Yards
$1/8$	10.42	0.39
$1/4$	20.83	0.77
$5/16$	26.04	0.96
$3/8$	31.25	1.16
$1/2$	41.67	1.54
$5/8$	52.08	1.93
$3/4$	62.50	2.31
1.0	83.30	3.09

CULTIVATION

This is an optional but sometimes very important step in the renovation process. Severe compaction of the soil surface or the presence of soil layers differing in texture in the surface two inches are conditions that require core cultivation or aerification. This will improve aeration and water penetration, and reduce surface layering problems. Grooving and slicing are also used in cultivation. Any of these procedures are preferred to spiking since they bring soil to the surface and penetrate to a greater depth. From two to five repeat cultivations may be necessary. If core cultivation (aerifying) is done, vertical mowing or dragging of the area with a steel dragmat may be necessary to break up the cores and scatter the soil over the surface. Core cultivation does not remove excessive thatch and should complement, not substitute, for vertical mowing.

PLANTING

In thinned areas of grass, reseeding or vegetative replanting should be performed at this time. Procedures for reestablishment into these areas are the same that would be followed for a new turf area. Sprigs removed during vertical mowing are an excellent source of vegetative material.

FERTILIZATION AND pH CORRECTION

Soil test for pH, phosphorous (P) and potassium (K) levels. Correction of pH should be done at this time if necessary. Renovation is a temporary setback to actively growing turf because it reduces the turf's ability to synthesize plant food due to removal of green grass blades.

Recovery is more rapid if the turf is properly fertilized immediately following renovation. A 16-4-8 fertilizer with micronutrients is one of the best formulations, but any fertilizer is better than none.

Include phosphorous and potassium rates suggested by soil test results, if available, and a minimum of 1 pound of readily available nitrogen per 1000 square feet. Make certain the fertilizer is watered into the soil immediately following the renovation procedure.

Except for irrigation, normal maintenance practices including mowing and control of insects and disease should be resumed immediately following renovation. Dead organic matter exposed in renovated areas dries quickly, becomes hydrophobic (water repelling) and further stresses renovated turf. Thus, renovated turf should be treated as a new installation and irrigated two or three times daily until the turf is capable of surviving with less frequent, but deeper watering.

A good irrigation policy is to irrigate twice during the day. One-tenth inch of water or 62 gallons per 1000 square feet applied at 10:00 am and again at 2:00 pm should be adequate. The preceding water quantities should suffice under most conditions, but might require adjustment to better fit all local conditions.

Daily irrigation should be discontinued as soon as the turf becomes sufficiently rooted to withstand early morning watering only. Irrigation frequency and quantity should then be adjusted to avoid daytime wilting. Irrigate on an as-needed basis as soon as the renovated turf has fully recovered.

EQUIPMENT REQUIREMENTS

Table 3 is intended to serve as an equipment guide for small residential lawn maintenance companies or small commercial turf areas such as motels, hotels, and condominiums. Requirements for larger turf areas differ in that larger, high-speed equipment is required.

Table 3. Suggested equipment requirements.

Quantity	Description	Intended Use
1	Heavy duty, self-propelled, vertical mower, 10-12 HP.	Straight-line vertical mowing in open, readily accessible areas.
1	Medium duty, self-propelled vertical mower, 4-7 HP.	Close work around flower beds and other tight areas.
1	Heavy duty, self-propelled walk-behind or riding rotary mower with catcher.	Scalping and clipping removal prior to and following vertical mowing. Primarily for use in open, readily accessible areas. Mowing swath, HP, etc. to be determined primarily by size of areas normally selected for renovation.
1	Medium duty, self-propelled, walk-behind rotary mower with catcher.	Scalping and cleanup work around flower beds and other tight areas.
1	Self-propelled, walk-behind, or trailing brush-type sweeper.	Debris removal following vertical mowing.
1	Self-propelled, walk-behind vacuum sweeper.	Final cleanup and for removal of fine mat.
1	$1/2$- to 1-ton pickup with high sides.	Equipment and personnel transport. Haul away debris removed during renovation.
1	Rototiller	Prepare soil where areas need reestablishment.
1	Utility trailer with sides	Equipment transport and debris removal.
1	Aerifier	Core cultivation where compaction or layering is a problem.
–	Miscellaneous hand tools, (e.g., rakes, trash forks, brooms, etc.)	–

Low Temperature Damage to Turf

L. B. McCarty

Injury to warm-season turfgrasses often occurs when temperatures drop below 20°F (−6.7°C). In general, major winter injury to turf grass is caused by the following: 1) desiccation, 2) direct low temperature kill, 3) diseases and 4) traffic effects. For example, damage from the 1989-90 freeze can probably be attributed to poor cultural practices which weakened turf and made it more susceptible to injury or death from low temperatures. Subsequent damage may also have resulted from traffic on frozen turf.

REASONS FOR LOW TEMPERATURE DAMAGE

Most warm-season grasses have cold tolerance ratings as poor or very poor when compared to cool-season grasses. Cultural factors that tend to favor cold injury include: poor drainage (soil compaction); excessive thatch; reduced lighting; excessive fall nitrogen fertilization; and a close mowing height. The weather pattern preceding a severe and sudden cold wave also influences a turf's low temperature tolerance. In general, if turf has had several frosts prior to a drastic temperature drop, it has been better 'conditioned' to survive. The 1989–90 cold snap in much of north and central Florida was preceded by three to five frosts. These helped increase carbohydrates and protein constitutes in plants which enabled crown tissue to withstand cold temperatures without severe protoplasmic membrane disruption. The freezes in the early 1980s did not have these preconditioning periods; therefore, grasses were still mainly green, crown tissue was still succulent, and severe damage resulted.

Shade prevents normal daytime soil warming; therefore, these areas stay colder for longer periods of time, and more low temperature damage may occur. Shade (low light intensity) also reduces the plant's ability to produce carbohydrates needed for increased cold tolerance. Frozen turf crowns are easily damaged from traffic. Traffic should not be allowed on frozen turf until the soil and plants have completely thawed. Syringing the area lightly once temperatures are above freezing and prior to allowing traffic on it will help reduce frozen turf injury associated with traffic.

ASSESSING THE EXTENT OF INJURY

Symptoms of direct low temperature damage includes leaves that initially appear water-soaked, turning whitish brown and then progressing to a dark brown. Damaged leaves are not turgid and tend to mat over the soil. A distinct putrid (rotten) odor is frequently evident and areas hardest hit are usually poorly drained ones such as soil depressions.

Managers who think they have experienced cold damage should take several cup-cutter sized plugs from suspected areas and place them in a warm area for regrowth. A greenhouse or a warm window sill should suffice. Observe these for 30 days or until growth resumes. If good regrowth occurs, then little damage is assumed. If regrowth is absent or sporadic, then some degree of damage was sustained.

A second method is to remove the individual plant crowns, cut a slice through them with a razor blade and then examine them under a magnifying lens. Firm, white tissue with turgid cells indicates a healthy crown meristematic area that has survived. Crowns which are brownish or dark colored with a mush appearance have been injured. The plant can lose all its leaves and roots during cold periods and still recover if the basal crown was not injured.

REPAIRING WINTER DAMAGED TURF

Steps to minimize cold temperature damage to turf include:

❑ minimizing or diverting traffic from damaged areas,

❑ maintaining adequate soil moisture, especially in spring when roots are developing, and

❑ preparing to make an early assessment on the amount and spread of damaged areas.

An initial low mowing (scalping) of bermudagrass after the last expected frost date (approximately April 1 in Gainesville) will help to remove brown, dead overlying plant material. By removing this, sunlight can reach the surface better, resulting in earlier spring warm soil and corresponding green-up. If initial green-up indicates only small damaged spots (< 6 in diameter), then plan to aggressively encourage surrounding turf to refill these. Small areas on greens are easily repaired by plugging with a cup cutter. For those areas with wide-spread damage, replanting may be the quickest alternative. In either case, additional nitrogen, water and possible aerification may be necessary to encourage regrowth/reestablishment and should be planned and budgeted for.

For St. Augustinegrass and centipedegrass turfs, the factors influencing cold damage and ascertaining the amount are similar as for bermudagrass. However, these are inherently the least cold tolerant of grasses used, therefore they may have experienced more damage than in bermudagrass. If these are maintained at high levels of nitrogen prior to cold weather, increased damage can be expected. 'Centipedegrass decline' is a catch-all term describing poor winter survival of centipedegrass. Excessive nitrogen is consistently associated with the amount of decline expressed. Nitrogen rates above 2 lbs N/1000 sq ft the previous summer are consistently associated with decline development. The specific St. Augustine variety being grown also influences damage incurred. For example, Common/Roselawn, Floratine, Floratam, and Floralawn St. Augustinegrass varieties are less cold hardy. Bitterblue, Raleigh, Seville, and Jade St. Augustinegrasses tend to have better cold tolerance among the currently available varieties.

Recently planted (sprigged, sodded, or seeded) areas could expect more damage since rooting was not well developed. Seedlings less than four leaf stage are more succulent than older ones. In addition, lawn grasses tend to be subjected to more shade from trees and, therefore, may have more damage. If damage is suspected, sample and plan for reestablishment as mentioned above.

MINIMIZING FUTURE DAMAGE

In the future, reduce cold damage potential by:

❑ planting the most cold tolerant variety available;

❑ minimizing shade, soil compaction and poorly drained areas;

❑ using recommended amounts of nitrogen during the growing season with the last heavy application no later than late summer (middle of September);

❑ using a 4-1-2 or 3-1-2 type fertilizer ratio since these have been shown to promote cold tolerance;

❑ not planting warm-season grasses late in the summer as they do not have enough time (warm weather) to become properly established prior to winter; and

❑ mowing grass at highest height possible, especially the last several mowings prior to fall. Higher mowing height allows turf to produce and store more root carbohydrates late in the summer.

CHAPTER FOUR

Pest Management

Integrated Pest Management Strategies

L. B. McCarty

One of the most appealing aspects of a landscape is the beauty of the lawn. The responsibility for maintaining this beauty and acceptable conditions usually falls on the homeowner and/or contracted lawn maintenance firm. One method for meeting these objectives is the incorporation of a common sense approach to protecting the turf by information gathering, analysis, and knowledgeable decision making. Integrated Pest Management (IPM) utilizes the most appropriate cultural, biological and chemical strategies for managing plant pests.

Unfortunately, the pressures to maintain perfect conditions throughout the year have often forced lawn care managers to abandon sound agronomic practices for quick-fixes to get them through any current crisis. For example, too-close mowing heights, requests for perfect lawns with no scars or disruptions in consistency and growing grasses outside their natural range of adaptability have required increased use of fertilizer, water and pesticides. At the same time, public concerns over these inputs and restrictions on the availability of traditionally used resources, such as water, will require that many homeowners consider incorporating IPM programs into their total management scheme.

IPM BEGINNINGS

Modern IPM concepts and practices began to evolve in the late 1950s with apple production and was vastly expanded with cotton production in the 1960s. This evolved from the mid-1940s when the modern use of pesticides began to explode. Many felt at that time that pesticides were the "silver bullet" or ultimate specific weapon needed to control all pest problems. Many traditional pest and plant ecological studies were abandoned, as were non-chemical control alternatives. This led to a new generation of producers and scientists who had little experience with non-chemical approaches to pest or plant management. However, resistance to pesticides, especially insecticides, forced researchers and growers to seek alternative methods of pest control, thus, the birth of IPM.

In recent years, turf managers have begun to realize that their escalating dependence on pesticides and the lack of research and training in the pest management arena are now affecting their industry. For example, in the early 1980s, several very effective and relatively cheap pesticides were banned from the turf market. Two such pesticides were EDB (ethylene dibromide), a soil-injected nematicide, and chlordane, an insecticide. Managing the turf to withstand higher populations of nematodes or insects, particularly mole crickets and grubs, was not followed as long as EDB and chlordane were available. However, since the loss of these materials, nematodes, grubs and mole crickets have become the most serious turf pest problems in many areas. Researchers are currently trying to find alternative methods of management and control for these pests based on pest life cycle and the use of biological control agents. Obviously, additional time and research will be necessary to solve the problems that were basically ignored for more than 40 years.

STRATEGIES OF INTEGRATED PEST MANAGEMENT (IPM)

Strategy Development

Developing IPM strategies requires reliable information. Three main areas are:

❏ Knowledge concerning all normal inputs required for growing the turf—not only what they are but also why they are required. This is supplemented by knowing pest life cycles and which management practices disrupt or influence them to reduce pest numbers. Understanding the logic behind a management practice, rather than just doing it "because that is the way we have always done it," allows the homeowner to make decisions to alter these practices to reduce pest problems or encourage turf growth to overcome or tolerate the pest.

❏ Use of a monitoring system to carefully follow pest trends to determine if a pesticide will be necessary and, if so, when it would be most effectively applied. Ideally, monitoring systems are based on known economical or aesthetic threshold levels. Unfortunately, in many cases, these thresholds are not specifically known, thus are determined to reflect local conditions and threshold levels tolerated by clientele.

A professional scout, who may be employed by one or several lawn maintenance firms, is often used. Since these scouts visit several areas, pest trends are more easily recognized and information useful from one area can more easily be used to assist others.

Tools required for scouting vary with pest problems, scout training and clientele budget. A good set of eyes and an inquisitive mind are essential. These are supported by a standard 10X hand or pocket lens, soil profile probe, spade, cup cutter, pocket knife, tweezers, scalpel, collection vials and paper bags, and field identification guides. Soap and water also are necessary for insect monitoring.

Monitoring intensively maintained lawns includes scouting turf areas, adjacent ornamental plantings, flower beds and trees. Frequency of scouting reflects pest trends, desired level of aesthetics and, of course, economics. During periods of active turf growth or suspected pest activity, weekly scouting may be justified. During periods of inactive growth, scouting frequency can be extended.

Scouting begins by simply walking around the area to observe insect and disease activity as well as other pest and non-infectious symptoms. Specific techniques to detect or ascertain pest populations are described in detail elsewhere in the *Florida Lawn Handbook*. In order to better recognize specific pest damage such as disease symptoms and nocturnal insect feeding, early morning scouting is suggested.

❏ Maintenance of careful records to measure the effectiveness of the IPM strategies. Generally, it is important to stress to homeowners that elimination of pests is not ecologically or economically desirable. However, if necessary, the decision to apply a pesticide will be supported by maintaining careful records should it be questioned by regulatory officials or the public. In addition, an IPM program will constantly evolve as new control strategies, monitoring techniques and threshold information become available.

IPM Control Tactics

Tactics involved with these IPM control strategies can be divided into cultural controls, biological control and chemical control strategies. All are equally important in implementing a successful IPM program.

Cultural Controls

The following tactics are integral features of a good cultural control strategy for pest management:

❏ *Host-plant resistance.* Until recently, turfgrass breeders have been concerned primarily with improving the appearance and playability characteristics of grasses, including texture, density and growth habit. Breeding for pest resistance has been a secondary concern. However, one of the oldest means of pest control has been through careful breeding and selection of resistant or tolerant plants. For example, Floratam and FX-10 St. Augustinegrasses are noted for their resistance to chinch bugs.

❏ *Pest-free propagating material.* Another easy but often overlooked means of preventing pest

establishment in turf is the use of planting materials (seed or vegetative sprigs/sod) that are pest free. Each state has a certification program to provide pest free propagation material. Each bag of certified seed must provide information on purity and germination percentages. In addition, a weed seed listing must be provided, and no noxious weed seeds are allowed. If vegetative material such as sprigs or sod is being planted, inspect the turf for weeds, fire ants and other pests. If applicable, ask to see results from a nematode assay of the planting material before purchasing. Remember, these steps will help to prevent or reduce pest problems during and after establishment.

❏ *Site preparation.* Proper preparation of a planting site is an important step in pest management, primarily due to its effects on the health and viability of the turf. For turf managers, this includes planning and constructing highly utilized areas with irrigation and drainage systems capable of providing precise water management. If the soil remains saturated for too long, diseases and soil compaction eventually occur.

❏ *Basic agronomic practices.* Probably the best defense against pest invasion is providing a dense, healthy, competitive turf. This is achieved after establishment by providing cultural practices which favor turf growth over pest occurrence. Important cultural practices in IPM programs include proper irrigation, fertilization, mowing, aerification, verticutting, and topdressing. Prolonged use of incorrect cultural practices and lack of understanding concerning interrelationships of these practices weaken the turf, encourage pest activity or invasion and, quite often, result in excessive thatch development. Thatch harbors many insects and disease pathogens. It also binds pesticides and reduces the efficiency of an irrigation program.

Biological Controls

Pests in their native areas are usually regulated by predators and parasites that help keep populations at a constant level. Problems occur when pests, but not their natural enemies, are introduced into new areas and the pest populations increase unchecked. Biological pest control involves use of natural enemies to reduce pest populations, indigenous and introduced, to aesthetically acceptable levels.

One inherent principle concerning classic biological pest control, where the agent is introduced only once or on a limited basis for permanent establishment, is accepting that a minimum level of the target pest will always be present. This low pest population is necessary for the biological control agent to have a continual food source after the target pest has been reduced to an acceptable level. Thus, complete elimination of the pest is not feasible when integrating biological control measures into the overall pest management scheme. Homeowners must be educated to this fact and be willing to accept minor levels of pest pressure.

Various success stories have occurred using biological control agents involving parasites, predators or diseases to control another organism. However, only a few examples of biological control measures are currently being used in commercial turf production. *Bacillus popilliae*, a bacterium that causes the milky spore disease, has been used with variable success in the control of Japanese beetle grubs. Other potential agents for biological control of turf pests include endophytic fungi for insect control, various rust fungi (*Puccinia* spp.) for nutsedge control, several predacious nematodes for mole crickets and possible parasitic fungi and bacteria for turf nematode control. Research on antagonistic fungi and bacteria for biocontrol of diseases and fire ants also show promise. Other examples of non-synthetic pesticides include using soap flush for mole cricket control; the use of natural pyrethroid derived from chrysanthemums for foliage feeding insects; and the use of a mixture of copper and sulfur in the form of the Bordeaux Mixture for foliar diseases.

Biological control agents are complex, not totally effective and not always predictable. The concept of biological control has been so widely publicized that the general public views it as a viable and readily available alternative to all pesticides. Unfortunately, this is not the case, but this area currently is receiving much needed attention and hopefully will provide additional control agents in the future. The public must be informed that biological controls are not the answer to all pest problems, but may be a useful component of a good IPM program.

Chemical Controls

Not all pest problems can be solved by manipulating cultural practices in the plant environment or by the use of biological control agents. In these cases, pesticides become the second or third line of defense. In the IPM scheme, indiscriminate spraying is eliminated and only judicious use of pesticides is employed, minimizing damage to biological control agents and the environment. This requires knowledge of the ecological interrelationships between the pest, the host plant and the biological control agent. Judicious pesticide use involves making management decisions.

❑ The pest must be properly identified and monitored with reliable techniques to establish aesthetic thresholds. A determination then must be made on when or whether further action is necessary. These threshold levels have been referred to in other IPM programs as economic, damage or action thresholds. However, in turf management, economic and related threshold level terms mean little since an acceptable

aesthetic level, not crop yield, is the ultimate goal. An aesthetic threshold level deals with the amount of visual damage a particular turf area can withstand before action is required. Obviously, highly maintained lawns have a lower aesthetic threshold level before action is warranted than turf areas maintained at much lower levels.

❑ Best control of many insects and weeds occurs at a particular stage in its life-cycle, which is usually during the early stages of development. For example, mole crickets are most susceptible to chemical control when they are small, usually during the months of May or June. Chemical applications at other times are less effective.

❑ If use of a pesticide is necessary, select the one that is most effective but least toxic to non-target organisms or least persistent in the environment, whichever is more important in that location. Read the label completely and thoroughly. Spot treat, if possible, instead of applying blanket or wall-to-wall treatments. This requires effective scouting techniques and proper recording or mapping of pest outbreaks.

STARTING AN IPM PROGRAM

Pest problems are going to occur in turf and even the best management program cannot guarantee that pest damage will not occur. The following steps have proven successful in developing IPM programs and should provide a good starting point for those who are innovative enough to try such an approach.

❑ Define the role and responsibility of all people who will be involved in the IPM program. This includes establishing good communication between homeowners and maintenance staff. Emphasize and explain to these individuals exactly what will be involved and why. Do not lead anyone to expect perfection–either on the lawn, or in the IPM program as there will probably be as many problems as successes, especially during the development stages of the program.

Scouts who are conscientious and trained to recognize turf pest problems provide the base of a successful monitoring program. The field technician will probably want to begin as the primary scout until a feel for IPM strategies is attained. Once this occurs, the responsibility might be delegated to an assistant. However, it should be emphasized that all employees, especially those who regularly mow the lawn, should play an important role in recognizing pests and/or damage symptoms.

❑ Determine management objectives for specific areas of the lawn and correct all practices which favor pest development or place undue stress on the turf. Before

Table 1. Field history report form used for lawn IPM programs.

TURF IPM FIELD HISTORY REPORT FORM

Location _____   Owner _____   Phone Number _____

Scout _____   Phone Number _____   Date _____

Site	Plant Species	Area	Mowing Height/ Schedule	Soil Analysis			Soil Drainage	Fertilization					Irrigation Scheduling
				pH	P	K		Amount (N/1000 sq ft)				Frequency	
								Spring	Summer	Fall	Winter		
Lawn													
Trees			—										
Ornamentals			—										
Flower Beds			—										
Other													

Comments on specific topics such as shade, overseeding, nitrogen carrier, weather, irrigation salinity levels, etc.:

_____

_____

_____

_____

Table 2. Field infestation report form used for lawn IPM programs.

TURF IPM FIELD INFESTATION REPORT FORM

Location _____ Owner _____ Phone Number _____

Scout _____ Phone Number _____ Date _____

Site	Mowing Height	Soil Moisture	Weeds Species	No. or %	Diseases Species	No. or %	Insects Species	No.	Nematodes Species	No.
Lawn										
Trees		—								
Ornamentals		—								
Flower Beds		—								

Notes:

Weeds
1. Goosegrass
2. Crabgrass
3. Thin Paspalum
4. Dollarweed
5. Florida Betony
6. Matchweed
7. Doveweed/dayflower
8. Beggartick
9. Pusley
10. Nutsedge (Yellow, Globe, Purple, Annual, Kyllinga)
11. Other

Diseases
1. Dollar Spot
2. Leaf Spot
3. Pythium Blight
4. Pythium Root Rot
5. Fairy Ring
6. Brown Patch (R. solani)
7. Algae/Moss
8. Centipedegrass Decline
9. St. Aug. Take-all Root rot
10. Rhizoctonia Leaf and Sheath Blight (R. zeae)
11. Other

Insects
1. Mole Crickets
2. Sod Webworms
3. Armyworms
4. Cutworms
5. White Grubs
6. Fire Ants
7. Mites
8. Grass Scales
9. Billbugs
10. Spittlebugs
11. Other

Nematodes
1. Sting
2. Lance
3. Stubby-Root
4. Root-Knot
5. Cyst
6. Ring
7. Spiral
8. Sheath
9. Other

implementing the IPM program, inspect and map each site. This will provide the foundation on which all management decisions can be based. For each lawn, information that should be obtained includes:

○ turf species,

○ mowing height and schedule,

○ irrigation amount and frequency,

○ soil drainage,

○ complete soil analysis,

○ fertilizer program, traffic patterns, and

○ shade and air circulation concerns.

A field history form similar to the one shown in Table 1 can be used to record such foundation data.

Be prepared to improve the existing problems which weaken the turf, such as a poor irrigation or drainage system or severe tree effects. Improve these conditions before the IPM program is implemented. Otherwise, the potential success of the IPM program will be greatly reduced. Again, communicate openly with the homeowner.

❑ Monitor local weather patterns closely. This will provide detailed, localized data on rainfall, soil temperatures, humidity and sunlight indexes and evapotranspiration rates. Climatic conditions usually play the most important role in specific turf growth patterns and pest problems.

❑ Establish aesthetic or action threshold levels and begin monitoring and recording pest levels. A form similar to the one shown in Table 2 may be used to record such levels. Threshold levels will vary according to location of the lawn, the specific pest being scouted, use of the turf area, expectations of the owners and budget constraints. Table 3 lists suggested aesthetic or action thresholds for several common turf insects. In addition to recording pest levels on forms, pinpoint pest problem areas on a map for each lawn. For example, mole crickets usually lay eggs in the same location each year. This may allow for spot treatment rather than a blanket pesticide application. Over time, these maps can indicate where pest problems annually

occur and possibly allow management or environmental variables influencing this occurrence to be corrected. These maps also allow new crew members a visual aid in examining and treating problem areas. Computer programs are available that allow one to draw or paint such maps.

❑ Use pesticides correctly and only when threshold limits are reached. One of the goals of IPM is intelligent and prudent pesticide use. Pesticide use may not necessarily be reduced by an IPM program, although it often is, but it will allow for more efficient and effective use of pesticides. For example, by monitoring pest development, the pesticide can be used during the most susceptible stage of its life cycle. Utilize the safest, most effective pesticide available for the particular pest. Spot treat whenever possible.

❑ Evaluate the results of the cultural modifications and pesticide treatments by periodically monitoring the site environment and pest populations. Keep written records of site pest management objectives, monitoring methods, data collected, actions taken, and the results obtained. This will provide additional information for owners who do not necessarily understand the IPM program but do understand desirable results. It will also aid in demonstrating that lawn maintenance firms are striving to reduce the inputs in maintaining the turf and to obtain an ecological balance between man and nature.

Table 3. Common turf insects, their aesthetic thresholds, and inspection/detection methods.

Insect	Aesthetic Threshold for Lawns	Insepection/ Detection Method
Armyworms	3 to 4 per sq ft	Visual + soap flush
Billbugs	6 per sq ft	Visual
Chinch bugs	20 per sq ft	Water float
Cutworms	1 per sq ft	Visual + soap flush
June beetle grubs	3 to 4 per sq ft	Visual + soil inspection
Masked chafer beetle grubs	4 per sq ft	Visual
Mole crickets	2 to 4 per sq ft	Visual + soap flush
Sod webworms	10 to 12 per sq ft	Visual + soap flush

CHAPTER FIVE

Weed Control

Weed Control Guide for Florida Lawns

L. B. McCarty

Weeds can simply be defined as unwanted plants or plants growing out-of-place. The proper identification and an understanding of growth habits of weeds are important in understanding the biology and best control strategy. Knowledge of whether or not weeds were previously present in a particular area will also help the homeowner prepare for control procedures in the future.

PROPER MANAGEMENT FIRST

The first and best method of weed control begins with proper management practices which encourage a dense, thriving turf. Healthy turf shades the soil so sunlight can't reach weed seeds ready to germinate. A thick turf also minimizes the physical space available for weeds to become established. There are several management tools to consider when attempting to grow healthy grass.

Proper Cultivar Selection

The first management decision is whether the best turf species or variety is being grown for a particular area. For example, areas heavily shaded will support only a few turfgrass species. Growing bermudagrass or bahiagrass under any shade will result in thin, weak turf which is very susceptible to weed invasion. Alternate grass choices for shady conditions would be specific cultivars of zoysiagrass, St. Augustinegrass, or centipedegrass or the use of a groundcover or mulch.

Proper Cultural Practices

A desirable turf stand requires proper fertilizing, watering, mowing, and other pest control measures. If a turf is overwatered and fertilized or mowed too low or too infrequently, the turf is weakened and cannot outcompete weeds. Damaged areas resulting from using unsharpened mowers increase the time needed for turf recovery.

Traffic Control

Turf damaged by foot or vehicle traffic invites weeds. Turf compacted by excess traffic, especially when the soil is water saturated, cannot extract oxygen as well as under better growing conditions. Goosegrass, annual bluegrass, and certain sedges are weeds which grow well in compacted and/or continuously wet soil.

Other Pest Control

Turf damaged by pests such as insects does not always recuperate quickly enough to outcompete germinating weeds. Specifically, tunneling from mole crickets disrupts the soil surface, and chinch bugs and St. Augustinegrass Take-All Root Rot thin the turf, enabling weed seeds to readily germinate and become established. Other insects and diseases can cause large patches of bare turf. These open areas are usually slow to recover, thus enabling weeds to become established. High nematode populations also thin the turf and make it less able to recuperate from environmental stresses. Weeds that often become established in nematode infested soil include spotted spurge and Florida pusley.

WEED CONTROL

Areas adjacent to fine turf areas which are hard to mow such as fence rows or ditch banks often support a weed population. These weeds normally produce seed which reinfests the nearby turf. These areas should also receive weed control attention. Good sanitation practices should be followed, such as planting only certified seed, using weed-free sod, and the practice of washing off mowers used in weed infested areas before mowing in weed-free areas.

Weeds complete their life cycles in either one growing season (**annuals**), two growing seasons (**biennials**), or three or more years (**perennials**). Annuals that complete their life cycles from spring to fall are generally referred to as **summer annuals**, and those that complete their life cycles from fall to spring are **winter annuals**. Summer annual grasses, as a class, are generally the most troublesome weeds in turf. An excellent weed identification guide, *Weeds of Southern Turfgrasses*, SP 79, can be obtained through your local Cooperative County Extension office.

Methods

Encouraging turf growth. Refer to chapter "Selection and Adaptability" in this publication. If weeds become established, several methods of control are also available.

Mowing. If proper mowing height and frequency are maintained, many annual weeds will be eliminated. Mowing prior to weed seedhead formation will also reduce weed seed reserves.

Hand pulling or rogueing. If only a few weeds are present, it's simpler and less time consuming to physically remove the plant, but if weeds are a major problem, other alternatives should be considered.

Smothering. Smothering with nonliving material to exclude light is effective in certain areas, such as flower beds, foot paths, or nurseries, where turf is not grown. Materials used in such manner include straw, sawdust, hay, wood chips, and plastic film. Care must be taken to prevent mowing accidents due to movement of these materials into a maintained turf area. To be effective, a layer 2 to 3 inches deep is required when using natural mulch materials. Recently, synthetic mats impregnated with herbicides have been introduced to the landscape. These provide long-term weed control when properly used, but care must be taken to minimize desirable plant roots from encountering these layers.

Herbicides. A herbicide is any chemical which injures or kills a plant. Herbicides are safe and effective if product label instructions are followed. Label instructions include proper timing of application, proper rates, and dispersal methods. Timing of herbicide application during the plant's growth cycle also is important. For example, weeds not controlled prior to seedhead formation are harder to control and are able to deposit new seeds for future problems.

Types of Weeds

Broadleaves. Broadleaves, or dicotyledonous plants, have net-like veins in their true leaves and usually have showy flowers. Examples include clovers, lespedeza, plantain, henbit, chickweed, Florida pusley, beggarweed, matchweed, and others, such as

Plate 40.	Southern Sida (*Sida acuta*)
Plate 41.	White Clover (*Trifolium repens*)
Plate 42.	Alternanthera (*Alternanthera paronychioides*)
Plate 43.	Garden Spurge (*Chamaesyce hirta*)
Plate 44.	Ground-ivy or Creeping Charlie (*Glechoma hederaces*)
Plate 45.	Brazilian Pusley (*Richardia braziliensi*)
Plate 46.	Asiatic Hawksbeard (*Youngia japonica*)
Plate 47.	Slender Amaranth (*Amaranthus viridus*)
Plate 48.	Hairy Beggar's-tick (*Bidens alba*)
Plate 49.	Spreading Dayflower (*Commelina diffusa*)
Plate 50.	Pennywort or Dollarweed (*Hydrocotyle* spp.)
Plate 51.	Creeping Indigo (*Indigofera spicata*)
Plate 52.	Cutleaf-evening-primrose (*Oenothera laciniata*)
Plate 53.	Yellow Woodsorrel (*Oxalis stricta*)
Plate 54.	Matchweed, Mat Lippia or Match-head (*Phyla nodiflora*)
Plate 55.	Niruri or Chamberbitter (*Phyllanthus urinaria*)
Plate 56.	Florida Pusley (*Richardia scabra*)
Plate 57.	Florida Betony or Rattlesnake Weed (*Stachys floridana*)
Plate 58.	Puncturevine (*Tribulus terrestris*)

Grasses. Grasses are monocotyledonous plants that have only one seed cotyledon present when seedlings emerge from the soil. Grasses have hollow, rounded stems with nodes (joints), and parallel veins in their true leaves. Examples include crabgrass, goosegrass, crowfootgrass, dallisgrass, bullgrass, annual bluegrass, alexandergrass, cogongrass, torpedograss, and smutgrass.

Plate 59.	Sandspur (*Cenchrus* spp.)
Plate 60.	Crowfootgrass (*Dactyloctenium aegyptium*)
Plate 61.	Blanket or Rabbitt Crabgrass (*Digitaria serotina*)
Plate 62.	Goosegrass (*Eleusine indica*)
Plate 63.	Thin or Bull Paspalum (*Paspalum setaceum*)

Sedges/Rushes. These generally either have stems which are triangular-shaped and solid (sedges) or round and solid (rushes) and favor a moist habitat. Economically important members include yellow and purple nutsedge and, to some degree, globe, Texas, annual, and water sedge, plus path and beak rush and perennial kyllinga.

Plate 64.	Nutsedge (*Cyperus* spp.)
Plate 65.	Perennial Kyllinga (*Cyperus brevifolia*)
Plate 66.	Globe Sedge (*Cyperus globulosus*)
Plate 67.	Purple Nutsedge (*Cyperus rotundus*)

Herbicide Types

Selective. A selective herbicide controls certain plant species without seriously affecting the growth of other plant species. The majority of herbicides used are selective herbicides.

Nonselective. Nonselective herbicides control green plants regardless of species. These are generally used to kill all plants, such as in the renovation or establishment of a new turf area or as spot treatment or as a trimming material along sidewalks, etc. Glyphosate (Roundup Pro) is an example of a nonselective herbicide.

Contact. Contact herbicides affect only the portion of green plant tissue that is contacted by the herbicide spray. These herbicides are not translocated or moved in the vascular system of plants. Therefore, these will not kill underground plant parts, such as rhizomes or tubers. Usually repeat applications are needed with contact herbicides to kill regrowth from these underground plant parts. Examples of contact herbicides include the organic arsenicals (MSMA, DSMA), bentazon (Basagran T&O), glufosinate (Finale), and diquat (Reward).

Systemic. Systemic herbicides are translocated in the plant's vascular system. The vascular system transports the nutrients and water necessary for normal growth and development. Systemic herbicides kill plants over a period of days. Examples of systemic herbicides include glyphosate (Roundup Pro), 2,4-D, dicamba (Vanquish), imazaquin (Image), and sethoxydim (Vantage).

Timing of Application

Two herbicide types in reference to timing of application are important.

Preemergence. Preemergence herbicides are applied prior to weed seed germination. Knowledge of weed life cycles is important, especially when herbicide application timing for preemergence control is attempted. If chemical application is after weed emergence, preemergence herbicides are generally ineffective. This narrow window of application timing is a potential disadvantage for many lawn care companies and homeowners, who often wait too late in the spring to correctly apply the preemergence herbicide. A general rule of thumb for preemergence herbicide application is February 1 in south Florida, February 15 in central Florida, and March 1 in north Florida (day temperatures reach 65° to 70°F for 4 or 5 consecutive days). These application timings generally coincide with blooming of garden plants such as azalea and dogwood. If goosegrass is the primary weed species expected, wait 3 to 4 weeks later than these suggested application dates, since goosegrass germinates later than most summer annual grasses. For preemergence control of winter annual weeds such as annual bluegrass (*Poa annua*), apply herbicide when nighttime temperatures drop to 55° to 60°F for several consecutive days (early October for north Florida, late October to early November for central and south Florida).

The timing of aerification and dethatching in the form of spiking, coring, or slicing should be prior to preemergence herbicide application. Preemergence herbicides form a uniform soil barrier. Disturbing the treated soil layer by methods such as aerification may disrupt the herbicide barrier and deposit a fresh supply of weed seeds on the soil surface. Therefore, herbicide effectiveness may be reduced. Adequate soil moisture before and after application is necessary to activate most preemergence herbicides. Preemergence herbicides are generally effective in controlling weeds from 6 to 12 weeks following application. For season-long control, an additional application should follow 9 weeks from the initial one. Refer to Table 1 for preemergence herbicides for use in Florida.

Postemergence. Postemergence chemicals are active on emerged weeds. Normally, *the younger the weed seedling, the easier it will be controlled.* Postemergence herbicide effectiveness is reduced when the weed is under drought stress, has begun to head-out (produce seeds), or mowed before the chemical has time to work (several days after application). Avoid application when these detrimental growing conditions exist. Refer to Table 2 for postemergence herbicides for use in Florida.

Fertilizer/Herbicide Mixtures

Many herbicides are formulated with a fertilizer as the carrier. Fertilizer/herbicide mixtures enable a "weed-n-feed" treatment in the same application or trip over the turfgrass. When using these products, it is important to determine if the manufacturer's recommended rate of the product supplies the amount of fertilizer needed by the turfgrass and the amount of herbicide that is required for weed control. Supplemental applications of fertilizer or herbicide may be required if the fertilizer/herbicide product does not supply enough fertilizer or herbicide to meet the fertility needs of the turfgrass or the amount of herbicide needed for weed control.

Turfgrass fertilizer/herbicide products should be used with caution near ornamentals. Products that contain dicamba, metsulfuron, or atrazine can be absorbed by the roots of ornamentals and cause severe injury. Do not apply products that contain these over the root zone of ornamental trees and shrubs.

Adjuvants

An adjuvant is a spray additive that enhances the performance or handling characteristic of a herbicide. Adjuvants include surfactants, crop oils, crop oil concentrates, antifoaming agents, drift control agents, and compatibility agents. Surfactants, crop oils, and crop oil concentrates are added according to label directions since indiscriminate use may result in severe turfgrass injury or decreased herbicide performance. These additives do not improve the performance of preemergence herbicides and are used only with postemergence herbicides. Surfactants, crop oils, and crop oil concentrates are not always added to postemergence herbicides. Some herbicide formulations have premixed surfactants and no additional surfactant is necessary. Commonly used agricultural surfactants are Surfactant WK, X-77, Kinetic, and Triton AG98.

WEED CONTROL PRIOR TO TURF ESTABLISHMENT

Preplant Treatment

The best preplant weed control available for new turf sites is fumigation. Fumigating chemicals kill most weed seeds, insects, and nematodes. It is much easier to prevent weed establishment than try to eradicate them after emergence. Dazomet (Basamid Granular) may be used by homeowners as a preplant herbicide treatment. This may be used with and without a plastic cover. If a cover is not available, cultivate the soil and keep moist for 1 week. Apply Dazomet at 8 to 13 ounces of product per 100 square feet. Immediately irrigate to the depth control desired. If a cover is available, treat the soil in front of a

Table 1. Preemergence herbicides for weed control in turf.

Turfgrasses	Weeds Controlled	Herbicide	
		Common Names	(Trade Name Examples)
St. Augustinegrass, bahiagrass, centipedegrass, bermudagrass, zoysiagrass	Crabgrass, goosegrass, crowfootgrass, annual bluegrass, and some annual broadleaf weeds such as spurges	Benefin DCPA Napropamide Bensulide Oryzalin Benefin + oryzalin Benefin + trifluralin Pendimethalin Dithiopyr Prodiamine	(Balan) (Dacthal) (Devrinol) (Betasan, PreSan) (Surflan) (XL) (Team) (Pre-M) (Dimension) (Barricade)

Remarks: Follow label instruction for a specific product. Do not apply to immature turf, sodded, or newly sprigged areas. For continued summer weed control, repeat application 9 weeks after the initial. Delay reseeding 6-16 weeks after application. Several of these are also available on a fertilizer carrier. Do not overtreat by making several trips around trees and shrubs, and do not use these mixtures each time the lawn needs fertilizer. Do not use weed/feed fertilizers once weed seedlings germinate. Use a straight fertilization source when fertility is the objective at this time.

Turfgrasses	Weeds Controlled	Herbicide	
St. Augustinegrass, bermudagrass, zoysiagrass	Crabgrass, goosegrass, purslane, woodsorrel, carpetweed, annual bluegrass	Oxadiazon	(Ronstar)

Remarks: For use by commercial turf and landscaping personnel only. May cause temporary turf discoloration. Do not apply to wet turf. Irrigate after application to increase effectiveness. Do not apply to newly established turf. Delay reseeding for 4 months following treatment. Oxadiazon is the safest preemergence herbicide to use on newly sprigged or sodded areas.

Turfgrasses	Weeds Controlled	Herbicide	
Centipedegrass, St. Augustinegrass, zoysiagrass	Annual bluegrass, crabgrass, corn speedwell, chickweed, henbit, hop clover, spurweed, pennywort, and other broadleaf weeds	Atrazine Isoxaben	(Aatrex & others) (Gallery)

Remarks: Atrazine may be applied for pre- and postemergence broadleaf weed control in St. Augustinegrass, centipedegrass, and zoysiagrass. Avoid application during greenup. May be used in newly sprigged, sodded, or plugged turf areas with minimum retardation of growth resulting. Do not use under the drip line of trees, shrubs, palms, and ornamentals. May cause yellowing of bahiagrass. For pennywort control, apply in fall and repeat 3-4 weeks later. Complete control may take more than 1 year. A pre-packaged mixture of atrazine and bentazon is available as Prompt. Prompt generally provides superior control over atrazine alone once weeds have emerged. Repeat applications spaced 3 weeks apart may be necessary for complete control.

Isoxaben provides preemergence control of many broadleaf weeds but must be tank-mixed with other herbicides to control annual grassy weeds. It is also labeled for bermudagrass and bahiagrass.

NOTE: Numerous commercial trade names may be available to the homeowner other than those listed. Some of the herbicides listed are Restricted Use Products and require a pesticide license to buy and use. Some herbicides listed are not available in small quantities. The homeowner is advised to consult a pest control operator for commercial application.

rotary tiller and cover the soil for 2 days after treatment. Planting may take place 14 to 21 days after treatment. *Read and follow all label recommendations to the letter.*

Existing weeds such as bermudagrass or nutsedge may be killed prior to grass establishment by using a nonselective material such as glyphosate (Roundup Pro, Kleenup). Only emerged plants will be controlled with this chemical. Glyphosate has no soil residual effect and will have no activity on nongerminated seeds. Glyphosate (Roundup Pro 4 pounds per gallon) is applied at 2 to 5 ounces per gallon of water and may require repeat treatments for complete control of perennial weeds such as bermudagrass. Glyphosate is a nonselective material and will injure most plants encountered. Use extreme caution when applying glyphosate around desired plants.

Seeded Areas

Do not apply preemergence herbicides prior to or immediately following seeding of grasses such as common bermudagrass, bahiagrass, centipedegrass, or ryegrass. Due to their root pruning or seedling kill mode of action, preemergence herbicides may be applied only after seeded grasses have emerged and are well established. A rule of thumb for timing is to make an application after the desired grasses are 2 to 3 inches tall or have begun to spread by runners (stolons). At this time, *half* the normal preemergence herbicide rate (Table 1) may be applied. Postemergence herbicides (Table 2) may also be applied at *one-half* rates at the same growth stage.

If a prior preemergence herbicide has been applied, wait 9 weeks before attempting seeding. Use a small test

Table 2. Herbicides for postemergence weed control in turf.

Turfgrasses	Weeds Controlled	Herbicide	
		Common Names	(Trade Name Examples)
Centipedegrass	Crabgrass, goosegrass, and other annual grasses	Sethoxydim	(Vantage)
Remarks: Apply before weedy grasses exceed 4 inches in height. **Do not** apply to any desirable turfgrasses except **centipedegrass**. For bahiagrass and bermudagrass suppression, repeat treatment 10-14 days after the first application. Do not mow within 7 days before or after application, nor make more than 2 applications per season. Do not apply to grass under moisture, mowing (scalping), or cold temperature stress.			
Bermudagrass, zoysiagrass	Crabgrass, goosegrass, dallisgrass, and nutsedge	**MSMA** **CMA**	(Many formulations and trade names are available)
Remarks: Repeat applications at 7- to 10-day intervals are necessary. Discoloration of Tifgreen 328 and Tifdwarf will occur. Use only when soil moisture is adequate and temperatures are below 85°F. **Do not** use on St. Augustinegrass, centipedegrass, or bahiagrass turf.			
Tifway (419) bermudagrass, St. Augustinegrass	Crabgrass, goosegrass, bullgrass, sandbur	Asulam	(Asulox)
Remarks: Do not apply to freshly mowed turf or turf under moisture or mowing (scalping) stress. Application during hot (>80°F), dry weather normally results in turf phytotoxicity and should be avoided.			
Bermudagrass, zoysiagrass, bahiagrass, centipedegrass	Wild garlic/onion, dandelion, clover, plantains, and other broadleaf weeds	2,4-D amine + dicamba + MCPP and/or 2,4-DP	(Many formulations and trade names are available)
Remarks: Apply to young, actively growing weeds. Repeat application at 2 weeks, if necessary. Do not spray in temperatures above 80°F. Avoid drift. For wild garlic/onion control, add a commercial surfactant and treat in early December. Follow with a repeat application in February and schedule this for 3 consecutive years. <u>Caution:</u> use only when there is no air movement. <u>Do not</u> use within the root zone of ornamentals. Most woody shrubs, ornamentals, and trees are highly sensitive to these materials. Read and follow all instructions and warnings on product labels before use. Although labeled for use on St. Augustinegrass, 2,4-D has caused considerable injury to it, especially during periods of hot weather. Therefore, it is suggested not to use products containing 2,4-D on St. Augustinegrass unless some degree of turf injury is acceptable. The addition of dicamba, MCPP and/or 2,4-DP to 2,4-D will increase weed control but also increase the potential of turf discoloration. Refer to information on atrazine in Table 1 for broadleaf weed control in St.Augustinegrass, centipedegrass, or zoysiagrass as this should be the first herbicide used for broadleaf weed control in these turfgrasses.			
Bahiagrass, bermudagrass, centipedegrass, St. Augustinegrass	Yellow nutsedge, globe sedge, annual sedge	Bentazon	(Basagran T&O)
Remarks: Apply to actively growing yellow nutsedge under good moisture conditions. Repeat application may be necessary. Do not mow 3-5 days prior to or after application. Will also control other nutsedges, except purple nutsedge.			
Bermudagrass, centipedegrass, St. Augustinegrass, zoysiagrass	Purple nutsedge, sandbur, wild garlic	Imazaquin	(Image)
Remarks: Do not apply to newly seeded, sodded, or sprigged areas, or golf greens. Not labeled for use on bahiagrass. Use only on well-established, green, actively growing turfgrass.			
Bahiagrass, bermudagrass, centipedegrass, St. Augustinegrass, zoysiagrass	Most sedges and kyllinga species	Halosulfuron	(Manage)
Remarks: Note the low use rate on the label. Weeds should be actively growing when treated. Repeat application(s) 3 to 4 weeks apart will be needed for complete control.			

area to determine when the herbicide residues permit seedling growth.

Sprigged, Sodded or Plugged Areas

Preemergence herbicides should be applied following signs of new growth at *half* the normal rate recommended for established grasses. Water should be applied to treated areas immediately to activate the herbicide. If herbicide is not applied soon after planting, weed seedlings will emerge and will be unaffected by preemergence herbicides. If over half the recommended herbicide rate is applied, severe root pruning may result to the desirable turf.

Atrazine 4EC is recommended at 1.5 fluid ounces per 1000 square feet as a preemergence treatment, but only for centipedegrass and St. Augustinegrass. Atrazine will provide good weed control and minimal damage to these grasses but will severely stunt or kill other lawn turf species.

Postemergence herbicides, in general, should not be applied until the grass is visibly growing and spreading. Mowing will help control most broadleaf weeds until the lawn is well established. Spot spraying of weeds should be practiced until establishment occurs. Use only half the recommended rate of atrazine or simazine until the turf has matured.

APPLICATION PROCEDURES

Herbicides

Proper rates. To avoid injury to turfgrasses and ornamentals, apply proper rate of herbicide. Mark off 1000 square foot areas to apply herbicides. Apply herbicides in $1/2$ to 1 gallon of water per 1000 square feet (approximately 20 to 40 gallons per acre).

Applicators. For increased application accuracy, air pressure type sprayers are preferred over hose-end type sprayers. For herbicides formulated as a granular, use a spreader and calibrate properly.

Vapor drift. Volatile vapor drift from 2,4-D esters or spray drift from 2,4-D amines, dicamba, or other phenoxy or benzoic acid compounds may damage sensitive plants such as ornamentals, trees, vegetables, or fruits. Amine forms of phenoxys can be used with greater safety near sensitive plants.

Equipment. Do not apply insecticides or fungicides or other herbicides with equipment used for 2,4-D, due to the difficulty of removing this herbicide from most sprayers.

PESTICIDES

Labels. Observe all directions, restrictions, and precautions on pesticide labels. It is dangerous, wasteful, and illegal to do otherwise.

Storage. Store pesticides behind locked doors in original containers with labels intact, separate from seed, fertilizer, and other pesticides.

Dosage. Use pesticides at correct dosage and intervals to avoid illegal residues or injury to plants and animals.

Disposal. Dispose of used containers in compliance with label directions so that contamination of water and other hazards will not result.

Clothing. Always wear protective clothing when applying pesticides. At a minimum, wear a long-sleeved shirt, long-legged pants, rubber gloves, boots (never go barefoot or wear sandals), eye protection, and a wide-brimmed hat.

Handling. Never eat, drink, or smoke when handling pesticides, and always wash with soap and water after use.

Rinsing. Triple rinse a container that has been emptied into the spray tank. Never pour pesticides down a drain or into an area exposed to humans, animals, or water.

USEFUL CONVERSIONS

gallon/acre = 2.93 oz/1000 sq ft

1 acre = 43,560 sq ft

100 gal/acre = 2.3 gal/1000 sq ft = 1 qt/100 sq ft

1 liter = 1000 milliliters (ml) = 1.058 qts

100 lbs/acre = 2.3 lbs/1000 sq ft

1 lb = 453.6 grams = 16 oz

1% by volume = 10,000 ppm = 10 grams/liter = 1.33 oz by weight/gallon of water

1 kilogram (kg) = 1000 grams (g) = 2.2 lbs

❧ CHAPTER SIX ❧

Insect
Problems

Management Guide for Insects and Related Arthropods in Lawns and Other Turfgrass Areas

D. E. Short

This guide suggests pesticides and cultural practices for controlling insect pests in turfgrass. Certain pesticides listed herein can be applied only to commercial turf areas such as golf courses and sod farms; others may be applied to lawns and other non-commercial turf, but only with certified applicators; still others are over-the-counter pesticides available to the general public for purchase and application.

Monitor the turf area regularly. If a pest problem is present, diagnose it correctly and select the proper pesticide. Read, understand and explicitly follow the pesticide label directions. Be familiar with and obey all federal, state, and local pesticide laws and regulations.

Insects listed in this publication include:

❏ Chinch Bugs (Table 1)

❏ Sod Webworms, Armyworms, and Grassloopers (Table 2)

❏ Mole Crickets (Table 3)

❏ White Grubs and Billbugs, and Spittlebugs (Table 4)

❏ Grass Scales and Bermudagrass Mites (Table 5)

❏ Nuisance Pests (Table 6)

❏ This publication is revised at least once each year. Contact your local county cooperative extension office for the most current version.

For information on identification, biology, symptoms of damage and integrated pest management practices, order the illustrated color publication entitled *Insects and Related Pests of Turfgrass in Florida* (SP 140). Single copies may be purchased from Publications, IFAS Building 664, P.O. Box 110011, Gainesville, FL 32611-0011.

Table 1. Chinch Bugs.

Follow directions and precautions on pesticide container labels carefully. Be sure the formulation of pesticide you use is labeled for use on turfgrass.

CHEMICAL CONTROLS	
Pesticide Formulation[1]	Amount of Formulation for 1,000 Sq Ft
Crusade 5 G[2]	1.5 - 1.8 lb
Diazinon[3,6]	See label.
Dursban[3]	See label.
Oftanol 2	3 fl oz
Oftanol 1.5 G[3]	See label.
Orthene turf, tree & ornamental spray[3]	1.2 - 2.4 oz
Pounce 3.2 EC[4]	0.7 - 0.9 fl oz
Scimitar WP[4]	See label.
Tempo 2[4]	See label.
Triumph 4 E[5]	$3/4$ fl oz

Granulated formulations of the above materials are equally effective. Apply as directed on the label.

Cultural Controls: Consult other sections in this book for minimal fertility recommendations for St. Augustinegrass. Using less nitrogen will reduce chinch bug problems. Also, water-insoluble nitrogen causes less damage than do water-soluble sources. Mow St. Augustinegrass to correct height: 3 inches in sunny areas and 4 inches in shaded areas. Keep mower blade sharp. Controlling thatch will reduce chinch bug numbers, and pesticides, if required, will be more effective where thatch is not allowed to build up. To preserve beneficial arthropod numbers, monitor turf area regularly and spot treat damaged area and a 5-foot area surrounding it. Recheck for control in 2 to 3 days. Spot treat again if necessary. Chinch bugs are especially troublesome during dry-weather periods.

[1] Only a few formulations of recommended insecticides are listed as examples. Many others are also available. **Read container labels carefully for directions, application techniques, irrigation requirements, and precautions.**

[2] Not labeled for lawns.

[3] Certain formulations of Diazinon, Dursban, Orthene, and Oftanol 1.5G are over-the-counter products available to the general public. The remaining products must be applied by a certified pest control operator.

[4] Several pockets of chinch bugs resistant to organic phosphate have occurred in south Florida. If one of the above organic phosphate insecticides does not provide control, apply Pounce, Tempo or Scimitar or replace grass with Floratam, Floralawn or a grass other than St. Augustine.

[5] For restrictions on the use of Triumph, see Table 3 (Mole Crickets).

[6] Do not apply Diazinon on golf courses or sod farms.

Table 2. Sod Webworms, Armyworms and Grassloopers.

Follow directions and precautions on pesticide container labels carefully. Be sure the formulation of pesticide you use is labeled for use on turfgrass.

CHEMICAL CONTROLS	
Pesticide Formulation[1]	Amount of Formulation for 1,000 Sq Ft
Bacillus thuringiensis [2,4]	See label.
Crusade 5 G[5]	1.5 - 1.8 lb
Diazinon[4,8]	See label.
Dursban[4]	See label.
Dylox or Proxol 80% WP	1$\frac{1}{2}$ - 3$\frac{3}{4}$ oz
Mocap 10 G[6]	1.15 lb
Orthene turf, tree & ornamental spray[4]	See label.
Pounce 3.2 EC[3]	0.35 - 0.45 fl oz
Scimitar WP	3 - 6 g
Tempo 2	See label.
Triumph 4 E[7]	$\frac{3}{4}$ fl oz
Turcam 76% WP	$\frac{1}{2}$ - 1 oz
Cultural Controls: The same cultural controls used for chinch bugs apply to these caterpillars on all turfgrasses.	

[1] Only a few formulations of recommended insecticides are listed as examples. Many others are also available. **Read container labels carefully for directions, application techniques, irrigation requirements, and precautions.**

[2] Not recommended for armyworms.

[3] Use chinch bug rate for armyworms.

[4] Certain formulations of *Bacillus thuringiensis*, Diazinon, Dursban, Orthene, and Sevin are over-the-counter products available to the general public. The remaining pesticides must be applied by a certified pest control operator.

[5] Not labeled for lawns.

[6] Mocap only labeled for golf courses.

[7] For restrictions on the use of Triumph, see Table 3 (Mole Crickets).

[8] Do not apply Diazinon on golf courses or sod farms.

Table 3. Mole Crickets.

Follow directions and precautions on pesticide container labels carefully. Be sure the formulation of pesticide you use is labeled for use on turfgrass.

CHEMICAL CONTROLS	
Pesticide Formulation[1]	Amount of Formulation for 1,000 Sq Ft
Crusade 5 G[2]	1.8 lb
Dursban Bait[4]	See label.
Mainstay 2 G	4 - 4.6 lb
Mocap 10 G[3]	1.7 - 2.3 lb
Oftanol 2	3 fl oz
Oftanol 5% G	0.9 lb
Oftanol 1.5 G[4]	3 lb
Orthene turf, tree & ornamental spray[4]	See label.
Triumph 4 E[5]	$1^{1}/_{2}$ fl oz
Turcam 2 1/2 G	1.9 - 3.7 lb

Cultural Controls: To ensure better damage tolerance, do not mow grass shorter than recommended heights and be sure blade is sharp. Do not allow turf to dry out excessively. For optimum root growth, be sure potassium, other macro- and minor nutrients and pH are maintained at optimum levels. To encourage a healthy root system, irrigate with $^{3}/_{4}$ inch of water when grass begins to wilt. Do not irrigate again until grass begins to wilt.

NOTE: Sprays and granules should be applied during mid- to late June (Orthene and baits in mid-July and later). When insecticides are applied later in the year (August to October), more damage will have occurred and the crickets are more difficult to control. Apply pesticides during late afternoon or early evening hours. Irrigate with $^{1}/_{2}$ inch of water immediately after applying sprays or granules (except Orthene). Apply baits as late as possible in the afternoon and do not irrigate following application for 2 to 3 days if possible. If soil is not moist, it is important to irrigate before applying sprays, granules and baits.

Overwintered mole crickets become active in March, April, and May. Treatment at this time is optional except in highly maintained turf areas or sod fields. Orthene is suggested if a pesticide is needed for adult cricket control in the spring. Treatment at this time may reduce tunneling damage but does not replace treatment later in the season. If possible, it is important to keep damaged grass rolled (packed down), watered and properly fertilized to minimize damage.

An assessment of spring tunneling (egg-laying) activity on golf courses, sod farms and other large turf areas can help reduce the area treated and decrease pesticide usage when nymphs hatch later. Map areas in the spring (April through May), showing areas of overwintered mole cricket activity. Maps of fairways or fields can be made by using landscape plantings or distance markers as landmarks. Target these sites for treatment in June. Mapping saves labor, reduces the amount of pesticide applied and limits possible environmental contamination.

[1] Only a few formulations of recommended insecticides are listed as examples. Many others are also available. **Read container labels carefully for directions, application techniques, irrigation requirements, and precautions.**

[2] Not labeled for lawns.

[3] Mocap only labeled for golf courses.

[4] Oftanol 1.5 G, Orthene and various baits are over-the-counter products available to the general public. The remaining pesticides must be applied by a certified pest control operator.

[5] Triumph is restricted to certain soil types and several application techniques must be followed. It is labeled for use on lawns (by certified pest control operators only), sod farms and golf courses. On golf courses treat only tees, greens and aprons. A maximum of one application per year is permitted for the 1.5-fl-oz. rate and a maximum of two applications per year, at least 60 days apart, for the $^{3}/_{4}$-fl-oz. (chinch bug, webworm) rate.

Table 4. White Grubs and Billbugs, and Spittlebugs.

Follow directions and precautions on pesticide container labels carefully. Be sure the formulation of pesticide you use is labeled for use on turfgrass.

CHEMICAL CONTROLS	
Pesticide Formulation[1]	Amount of Formulation for 1,000 Sq Ft
White Grubs and Billbugs	
Crusade 5 G[2]	18 lb
Diazinon[3,5]	See label.
Dylox or Proxol 80 WP	3³/₄ oz
Mainstay 2G	4 - 4.6 lb
Mocap 10 G[6]	1.15 lb
Oftanol 2	3 fl oz
Oftanol 5 G	0.9 lb
Oftanol 1.5 G[3]	3 lb
Sevin[3]	See label.
Triumph 4 E[4]	1¹/₂ fl oz
Turcam 2 1/2 G	1.9 - 3.7 lb
Spittlebugs	
Diazinon[3,5]	See label.

[1] Only a few formulations of recommended insecticides are listed as examples. Many others are also available. **Read container labels carefully for directions, application techniques, irrigation requirements, and precautions.**

[2] Not labeled for lawns.

[3] Certain formulations of Diazinon, Sevin, and Oftanol 1.5 G are over-the-counter products available to the general public. The remaining pesticides must be applied by a certified pest control operator.

[4] For restrictions on the use of Triumph, see Table 3 (Mole Crickets).

[5] Do not apply Diazinon on golf courses or sod farms.

[6] Mocap labeled only for golf courses.

Table 5. Bermudagrass Mite.

Follow directions and precautions on pesticide container labels carefully. Be sure the formulation of pesticide you use is labeled for use on turfgrass.

CHEMICAL CONTROLS	
Pesticide Formulation[1]	Amount of Formulation for 1,000 Sq Ft
Bermudagrass Mite	
Mavrik Aquaflow	See label.
Diazinon 25% EC[2]	See label.
Diazinon AG500[2]	See label.
Cultural Controls: Collect and destroy grass clippings to help prevent mite dispersal. In general, as mowing height is decreased, mite infestations are decreased. Keep all areas of bermudagrass mowed as short as is practical. Infestations usually develop in taller grass (in rough areas, around sand traps, along canals, and fence rows, etc.).	

[1] Using a wetting agent in the spray mixture will improve results. Apply a second treatment in 7 to 10 days.

[2] Do not apply Diazinon on golf courses or sod farms.

Table 6. Nuisance Pests: Ground Pearls, Fire Ants, Ants, Millipedes and Sowbugs, Chiggers, Fleas and Ticks.

Follow directions and precautions on pesticide container labels carefully. Be sure the formulation of pesticide you use is labeled for use on turfgrass.

CHEMICAL CONTROLS		
Pest	Pesticide Formulation*	Amount of Formulation for 1,000 Sq Ft
Ground Pearls	—	—
Cultural Controls: All approved fertilization, mowing and watering practices should be followed to keep grass growing below the damage. No practical, effective insecticide is currently available.		
Fire ants	Amdro Bait	Follow label directions. Use one of the baits and follow up with Dursban spray in 5 days to control the remaining workers.
	Award Bait	
	Dursban	
	Oftanol 2	See label.
	Oftanol 1.5 G	See label (mound treatment only).
Ants	Diazinon	See label.
	Dursban	See label.
	NOTE: 2 % Diazinon, %5 Malathion, 5% Sevin dust, or 2% Diazinon granules may also be used for ant control. Do not apply Diazinon on golf courses or sod farms.	
Millipedes and Sowbugs	Diazinon	See label.
	Sevin	See label.
Chiggers	Diazinon	See label.
	Dursban	See label.
Fleas	Diazinon	See label.
	Dursban	See label.
	Orthene turf, tree & ornamental spray	See label.
	Tatic 25 WP	
Ticks	Diazinon	See label.
	Dursban	See label.
***Read container labels carefully for directions, application techniques, irrigation requirements, and precautions.**		

Management of Insects in Lawns

D. E. Short, R. J. Black and L. B. McCarty

Several insects and related pests are common in Florida lawns. Southern chinch bugs, spittlebugs, grass scales, and bermudagrass mites suck plant juices. Mole crickets, white grubs, and billbugs live in the soil and damage the grass roots. Other pests, including sod webworms, grass loopers, and armyworms, eat the grass leaves. Additional insects and related pests such as fleas, millipedes, chiggers, sowbugs, and snails do not damage the lawn but may become nuisances by biting people or crawling into houses, garages and swimming pools.

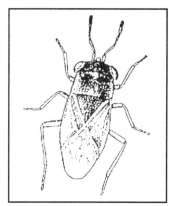

Figure 1. Big-eyed bug.

One group of insects often confused with these pests is actually beneficial. This group includes big-eyed bugs (Figure 1), anthocorids, and nabids that resemble chinch bugs, but actually feed on chinch bug eggs and nymphs. The *Labidura* earwig, ground beetles, and spiders search through the grass and feed on chinch bugs, webworms, and several other lawn pests. The presence of these beneficial organisms will often prevent the insect pests from reaching damaging levels. It is necessary that a small population of pests be present to maintain these beneficial organisms. Preventative treatments (pesticide applications every 4 to 8 weeks) may reduce these beneficial organisms and actually contribute to a persistent chinch bug, sod webworm, or other pest problem. Apply pesticides only when damage is apparent.

Studies throughout Florida over the past several years have demonstrated that the need for pesticide applications to control chinch bugs, sod webworms, and armyworms can be drastically reduced by following certain management practices.

MONITORING

Inspect the lawn weekly during the spring, summer, and fall months and biweekly during the winter months, as outlined in the sections of this publication relating to the various pests to determine if damage is beginning to occur and if insects are the problem.

CULTURAL PRACTICES

Cultural practices can influence the susceptibility of lawn grasses to chinch bugs and turf caterpillars. Attention to the following practices will reduce pesticide use, leading to energy conservation and less contamination of the urban environment. Rapid succulent growth, resulting from frequent or high applications of water-soluble inorganic nitrogen fertilizers, acts as an attractant and substantially increases the chances of insect attack. Incidence of damage from these pests can be greatly reduced with applications of minimal amounts of slow-release nitrogen fertilizers in combination with other macro- and micronutrients. Contact your local county Cooperative Extension office or refer to the appropriate sections in this book for fertility recommendations and sources of slow-release nitrogen fertilizer for each of the turfgrass species in your particular area of the state.

Improper mowing and excessive watering and fertilizing can cause lawngrasses to develop a thick, spongy mat of live, dead and dying shoots, stems, and roots which accumulate in a layer above the soil surface. This spongy mat, referred to as thatch, is an excellent habitat for chinch bugs and turf caterpillars, and chemically ties up insecticides, therefore reducing their effectiveness. When a serious thatch problem exists, it may be necessary to remove the thatch mechanically (vertical mowing, power raking, etc.).

Proper mowing practices can make the grass more tolerant to pests and greatly improve the appearance of a lawn. The best recommendation on mowing is to mow often enough so that no more than one-third of the leaf blade is removed at each mowing. Insects are only a few of the many causes of yellowish or brownish areas in grass. Disease, nematodes, dry weather, and nutritional disorders are sometimes responsible for such injury. It is important that homeowners be sure of the cause so the proper treatment can be applied to correct the trouble without the needless use of pesticides and extensive damage to the grass.

An effective way to survey for chinch bugs, lawn caterpillars, mole crickets and beneficial insects is by the use of a soap mixture applied with a 2-gallon sprinkling can. (This mixture is not effective in surveying for white grub or billbug larvae.) Mix 1½ fluid ounces of dishwashing detergent in a 2-gallon sprinkling can full of water, and drench 4 square feet with this solution. Observe the area for about 2 minutes. If the above pests are present, they will emerge to the grass surface and can be detected. If no insects are found in the first area checked, examine at least three or four other places in the suspected areas.

MOLE CRICKETS

Several species of mole crickets are prevalent in Florida. These include the southern and the tawny (Plate 68). Adults are about 1 inch long, light brown in color, and have forelegs which are well adapted for tunneling through the soil. Both species are believed to have been introduced around 1900 at the seaport of Brunswick, Georgia in the ballast material of ships from the Atlantic Coast of South America. They have become a serious statewide turf pest in Florida in recent years because they have few natural enemies, there are millions of acres of their favorite host grasses (bermuda and bahia), and Florida's sandy soils favor their development and proliferation.

Mole crickets (Figure 2) damage turfgrass in several ways. They tunnel through the soil near the surface and this tunneling action loosens the soil so that the grass is often uprooted and dies due to the drying out of the root system (Plate 69). They also feed on grass roots, causing thinning of the turf, eventually resulting in bare soil (Plate 70).

Mole crickets deposit their eggs in chambers hollowed out in the soil. Most chambers are found in the upper 6 inches of soil but cool temperatures and/or dry soil result in the chambers being constructed at a greater depth. An average female will excavate three to five egg chambers and deposit approximately 35 eggs per chamber.

In north and central Florida, egg laying usually begins in the latter part of March and reaches a peak in May through mid June. Approximately 75% of the eggs are laid during these months. In south Florida, based upon studies in Ft. Lauderdale, egg laying continues throughout the year. Eggs deposited in May and June require about 20 days to hatch; a longer time is required during cooler periods. Peak egg hatching normally occurs during the first half of June in northern Florida and continues through August in southern Florida. A lesser peak of egg hatching occurs in late January to mid-February for the southern mole cricket in south Florida. The young nymphs escape from the egg chamber and burrow to the soil surface to begin feeding on roots, organic material and on other small organisms, including insects.

Most mole cricket feeding occurs at night after rain showers or irrigation, during warm weather. Some surface feeding has been noted when the soil is dry, but feeding is greatly reduced. All nymphal stages as well as adults come to the surface at night to search for food. Tunneling of more than 20 feet per night has been observed. During the day the mole crickets return to their permanent burrows and may remain there for long periods of time when the weather is unfavorable. Adult mole crickets are strongly attracted to lights during their spring dispersal flights.

When mole crickets come to the soil surface, they are subject to predators including fire ants, ground beetles, *Labidura* earwigs, and *Lycosa* spiders. Larger animals including raccoons, skunks, red foxes, armadillos, and several toads also feed on mole crickets, but often damage turf areas when searching for them. Research is underway concerning the introduction of several insect and nematode parasites from other countries as biological control agents.

June is the optimum time for controlling mole crickets. At this time the nymphs are small and visible damage will not usually be noticed due to their small size. To determine if the mole crickets are present, use the soap flush as described earlier in this chapter. Check several places in the lawn; if an average of two to three per square foot is detected, a treatment should be applied.

CHINCH BUGS

The southern chinch bug is the most important insect pest of St. Augustinegrass in Florida. Adults are about 1/5 inch long, and black, with white patches on the wings (Plate 71). The young (nymphs) range from 1/20 inch long to nearly adult size. The small nymphs are reddish with a white band across the back, but become black in color as they approach adult size. Sometimes adults hibernate in the winter in northern Florida, but all stages are present year-round in most of the state. Eggs are laid in sheaths or pushed into soft soil and protected places. In summer, eggs hatch in 10 days and the young develop to adults in 3 weeks. Chinch bugs pass through three generations per year in north Florida and seven to ten in south Florida.

Chinch bugs (Figure 3) are seriously damaging only to St. Augustinegrass but will feed on other grass species. This insect sucks the plant juices through its needle-like beak and also apparently causes other internal injury to

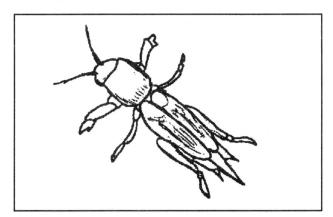

Figure 2. Mole cricket.

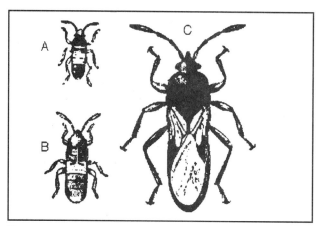

Figure 3. Chinch bugs: A, first stage or red nymph; B, second stage nymph; C, winged adult.

the grass, resulting in yellowish to brownish patches in lawns (Plate 72). These injured areas frequently are first noticed along concrete or asphalt paved edges or in water-stressed areas where the grass is growing in full sun. In south Florida, chinch bugs may cause economic damage from March through October; in north Florida, it is usually from April through September.

When chinch bugs are present in sufficient numbers to cause yellow or brown areas in lawns, they can be found by parting the grass runners in the yellowed areas and observing the soil surface. All stages of chinch bugs will be seen moving through the loose duff on the soil surface. In extremely heavy infestation some of the chinch bugs can be seen crawling over grass blades, sidewalks and outside walls of houses.

If no chinch bugs are seen by this method, their presence or absence can be confirmed by using the soap flush described earlier, or by using a metal can such as a three-pound coffee can with both ends cut out. Place one end of the can on the grass in an area where the grass is yellow and declining. Cut the grass runners around the bottom edge of the can with a knife. Twist and push the bottom end of the can an inch or two into the soil and fill the can with water. If chinch bugs are present they will float to the surface within 5 minutes. It may be necessary to add more water to keep the water level above the grass during this 5-minute period. If no chinch bugs are found in the area checked, examine at least three or four other places in the suspected areas. Treatment may be necessary if 20 chinch bugs are found per square foot.

The St. Augustinegrass varieties Floratam, Floralawn, and Floratine provide various degrees of resistance to chinch bug feeding. Most chinch bugs cannot complete their development when attempting to feed on Floratam and Floralawn. In comparison studies with other varieties (Bitterblue, Roselawn, Raleigh, Seville and common St. Augustinegrass), Floratam, Floralawn, and Floratine showed very little damage. Adult chinch bug mortality on

Floratam and Floralawn averaged 60% compared to less than 10% of the chinch bugs on the other named varieties. Floratam and Floralawn exhibit true resistance to chinch bug injury, while Floratine is only tolerant to low populations. Recently, chinch bug feeding has been noted on Floratam. This is believed to be a strain of chinch bug which can feed on the grass without death.

LAWN CATERPILLARS

Several kinds of caterpillars, the immature or larval stage of moths, including sod webworms, armyworms, cutworms, and grass loopers may cause damage to all turfgrasses (Plate 73). Bermudagrass is their favorite grass while bahiagrass is the least desirable. The most damaging caterpillar is the tropical sod webworm. The larvae are greenish with many black spots. Adults are dingy brown moths with a wingspread of about 3/4 inch. Eggs are deposited on the grass blades and hatch in about 1 week. Larvae feed on the grass blades and cause noticeable injury within 2 weeks. There may be rather extensive damage within the next 1 to 1 1/2 weeks until pupation. Adults appear about 1 week later. They complete their life cycle in 5 to 6 weeks and have several generations each year. Other sod webworms species, fall armyworms, cutworms, and grass loopers are also damaging to turfgrasses in Florida. Armyworms, cutworms, and looper larvae are brown to greenish in color and have stripes along their sides. Sod webworms are usually not present in sufficient numbers to damage grass before June in south Florida, July in central Florida, and August in north Florida. Armyworms (Figure 4) and loopers may be present during the spring, summer or fall.

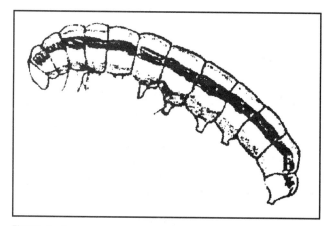

Figure 4. Armyworm.

Sod webworms differ from armyworms and loopers in size and feeding habits (Figure 5 and Plate 74). The webworms feed primarily at night and remain in a curled position on or near the soil surface during the day. This habit makes them difficult to find. Newly hatched caterpillars cause very little visible damage to grass. It is

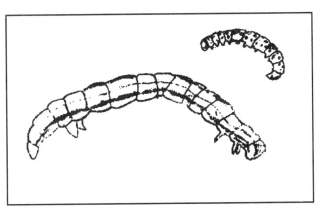

Figure 5. Top: Sod webworm. Center: Grass looper.

not until they are almost full grown, nearly ³/₄ inch long, that their feeding becomes noticeable, and then it appears to show up almost overnight. This, along with their night feeding habit, explains how extensive damage may occur before it is noticed.

Injured grass has notches chewed along the sides of the blades, which are also eaten back unevenly (Plate 75). The foliage may be almost completely stripped off in patches, and these close-cropped areas soon become yellowish to brownish.

The soap flush technique (described earlier) is a good way to detect sod webworms. They may also be found by parting the grass and looking for the small green "worms" curled up on the soil surface and for small green pellets of grass or excrement. A flashlight used at night will reveal the caterpillars feeding in the grass foliage.

Armyworms, cutworms, and loopers grow to about 1¹/₂ inches in length, or about twice the length of the full grown sod webworm. Armyworms and loopers feed during the day and do not rest in a curled position while cutworms feed during the night and remain concealed during the day like webworms.

BILLBUGS AND WHITE GRUBS

Like mole crickets, these insects are soil dwellers. The hunting billbug sometimes causes severe injury to grass in Florida, especially zoysiagrass and bermudagrass. As the name suggests, the adult beetle has a bill or snout and is dark brown and about ³/₈ inch long (Plate 76). The larva or grub, which is legless and grows to about ³/₈ inch in length, is white with a yellowish brown head. This stage causes most of the damage to grass by feeding on the roots and causing dead areas in lawns and other turf (Plate 77). Treatment may be necessary if 10 to 12 billbugs are found per square foot.

Several species of white grubs damage grass (Plate 78). These pests are the larval stage of beetles such as June beetles (*Phyllophaga* sp.) and masked chafers (*Cyclocephala* spp.). Unlike billbug larvae, white grubs

have three pairs of small legs near the head. They are white, with brown heads and a dark area at the rear of the abdomen. They rest in a C-shaped position. Depending on the species, 1 to 4 years are required to complete their life cycle. Grubs damage the grass by feeding on the roots. Yellowish areas develop in the turf and grass can be killed. In severe cases roots are pruned to the extent that the turf mat can be rolled back like a carpet. Adult beetles do not damage grass but usually feed on flowers and foliage of ornamental plants upon emergence in the spring. They are generally distributed in Florida and have become more of a problem in recent years.

If grass consistently wilts in an area of the turf even though adequate water is available, an infestation of root-feeding grubs or billbugs should be considered. To check for grubs and billbugs, use a spade to cut three sides of a 1-foot square piece of sod about 2 inches deep at the edge of one of the off-color or yellowed areas in the lawn. Force the spade under the sod and lay it back. See if the grass roots are chewed off and sift through the soil looking for the larvae (Plate 79). Replace the strip of sod. Check several places in the turf area. As a rule of thumb, if an average of 3 to 5 grubs or 10 billbugs are found per square foot, apply an insecticide.

BERMUDAGRASS MITE

The bermudagrass mite is a serious pest of bermudagrass throughout Florida. Generally speaking, the most severe damage occurs to the coarser varieties of bermudagrass like common and Ormond. The mites are extremely small, only about ¹/₁₃₀ inch long, yellowish-white, and somewhat wormlike in shape. A microscope is needed to find them on infested grass. They multiply very rapidly, requiring only about 7 days to complete their life cycle.

Since the bermudagrass mite is so small and remains hidden beneath the leaf sheath, it can more easily be identified by symptoms of damage to the grass. The mites cause a characteristic type of damage. The grass blades turn light green and curl abnormally, the internodes shorten, tissues swell, and the grass becomes tufted so that small clumps are noticed (Plate 80). The grass loses its vigor, thins out, and may die. Injury is more pronounced during dry weather and especially when the grass is stressed due to poor maintenance.

BANKS GRASS MITE

This spider mite has previously been reported as an economic pest of wheat, corn, sorghum, sugarcane, bluegrass, and bermudagrass in other states. However, in Florida it has become a pest of St. Augustinegrass.

These are small spider mites (less than ¹/₅₀ inch) and deep green in adult stage. The mite's color and small size makes it difficult to detect in St. Augustinegrass. The length of their life cycle varies from 8 to 25 days depending on the temperature. Damage appears as leaf stippling which then turns yellow. The stippling effect is also produced by mildew and SAD virus, so if there is any doubt, samples of grass should be sent to an Extension specialist.

The mite has currently been reported in the central area of Florida and along the southeastern coast. Research is currently underway to determine the best acaricide for control.

GROUND PEARLS

These are mealybugs that live in the soil and suck juices from grass roots. They are spherical and range in size from a grain of sand to about $1/8$ inch diameter (Plate 81). They are yellowish-purple in color and look very much like pearls. Eggs are laid in the soil from March to June. The life cycle from egg to adult requires at least 1, possibly 2 years. They most commonly infest centipedegrass in north and northwest Florida, but they will infect all turfgrass throughout Florida. Severely infested grass turns yellow, then brown.

GRASS SCALES

The rhodesgrass mealybug has been the most frequently encountered scale, but the bermudagrass scale may occasionally be found, especially on bermudagrass (Plate 82). Both scales may be found on several grass species. The body of the rhodesgrass mealybug is roughly spherical, dark but covered with a white cottony secretion, and about the size of a BB. The bermudagrass scale is oval or nearly circular in outline, and is $1/25$ to $1/15$ inch in diameter. Often bermudagrass scales and bermudagrass mites are found infesting the same turf area. Scale insects suck plant juices and the infested grass turns yellow and thins out. The grass may be killed if scales are not controlled.

SPITTLEBUGS

Spittlebugs (Plate 83) are an occasional pest of turfgrasses. The nymphs are white and live within a white frothy mass or "spittle" (Plate 84). They feed by sucking juices from the grass. Infested grass will have spittle masses present, and tips of the grass will turn yellow, followed by browning and curling (Plate 85). Centipedegrass seems to be the grass most often damaged by spittlebugs.

PREDATORS AND PARASITES

Several predatory and parasitic insects are often associated with chinch bugs and webworms. The most

prominent predator of chinch bugs is the big-eyed bug. One of the earwigs (*Labidura*) is a very good predator of both chinch bugs and webworm larvae as well as several other turfgrass insects (Figure 6). It is known to eat as many as 50 adult chinch bugs in one night. Spiders and ground beetles are efficient predators of several harmful lawn insects and are considered extremely beneficial. An ichneumonid wasp is also a very common parasite of webworm larvae and

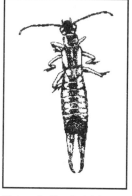

Figure 6. The *Labidura* earwig.

can be seen hovering over grass infested by webworms. Big-eyed bugs, some lygaeids, and anthocorids (another group of predators) are about the same size as chinch bugs and are often confused with them. Quite often these beneficial insects are misidentified as being harmful and a pesticide is applied when it is not needed. Consult the Beneficial Insects Handbook at your County Extension office for more specific information.

NOTES ON CONTROL

Apply insecticides properly. Read and understand all directions on the container label regarding dosage rates, application information, and precautions. When a spray is applied for controlling insects, it is important to apply the insecticide in a large amount of water. The jar attachment to a garden hose is the suggested application device for lawns. The type that requires 15 to 20 gallons of water passing through the hose to empty the quart size jar is recommended. Put the amount of insecticide in the jar as directed on the label for 1000 square feet. Fill the jar the rest of the way with water. Spray the contents over 1000 square feet. To ensure even coverage, spray back and forth across the measured area; then turn at right angles and spray back and forth across the same area.

When spraying for control of soil insects (mole crickets, white grubs and billbugs), the turf should be moist at the time of application. Immediately after spraying the insecticide, irrigate with about $1/2$ inch water to leach the insecticide into the soil where the insects are feeding. For control of surface feeders (chinch bugs, lawn caterpillars, bermudagrass mites, grass scales and spittlebugs), do not irrigate after application.

Granular formulations for the recommended insecticides may be substituted for sprays in controlling chinch bugs, webworms, mole crickets, white grubs, or billbugs. If applied for soil insects (mole crickets, white grubs, or billbugs), irrigate with about $3/4$ inch of water immediately after applying.

To help prevent unnecessary environmental contamination and reduction of beneficial insects, spot treatments can be applied when infestations are first noticed and the damaged area is small. Treat the off-color area and about a 10-foot buffer area surrounding it.

If damage is widespread over the yard or if many infested areas are detected, the entire yard should be treated. Inspect the area two to three times at biweekly intervals to determine if infestation is under control.

If a bait is used for mole crickets, irrigate before application, but do not irrigate after applying the bait. Apply late in the afternoon or in early evening. It is very important to scatter the bait evenly over the soil surface. A few particles should fall on every square inch of the infested area.

PRECAUTIONS

Insecticides are poisons and should be handled as such. Read the manufacturer's label carefully before opening the container and observe all instructions and precautions. Wear rubber gloves when handling and applying insecticides. Do not spill sprays on skin or clothing. Do not breathe mists or fumes. Wash exposed parts of the body with soap and water immediately after using insecticides.

The Bermudagrass Mite and Its Control

D. E. Short

The bermudagrass mite can be a serious pest of bermudagrass lawns throughout Florida. The most severe damage occurs to the coarser varieties of bermudagrass - Common, Ormond, and St. Lucie. Damage is usually not as evident on varieties such as Tifway, Tiflawn, Tifdwarf, and Tifgreen.

The mites are extremely small, only about $1/130$th of an inch long, yellowish-white, and somewhat worm-like in shape. They cannot be seen with the naked eye, and a hand lens is of little help. A microscope is needed to find them on infested grass. They multiply very fast, requiring only about 7 days to complete their cycle from egg to adult at ideal temperature and humidity. The mites tend to develop between the grass stem and blade sheath; this area protects them and makes spray penetration into this area difficult. They remain for most of their life beneath the grass sheath, and large numbers in all stages of development may be found under infested sheaths.

Since the bermudagrass mite is so small, it can be identified only by the symptoms of damage to the grass (Figure 1) unless sufficient magnification is used. Fortunately, the mite causes a characteristic type of damage. The grass blades turn light green and curl abnormally. The internodes (the area between the joints of a stem) shorten, the tissues swell, and the grass becomes tufted so that small clumps are noticed. This produces small "cabbage heads" or "witches brooms" in the grass. With heavily infested grass, you can feel these clumps by moving your hand through the grass. The grass loses its vigor, thins out, and may die. Injury is more pronounced during dry weather and especially when the grass is stressed because it is not being well-maintained.

CONTROL

There are other factors such as diseases, drought, nutritional imbalance, and nematodes or insects that damage or discolor bermudagrass. The lawn should be examined carefully to determine what corrective measures are needed.

When it is established that bermudagrass mites are the problem, begin control measures as soon as possible. The recommended control is diazinon, applied as a spray. Jar attachments to garden hoses are excellent types of sprayers for homeowners to use when combatting lawn pests. Be sure to use a lawn hose attachment sprayer and not one that is for use on ornamental plants. Use the type which requires 15 to 20 gallons of water passing through the sprayer to empty the quart-sized jar. Put the amount of insecticide in the jar for 500 square feet (Table 1) and fill the remainder of the jar with water. Spray the contents of the jar over 500 square feet of lawn. To assure even coverage, spray from right to left across the measured area, then turn 90° and spray the same area from right to left. Refill the jar and move to another measured area, repeating this application procedure. Apply a second application 4 to 6 days later.

If you are following a minimal maintenance program, it is possible to closely mow the grass to a height of $3/4$ inch and dispose of all clippings, thus preventing further infestation by the mite. To reduce stress, water the lawn thoroughly for the next 3 days. This combination (mowing and watering) is an efficient control technique for small-scale infestations. Mite infestations are most frequently found on sloped ground where water drainage occurs, as well as near fence posts and other obstructions where mowing is minimal or where grass clippings are dumped.

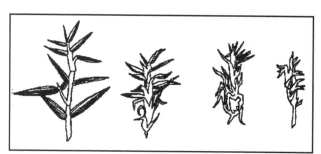

Figure 1. Bermudagrass mite symptoms on bermudagrass. L-R: normal, early symptoms, late symptoms, and final result.

Table 1. Insecticidal control of bermudagrass mites.

Pesticide	Amount per 500 sq ft of lawn
Diazinon 25% EC (2 lb/gallon)	6 tablespoons
Diazinon AG 500 EC (4 lb/gallon)	3 tablespoons
Mavrik Aquaflow	See label
NOTE: Do not use Diazinon on golf courses or sod farms.	

Irrigation, the proper use of fertilizers, and other approved maintenance practices to make the grass grow vigorously will greatly aid the appearance of infested bermudagrass.

PRECAUTIONS

Pesticides are poisons and should be handled as such. Read the manufacturer's label carefully before opening the container and observe all instructions and precautions. Wear rubber gloves and boots when handling and applying insecticides. Do not breathe mists or fumes or spill sprays on the skin. Change clothes and wash all exposed parts of the body immediately after using pesticides. Store pesticides in original labeled containers in a locked area out of the reach of children.

Southern Chinch Bug Management on St. Augustinegrass

D. E. Short, R. J. Black and L. B. McCarty

The southern chinch bug is the most injurious pest of St. Augustinegrass in Florida (Figure 1). It is not a serious pest on any of the other lawn grasses. In northern Florida, the eggs begin hatching about the middle of April each year. Three generations of southern chinch bugs with a partial fourth generation occur in north and central Florida. In south Florida, the eggs begin hatching in late February and there are seven generations per year. The nymphs (immature chinch bugs) are about the size of a pinhead when they hatch and they molt five times before reaching the adult stage. The small nymphs are bright red with a white band across the back. Late stage nymphs and adult chinch bugs are about $1/5$ inch long and black; the adults have white wings.

Figure 1. Chinch bug.

Southern chinch bugs suck the plant juices from grass resulting in yellowish to brownish patches in the lawns. These injured areas are often first noticed in water stressed areas along edges of lawns and in particular during dry periods.

Studies throughout Florida the past several years have demonstrated that certain management practices can drastically reduce the need for pesticide applications for control of southern chinch bugs. Attention to these practices will aid in alleviating excessive fertilizer and pesticide usage resulting in energy conservation and reduced contamination of the urban environment.

CULTURAL PRACTICES

Cultural practices can influence the susceptibility of St. Augustinegrass to chinch bugs. Rapid growth resulting from frequent applications of water soluble inorganic nitrogen fertilizers increase the chance of chinch bug attack. Chinch bug problems can be greatly reduced with minimum applications of slow release nitrogen fertilizers. Refer to other sections in this book for minimal fertility recommendations for St. Augustinegrass.

Prolonged periods of moisture stress can encourage southern chinch bug problems. Keep a close watch on the lawn and when the edges of the grass leaves start curling and appear to have a dull bluish-gray color, water the lawn immediately with $3/4$ inch of water. Do not irrigate again until wilting begins to occur.

Excessive water or fertilization can cause St. Augustinegrass lawns to develop a thick, spongy mat of live, dead and dying shoots, stems, and roots which accumulate in a layer above the soil surface. This spongy mat, referred to as thatch, is an excellent habitat for chinch bugs. The thatch provides a home for chinch bugs and chemically ties up insecticides and therefore reduces control. When a serious thatch problem exists, it may be necessary to remove the thatch mechanically (vertical mowing, power raking, etc.).

Proper mowing practices can make the grass more tolerant to chinch bugs and greatly improve the appearance of the lawn. St. Augustinegrass should be mowed to a height of 3 to 4 inches. It is very important to keep the mower blade sharpened. The grass should be mowed often enough so that no more than $1/3$ of the leaf blade is removed at each mowing. Do not remove the clippings.

MONITORING

Inspect the lawn every week during the spring, summer, and fall months. Look for off-color areas, especially in portions of the lawn that are not shaded by trees, and along sidewalks and driveways.

Usually, when chinch bugs are present in sufficient numbers to begin causing yellowish areas in lawns, they can be found by parting the grass at the margin of the yellowed areas and closely examining the soil surface and base of the turf. Several examinations should be made in suspect areas. In heavy infestations, the bugs may be seen crawling over the grass blades and sidewalks.

If no chinch bugs are noticed by visual inspection of the grass, their presence or absence can be confirmed by using a metal can such as a 2- or 3-lb coffee can with both ends cut out. Push one end about 2 or 3 inches into the soil at the margin of the yellowish areas of grass. If it is difficult to pass the can through the St. Augustinegrass runners, a knife may be used to cut a circle in the grass the size of the can. Fill with water and if chinch bugs are present, they will float to the surface within 5 minutes. It may be necessary to add more water to keep the level above the grass surface during the 5-minute period. If bugs are not found in the first area checked, examine at least 3 or 4 additional places in the suspected areas.

There are other factors such as disease, nutritional deficiencies, and drought that will cause off-color areas to occur in lawns. Therefore, the lawn should be carefully examined to determine what corrective measures are needed.

RESISTANT ST. AUGUSTINEGRASS VARIETIES

St. Augustine varieties Floratam, Floralawn and Floratine provide varying degrees of resistance to chinch bug feeding. Most chinch bugs cannot complete their development when attempting to feed on Floratam or Floralawn. If a new lawn is being established or an old one replaced, one should consider the use of Floratam or Floralawn. In comparison studies with other established varieties (Bitterblue, Roselawn, Scott's 1081, Seville, Raleigh and Florida common), Floratam and Floralawn showed resistance to the southern chinch bug. Floratam and Floralawn exhibit true antibiosis and are resistant to chinch bug injury, while Floratine is only tolerant to low populations.

BENEFICIAL INSECTS

Several predatory insects are often associated with southern chinch bugs (Figure 2). The most prominent predator of chinch bugs is the black big-eyed bug. A predacious earwig, *Labidura*, is also a very good predator on all stages of the chinch bug. An adult earwig has been observed to eat as many as 50 adult chinch bugs in one night. Big-eyed bugs and anthocorids (another group of predators) are about the same size as chinch bugs and are often confused with them. Quite often these beneficial insects are misidentified as chinch bugs, and a pesticide is applied when it is not needed.

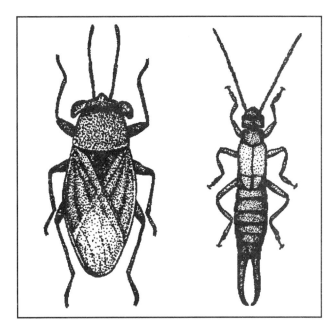

Figure 2. Big-eyed bug and earwig (*Labidura*).

CONTROL WITH PESTICIDES

When it is definitely established that chinch bugs are the problem and the damage threshold has been reached (20 to 25 chinch bugs per square foot) a pesticide should be applied. Products containing either Diazinon, Dursban or Othene are suggested for homeowner application.

Apply the insecticide properly. Read and understand all directions on the container label regarding dosage rates, application information, and precautions. When a spray is used, it is important to apply the insecticide in a large amount of water. The jar attachment to a garden hose is the suggested application device for homeowners. The type that requires 15 to 20 gallons of water passing through the hose to empty the quart-sized jar is recommended. Put the amount of insecticide in the jar as directed on the label for 1000 square feet. Fill the jar the rest of the way with water. Spray-out the contents over 1000 square feet of lawn. To ensure even coverage, spray back and forth across the same area. The treated grass should be irrigated lightly to flush the insecticide into the thatch layer where the chinch bugs are feeding.

Granular formulations of the recommended insecticides may be substituted for sprays. Granules should be applied with a drop-type spreader rather than the cyclone type to avoid getting granules on sidewalks and driveways. Irrigate lightly with about 1/8 inch of water. A correctly applied application should provide control of chinch bugs for 8 to 10 weeks.

To further avoid environmental contamination and reduction of beneficial insects, spot treatments can be applied when infestations are first noticed and the damaged area is very small. Treat the off-color area and about a 5-foot buffer area surrounding it. Inspect the area 2 to 3 times at biweekly intervals to determine if the infestation is under control. If damage is widespread over the yard or if many infested areas are detected, the entire yard should be treated.

In several areas of southern Florida, southern chinch bug populations have developed resistance to the organo-phosphate insecticides (Dursban and Diazinon). If one of the listed organo-phosphates does not provide control, apply a synthetic pyrethrin such as Tempo.

PRECAUTIONS

Insecticides are poisons and should be handled as such. Read the manufacturer's label carefully before opening the container and observe all instructions and precautions. Wear rubber gloves and boots when handling and applying insecticides. Do not breathe mists or fumes or spill sprays on the skin. Change clothes and wash all exposed parts of the body immediately after using pesticides. Store pesticides in original labeled containers in a locked area out of reach of children.

White Grubs and Billbugs in Home Lawns

D. E. Short

Grubs are the larval (immature) stage of several species of beetles including May or June beetles, and masked chafers. The adult beetles feed on the foliage of trees and other plants. The grubs are fat and commonly lie in a C-shaped position (Figure 1). They are dirty white in color with brown heads and with dark areas visible at the rear of the abdomen.

Figure 1. White grub.

Adult billbugs are snout beetles. The beetles are black and about $3/8$ inch long when mature. Billbugs are found most often on zoysiagrass, but also may attack Bermudagrass and other grasses. The larval stage (Figure 2) does the most damage, but both adults and larvae can be found in the soil.

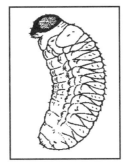

Figure 2. Billbug larva.

Grubs and billbugs damage the grass by feeding on the roots about an inch below the soil surface. Their feeding causes the grass to turn yellow and then brown. The damage may first appear as spots only a few inches in diameter, but these spots will gradually become larger as feeding continues. Heavy infestations completely destroy the roots, and the grass can be rolled back like a carpet. Moles, skunks, and armadillos feed on the grubs and may damage the lawn searching for them.

To inspect for grubs and billbugs, cut three sides of a 1 foot square piece of sod about 2 inches deep with a spade under the sod and lay it back. See if the grass roots are chewed off and sift through the soil to determine if larvae are present. Replace the strip of sod. Inspect several areas in the lawn. As a rule of thumb, if an average of three or four grubs or six to ten billbugs are found per square foot, apply an insecticide.

There are other factors such as disease, nutritional imbalance, and drought that will cause offcolor areas in lawns. The lawn should be examined carefully to determine what corrective measures are needed.

CONTROL

Apply insecticide properly. Read and understand all directions on the container label regarding dosage rates, application information, and precautions (Table 1). The jar attachment to a garden hose is the suggested lawn sprayer for homeowners. The type that requires 15 to 20 gallons of water passing through the hose to empty a quart sized jar is recommended. Put the amount of insecticide in the jar as directed on the label for 1000 square feet. Fill the remainder of the jar with water. Spray the contents over 1000 square feet. To ensure even coverage, spray back and forth across the same area.

Table 1. Insecticidal control of white grubs and billbugs.

Insecticide	Rate
Diazinon Oftanol Sevin Trichlorfon (Dylox or Proxol)	Apply as directed on the container label for controlling grubs and/or billbugs.

When spraying for control of white grubs, or billbugs, the turf should be moist at the time of application. Immediately after spraying the insecticide, irrigate with about $1/2$ inch of water to leach the insecticide into the soil where the insects are feeding.

Granular formulations of the recommended insecticides may be substituted for sprays. Irrigate with $1/2$ inch of water immediately after applying.

PRECAUTIONS

Insecticides are poisons and should be handled as such. Read the manufacturer's label carefully before opening the container and observe all instructions and precautions. Wear rubber gloves when handling and applying insecticides. Do not breathe mists or fumes or spill sprays on the skin. Wash exposed parts of the body immediately after using insecticides. Store pesticides under lock in original containers out of reach of children.

Management of Sod Webworms
and Other Lawn Caterpillars

D. E. Short and R. J. Black

Various caterpillars, primarily the tropical sod webworm (Figure 1) and fall armyworm, are pests of lawn grasses in Florida. Adults of the sod webworm are small, dingy brown moths with a wingspread of about ³/₄ inch. Larvae are small, greenish caterpillars with many black spots and range from ¹/₂₅ inch long when they first emerge from the egg to about ³/₄ inch long when mature. Laboratory studies indicate that at an average temperature of 78°F, 6 weeks is required for the insect to develop from egg to adult. At 72°F, development from egg to adult requires about 12 weeks.

Adults of the fall armyworm are light brown moths with a wingspread of about 1¹/₂ inch. The caterpillars are approximately 1¹/₂ inch long when mature. When first hatched, fall armyworm larvae are more grayish-green than webworms and have a stripe along their sides. When approaching maturity, they are pale brown to black with large stripes along their sides. On the front of the head is a yellow inverted "Y" marking. The length of the life cycle is about the same as that of the tropical sod webworm.

Webworm and fall armyworm larvae, as with other lawn caterpillars, feed on all species of warm season turfgrasses including bermuda, St. Augustine, centipede, zoysia, and bahiagrass. The newly hatched webworm larvae chew away tissue from the surface of the grass blades, leaving a colorless, membranous area on the

leaves. As larvae mature, the grass is progressively chewed off, and becomes ragged and yellowish to brownish in color. Damaged areas are often first noticed along hedges and flower beds. Injury normally begins in a few spots with the injured areas being only 2 or 3 inches across. These spots enlarge, fuse, and may encompass large areas of the lawn when heavy infestations are present. Severely damaged grass under stress due to hot, dry weather may be killed. However, if infested grass is not allowed to suffer from lack of moisture, it can recover from a large amount of webworm feeding.

Armyworm injury is similar to that of webworms; however, the damage is usually more scattered and not confined to patches as with sod webworm infestations. It is not unusual to have populations of armyworms, webworms, and other lawn caterpillars all feeding at the same time in the same location.

Studies throughout Florida during the past several years have demonstrated that pesticide applications to control lawn caterpillars can be drastically reduced by following certain management practices. Attention to these practices will result in energy conservation and less contamination of the urban environment by alleviating excessive fertilizer and pesticide use.

CULTURAL PRACTICES

Cultural practices can influence the susceptibility of lawn grasses to webworms and armyworms. Rapid growth, resulting from applications of water-soluble inorganic nitrogen fertilizers, substantially increase the chances of lawn caterpillar attack. The lush succulent growth attracts egg-laying female moths. Incidence of damage from these pests can be greatly reduced with minimum applications of slow-release nitrogen fertilizers. Refer to other sections in this book for fertilization recommendations for each of the turfgrass species.

Excessive watering or fertilization can cause lawn grasses to develop a thick, spongy mat of live, dead, and dying shoots, stems, and roots which accumulate in a layer above the soil surface. This spongy mat, referred to as thatch, is an excellent habitat for lawn caterpillars, and also chemically ties up insecticides, thereby reducing their effectiveness. When a serious thatch problem exists, it may be necessary to remove the thatch mechanically (vertical mowing, power raking, etc).

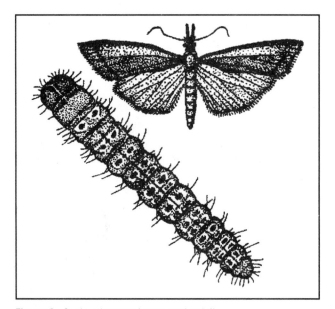

Figure 1. Sod webworm larva and adult.

Proper mowing practices can make the grass more tolerant to lawn caterpillars and greatly improve the appearance of the lawn. It is very important to keep the mower blade sharpened. The grass should be mowed often enough so that no more than $\frac{1}{3}$ of the leaf blade is removed at each mowing. Do not remove clippings.

MONITORING

Inspect the lawn every week during the spring, and especially during the summer and fall months. To check the lawn for caterpillars, examine grass in the off-color areas to determine if the blades have a chewed appearance. Part the grass in the suspect areas and closely examine the soil surface. Several examinations should be made in the off-color areas.

Sod webworm larvae rest in a curled position on the soil surface during the day and feed only at night or during cloudy or rainy periods. Small green pellets of excrement will be numerous on the soil surface when the insects are present. Armyworms do not rest in a curled position but feed during the day and may be seen crawling over the grass.

If no sod webworm or armyworm larvae are noticed by parting the grass, their presence or absence can be confirmed by applying a soap mixture. Mix $1\frac{1}{2}$ fluid ounces of dishwashing soap in a 2-gallon sprinkling can full of water and drench 4 square feet with this solution. Observe the area for about 2 minutes. If any caterpillars are present, they will emerge to the grass surface and can be detected. If no caterpillars are found in the first area checked, examine at least three or four places in suspected areas. Isolated areas of damage due to webworms may occur as early as April in south Florida, and populations move slowly northward as the season progresses. In north Florida, it is usually August before damage occurs. Some years, populations do not become damaging in north Florida. In spite of its name, the fall armyworm is usually the first species to be troublesome in lawns.

There are other factors such as disease, nutritional imbalance, and drought that will cause off-color areas in lawns. The lawn should be carefully examined to determine what corrective measures are needed.

BENEFICIAL INSECTS

A number of beneficial insects and spiders are extremely efficient in reducing lawn caterpillar populations. A predaceous earwig (*Labidura* sp.), several spiders (*Lycosa* spp.), ground beetles, and parasitic wasps are some of the more common predators and parasites found associated with lawn caterpillars. Quite often these are misidentified as pests, and are unnecessarily treated with pesticides. This elimination of beneficial organisms can lead to a caterpillar problem.

CONTROL WITH PESTICIDES

When it is definitely established that lawn caterpillars are the problem, and that the damage threshold has been reached (10 to 12 larvae per square foot), a pesticide should be applied. Products containing either *Bacillus thuringiensis*, diazinon, Dursban or Sevin are suggested for homeowner application. *Bacillus thuringiensis* is a biological control agent which only kills caterpillars.

Apply the insecticide properly. Read and understand all directions on the container label regarding dosage rates, application information, and precautions. When you use a spray it is important to apply the insecticide in a large amount of water. The jar attachment for a garden hose is the suggested lawn sprayer for homeowners. The type that requires 15 to 20 gallons of water passing through the hose to empty the quart-sized jar is recommended. Put the amount of insecticide in the jar as directed on the label for 1,000 square feet, fill the jar with water, and spray the contents over 1,000 square feet. To ensure even coverage, spray back and forth across the same area.

Granular formulations of the recommended insecticides may be substituted for sprays. Granules should be applied with a drop-type sprayer rather than the cyclone type to avoid getting granules on sidewalks and driveways. After application of granules, irrigate lightly with about $\frac{1}{8}$ inch of water.

To further avoid environmental contamination and reduction of beneficial insects, spot treatments can be applied when infestations are first noticed and the damaged area is very small. Treat the off-color area and about a 5-foot buffer area surrounding it. When damage is widespread or many infested areas are detected, the entire lawn should be treated. Inspect the area two to three times at biweekly intervals to determine if the infestations are under control. Caution: Worms treated with *Bacillus thuringiensis* may require 2 to 5 days to die, but they are unable to feed after the first day.

PRECAUTIONS

Insecticides are poisons and should be handled as such. Read the manufacturer's label carefully before opening the container, and observe all instructions and precautions. Wear rubber gloves and boots when handling and applying insecticides. Do not breathe mists or fumes or spill sprays on the skin. Change clothes and wash all exposed parts of the body immediately after using pesticides. Store pesticides in original labeled containers in a locked area out of reach of children.

Mole Crickets in Lawns

D. E. Short

The two most destructive species of mole crickets in Florida are the tawny and southern. The short-winged mole cricket occurs in south Florida and the northern mole cricket can be found throughout Florida but is not numerous. Adults are about 1¹/₂ inches long and are light brown. The forelegs are short and stout and well adapted for tunneling through the soil. Tawny, southern, and short-winged mole crickets (Figure 1) are South American species that hitch-hiked to the United States in a ship's ballast. All three became established about 1900 at the seaport of Brunswick, Georgia.

Mole crickets are important pests for several reasons. The three pest species from South America had no native insect parasites in the U.S. to limit their development and spread. In Florida there are about 4.4 million acres of bahiagrass, which is their favorite host. Much of this is in pasture or roadsides, which are not highly managed. Lastly, Florida's sandy soils provide them with an ideal habitat. Since 1978, concentrated research has been conducted by University of Florida researchers in the following areas: biology, biological control, resistant grass varieties, and chemical control.

Mole crickets damage turfgrass in several ways. They tunnel through the soil near the surface. This tunneling action loosens the soil so that the grass is often uprooted and dies due to desiccation of the root system. Both species of mole crickets damage grass roots causing thinning out of the turf and, eventually, completely bare soil.

Bahiagrass has a very open-growth habit which seems to accentuate the damage by allowing greater desiccation of the root system in the loosened soil. St. Augustinegrass is also damaged somewhat by mole crickets, but due to its more canopy-type growth habit and coarser root system, it does not exhibit as severe a response to mole crickets as does bahiagrass. Centipedegrass and zoysiagrass are not noticeably damaged.

Mole crickets deposit their eggs in chambers hollowed out in the soil. Most chambers are found in the upper 6 in of soil, but cool temperatures and/or dry soil cause the chambers to be constructed at a greater depth. An average female will excavate three to five egg chambers and deposit approximately 35 eggs per cell.

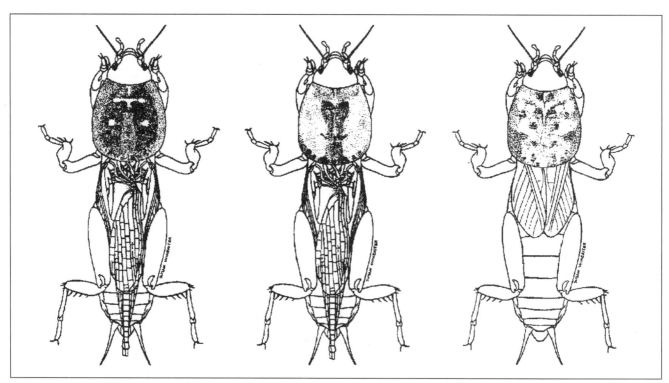

Figure 1. Left to Right: Southern, Tawny, and Short-winged Mole Crickets

In north and central Florida, oviposition by tawny and southern mole crickets usually begins in the latter part of March, with peak egg laying in May through mid-June. Approximately 75% of the eggs are laid during these months. Eggs deposited in May and June require about 20 days to hatch; a longer period is required during cooler periods. Peak egg hatching normally occurs during the first half of June in northern Florida, and continues throughout August in southern Florida with the southern mole cricket. The young nymphs escape from the egg chamber and burrow to the soil surface to begin feeding on organic material and on other small organisms including insects. The short-winged mole cricket lays eggs throughout the year. Its biology is in other respects similar to that of the tawny mole cricket.

Most mole cricket feeding occurs at night during warm weather, after rain showers or irrigation. All nymphal stages as well as adults come to the surface at night to search for food. Tunneling of more than 20 inches per night has been observed. During the day the mole crickets return to their permanent burrows and may remain there for long periods of time when weather conditions are unfavorable. Adult mole crickets are strongly attracted to lights during their spring dispersal flights.

INSPECTING FOR MOLE CRICKETS

Soap flush is an effective method for surveying mole cricket populations, especially in the late spring and early summer when the crickets are small and tunneling activity is not readily evident. Mix 1 1/2 fluid ounces of liquid dishwashing soap in 2 gallons of water and apply with a sprinkling can to 4 square feet of turf in several areas. If an average of two to four mole crickets appear on the surface within 3 minutes, then a treatment is probably needed.

CONTROL

Natural and Biological Control

Southern mole crickets are very cannibalistic and a high percentage of nymphs, especially early instars, may be lost in this manner. Young nymphs will devour each other and the unhatched eggs.

When mole crickets come to the soil surface they are subject to numerous predators, including fire ants, ground beetles, *Labidura* earwigs, and *Lycosa* spiders. Larger animals including raccoons, skunks, red foxes, and armadillos also feed on mole crickets, but often damage lawns when searching for them.

Concentrated research is under way concerning the introduction of several mole cricket parasites from South America. A parasitic nematode *Steinernema scapterisci* has been field-tested extensively since 1985. Results look very promising thus far. A parasitic fly is being evaluated and is now established in Florida. Laboratory and quarantine work is continuing with other natural enemies including fungal pathogens, a predatory larva of a beetle, and a pathogenic virus, all from South America.

Cultural Control

Proper mowing, irrigation, and fertility practices can encourage a deep, healthy root system which is more tolerant to soil-inhabiting insects such as mole crickets, white grubs and billbugs. Do not mow shorter than recommended heights. Keep the mower blade sharp. Do not allow turf to dry out excessively. When irrigation is required, apply 3/4 inch water. Do not irrigate again until grass begins to wilt. This encourages deep root growth. Fertilize according to the soil test for your particular type of grass. It is important to maintain optimum levels of potassium and minor nutrients as well as pH.

Chemical Control

If damage occurred the previous year or if excessive tunneling (egg-laying activity) was noticed in the spring months, a pesticide application will probably be required (Table 1). Mid to late June is the optimum time for an application in north and central Florida and probably during late May in south Florida. Before applying a pesticide, inspect the lawn for tunneling activity. If none is noticed, confirm the presence or absence of mole crickets by use of the soap and water technique described previously. Pesticides may also be applied in the early

Table 1. Insecticidal control of mole crickets.

Pesticide	Rate
Sprays	
Orthene Turf, Tree and Ornamental Spray	Apply as directed on the container label for mole cricket control.
Oftanol 2 Triumph	These are to be applied only by a certified Pest Control Operator.
Granules	
Oftanol 1.5% Turcam 2.5%	Apply as directed on the container label for mole cricket control.
Mainstay 2% Oftanol 5%	These are to be applied only by a certifed Pest Control Operator.
Baits	
Dursban 0.5%	Apply as directed on label.

spring or in July, August, and September. However, due to maturity of the crickets at these times of year, control will be reduced.

Mole crickets can be controlled by sprays, granules, or baits. Apply when the overnight temperature is expected to be 60°F or above. Make sure the lawn is moist when the treatment is applied. If it has become dry, irrigate the area to be treated by running sprinklers for about an hour. This aids in the penetration of the spray or granules into the soil, or in the case of baits, encourages the mole crickets to come to the surface to feed on the bait.

Be sure the pesticide is labeled for lawns. Read and understand all directions on the container label regarding dosage rates, application information, and precautions. When a spray is used, it is important to apply the insecticide in a large amount of water. The jar attachment to a garden hose is the suggested application device for homeowners. The type that requires 15 to 20 gallons of water passing through the hose to empty the quart-sized jar is recommended. Put the amount of insecticide in the jar as directed on the label for 1000 square feet. Fill the remainder of jar the rest of the way with water. Spray the contents over 1000 square feet of lawn. To ensure even coverage, spray back and forth across the same area.

After applying sprays or granules, irrigate immediately (except Orthene and Sevimol) for about 2 to 3 hours (or put on about $^1/_2$ inch of water to leach the insecticide into the top 1 to 2 inches of soil).

If a bait is used, apply it when it is not likely to rain overnight and preferably late in the afternoon. It is very important to scatter the bait thinly and evenly over the soil surface. A few flakes should fall on every square inch of soil in the treated areas.

Baits may be applied by hand. To insure even coverage, spread the bait back and forth across a measured area, then turn at right angles and spread back and forth across the same area again. If distributing by hand, be sure to wear rubber gloves. Do not irrigate after applying.

PRECAUTIONS

Insecticides are poisons and should be handled as such. Read the manufacturer's label carefully before opening the container and observe all instructions and precautions. Wear rubber gloves and boots when handling and applying insecticides. Do not breathe mists or fumes or spill sprays on the skin. Change clothes and wash all exposed parts of the body immediately after using pesticides. Store pesticides in original labeled containers in a locked area out of reach of children.

Ground Pearls in Lawns

D. E. Short

Ground pearls are scale insects that live in the soil and suck the juices from the grass roots. Centipedegrass is the grass most commonly attacked, but infestations have been found in Bahiagrass, St. Augustinegrass, and Carpetgrass.

The eggs are laid in the soil during April and May in north central Florida (Gainesville area). The eggs hatch into tiny crawlers which move about until they locate a feeding site, then they insert their tiny beaks into the grass roots and begin secreting a hard, yellow-brown scaly covering which completely encloses the body. They are round and range in size from a grain of sand to about $1/16$ inch in diameter (Figure 1). They look very much like small pearls, hence their name.

The adult egg-laying female which emerges from the "pearl" is about $1/16$ inch long, pink in color, and has well developed forelegs and claws to enable her to move through the soil. Adult males are rarely seen, but resemble tiny gnats. The life cycle from egg to adult takes at least 1 year and possibly 2 years.

SYMPTOMS OF INJURY

Symptoms attributed to ground pearl injury are first a yellowing of the grass, followed by browning. Ground pearl damage becomes most noticeable when the grass is under stress due to drought, nutritional deficiencies, etc. Under stress conditions, the grass may not be able to withstand the added effects of the pearls and the grass will die. On the other hand, properly watered and otherwise well managed lawns often do not show noticeable damage, even though they are heavily infested with these insects.

There are other factors such as disease, nutritional imbalances, drought, and nematodes (especially in Centipedegrass) that will cause off-color areas in lawns.

The lawn should be carefully examined to determine what corrective measures are needed.

CONTROL

All approved practices regarding fertilization, watering, and mowing should be carried out to keep the grass growing ahead of the damage. At the present time, it is felt that the benefits gained from an insecticide treatment for ground pearls is not sufficient to warrant an application. This is based on past research and grass response to insecticide treatments.

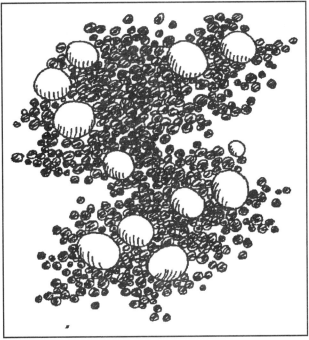

Figure 1. Ground pearls in soil.

Spittlebugs in Turfgrass

D. E. Short

Adult two-lined spittlebugs are black with red eyes and legs and have two orange transverse stripes across their wings (Figure 1). They are approximately $^1/_4$ inch long. The nymphs are yellow or white in color with a brown head. They are enveloped in a mass of white frothy spittle that they excrete for protection. Both adults and nymphs suck juices from the grass with their piercing-sucking mouthparts; however, research has shown that damage is caused primarily by the adults through the injection of phytotoxic salivary substances. Adults are most active during the early morning hours; during the heat of the day they retreat to the soil surface.

Spittlebugs are present throughout the entire state, but they are more prevalent in north and northwest Florida. They attack all turfgrass species but centipedegrass appears to be their favorite host. Adults also feed on ornamental plants, especially hollies.

Eggs are laid at the base of the grass in the thatch, in hollow grass stems, or behind the leaf sheaths. There are five nymphal stages and the life cycle requires about $2^1/_2$ months. There are two generations per year. Eggs laid by the second generation overwinter and hatch the following spring. Depending upon temperature and precipitation, most of the overwintering eggs hatch from late March to late April. The first generation adults are abundant in June. The adult population peaks again in early August to early September.

The majority of the spittle masses (see Figure 1) are not readily visible as they are usually located near the soil surface or in the thatch area. Infested turf wilts and the tips turn yellow and eventually brown then curl. Spittlebugs require high humidity conditions for optimum development. Thatch contributes to these conditions. Follow approved practices regarding mowing, fertilization, and irrigation to reduce thatch buildup. If a thatch problem exists, dethatching will reduce spittlebug problems.

CONTROL WITH PESTICIDES

To improve control, mow and dispose of clippings before an insecticide is applied. Irrigation before treatment will also aid in control. Diazinon is one of the more effective insecticides.

Read and understand all directions on the container label regarding dosage rates, application information, and precautions. When you use a spray, it is important to

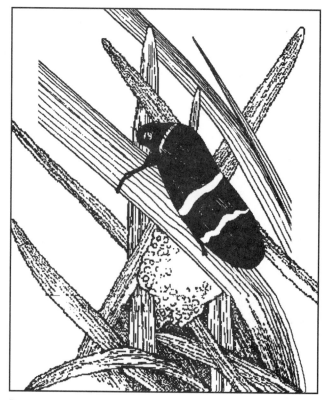

Figure 1. Adult spittlebug and spittle moss.

apply the insecticide in a large amount of water. The jar attachment for a garden hose is the suggested lawn sprayer for homeowners. The type that requires 15 to 20 gallons of water passing through the hose to empty the quart-sized jar is recommended. Put the amount of insecticide in the jar as directed on the label for 1000 square feet, fill the jar with water, and spray the contents over the 1000 square feet. To ensure even coverage, spray back and forth across the same area.

PRECAUTIONS

Insecticides are poisons and should be handled as such. Read the manufacturer's label carefully before opening the container, and observe all instructions and precautions. Wear rubber gloves and boots when handling and applying insecticides. Do not breathe mists or fumes or spill sprays on the skin. Change clothes immediately after using pesticides. Store pesticides in original labeled containers in a locked area out of reach of children.

CHAPTER SEVEN

Disease Problems

Turfgrass Diseases and Their Control

G. W. Simone and T. E. Freeman

Diseases of turfgrass frequently disfigure plantings around homes, recreational areas, and commercial grounds. Pathogens (organisms that cause diseases) are commonly present in turfgrass plantings, and the climate in Florida frequently favors disease development. Fortunately, grasses maintained by proper cultural practices (irrigating, mowing, fertilizing, etc.) are not likely to be as severely damaged as are grasses not receiving proper care. Cost and energy savings result from use of good cultural practices that enhance plant vigor and increase tolerance to disease. The need for costly pesticide applications is thereby reduced.

Generalities can be made about the more commonly found turfgrass diseases in Florida. Many of these diseases require similar environmental conditions to begin, as well as increase in severity. Chemical control measures, heavily relied upon in the past as the only disease control program, are now being used less frequently to supplement such non-chemical controls as host resistance and cultural management.

❏ Not every turfgrass problem is automatically a disease problem. Many of the nondescript disease symptoms of root and crown rot diseases, melting-out, etc., can be mimicked by improper cultural practices, misused pesticides, nematodes, or insect injury. Remember, diseases are continuous conditions that will not stay static but will increase and spread. It often is faster to rule out involvement of other factors than to verify the presence of disease.

❏ Some diseases, like Take-all Root Rot, represent complex developmental cycles involving one or more pathogens (i.e., fungus and nematode) or a pathogen and a cultural stress. Identifying one pathogen without the stress factor or the second invading microbe will not necessarily allow acceptable management of the problem.

❏ Suspected disease problems *cannot* be reliably diagnosed by "eyeballing" or "windshield" observations. Root and crown rot phases of many diseases necessitate laboratory diagnosis.

❏ Diseases can be expected to occur on poorly maintained turf. Imbalances in nitrogen and potassium levels, as well as thatch accumulation, will result in less vigorous, more susceptible turfgrass.

❏ Periods of high humidity, over-irrigation, rain, heavy dews, or fog will favor the incidence of many of the fungal diseases of turf. Free moisture is needed on the plant surface for infection to take place.

CULTURAL CONTROL

Turfgrass managers, including homeowners, should learn the cultural requirements of the grass species and cultivar they are maintaining. For example, the mowing height and mowing frequency for best health varies with each turfgrass species and cultivar. Improper mowing height and frequency can weaken the grass and lower its tolerance to disease. Dull mower blades inflict greater tissue damage than sharp blades. Damage is first evident as unsightly white to brown discoloration of the turf 1 to 2 days after mowing. Damaged tissue also provides an avenue for pathogens to infect the grass.

Diseases of turfgrasses are favored by prolonged periods of high humidity, rain, fog, or heavy dew because moisture on the plant surface is necessary for most pathogens to infect turfgrass. Turfgrass that enters the night period moist from irrigation is more inclined to become diseased. Little can be done to modify natural moisture conditions; however, irrigation can be timed to disfavor disease incidence. Irrigating early in the morning allows the grass to dry thoroughly before evening. This irrigation schedule reduces the time moisture is present on the leaves. Do not water turfgrasses lightly on a daily basis. Wait until the turf begins to show signs of wilt before irrigating. Refer to the section in this book on proper turfgrass water management for more information.

The susceptibility of turfgrasses to disease is also affected by nutrition. Properly fertilized grass is more resistant to disease and recovers faster if it should become diseased. In general, moderate fertilization and use of slow-release fertilizers should be practiced. However, turf managers should remember that each grass species and cultivar may have unique fertility or cultural requirements that should be provided for healthy growth.

Normal turfgrass maintenance activities also impact upon disease severity if not incidence. The debate over the merits of collecting and removing lawn clippings at mowing intervals still rages. The actual relationship between leaving or removing grass clippings and subsequent disease incidence is still unclear. However, when disease is *active* on an area of turfgrass, the lengthening of the mowing interval and the collection of clippings is encouraged. These practices will reduce the likely spread of the pathogen on infested clippings. Mowing equipment should be cleaned between lawn sites where active disease is involved. These efforts will improve the effectiveness of other control activities, especially fungicide use.

CHEMICAL CONTROL

Turfgrass diseases can be chemically controlled with proper use of fungicides. A uniform application over the entire planting is usually necessary and will be most effective if done early in disease development. Most fungicides are effective for a relatively short time, often not more than 14 days. Sunlight, rain, irrigation water, and mowing affect the rate at which the protective chemical is broken down and removed from the plant. Repeat applications are often necessary to control a disease during periods when weather conditions favor disease.

Fungicides should always be used in accordance with the manufacturer's instructions on the product label. Information on the label includes the diseases for which the fungicide is effective, proper rates, cautions with respect to mixing with other chemicals, frequency of application, and safety precautions.

Some of the fungicides are effective only for control of specific diseases so it is important to obtain an accurate diagnosis in order to select an appropriate fungicide.

Fungicides should be applied as needed for disease control as soon as possible after diagnosis. When applying fungicides:

❑ Follow label directions for proper rates, gallonage, spray intervals, and other instructions.

❑ Gallonage is normally 10 gallons per 1000 square feet except where label indicates otherwise.

❑ Use of a wetting agent will increase the effectiveness of the fungicide by improving coverage.

❑ Apply fungicide to entire area, not just the diseased areas, for most turf diseases. This is important as many disease-causing agents are either airborne, water-splashed or clipping-borne.

❑ Avoid mowing turfgrass immediately after fungicide application.

❑ Delay irrigations to fungicide-treated turf for as long as practical. The exception is where a root disease control product must be drenched into the root zone by irrigation to be effective.

Key for Identification of Turf Diseases

G. W. Simone

A. GRASS AFFECTED IN DISTINCT PATCHES

1. Affected areas 2 to 3 inches in diameter. Leaf spot-type lesions present. . . . . **Dollar spot**
2. Affected area usually larger than 2 to 3 inches in diameter. Leaf spot-type lesions not present.
   a. Ring or arc of lush growth or dead grass; mushrooms may be present. May be associated with localized dry areas. . . . . **Fairy ring**
   b. Patches not associated with ring of lush growth.
      i. Affected areas tend to be in streaks. Grass blades matted together (primarily on ryegrass and bermudagrass). . . . . **Pythium blight**
      ii. Affected area circular; often with wilted "smoke ring" margin. Grass blades not matted . . . . **Brown patch**
      iii. Affected areas appear as patches (8 to 24 inches in diameter) of chlorotic and necrotic grass. Roots short and black. . . . .

         . . . . **Bermudagrass decline**

         . . . **Take-all root rot of St. Augustinegrass**

3. Affected area usually larger than 2 to 3 inches in diameter. Leaf spot-type lesions are present. May appear as necrotic rings but **no** mushrooms are present and is not associated with dry areas.
   . . . . **Rhizoctonia leaf and sheath spot**

B. GRASS NOT AFFECTED IN DISTINCT PATCHES

1. Orange pustules present on leaf blades.. . . . . **Rust**
2. Orange pustules not present on leaf blades.
   a. Leaf Spots present.
      i. Primarily on ryegrass and bermudagrass
         . . . . **Helminthosporium leaf spot**
      ii. Primarily on St. Augustinegrass.
         (1) Leaf spots oval to irregular with brown borders and tan to gray centers.
            . . . . **Gray leaf spot**
         (2) Leaf spots linear with purple borders and tan to white centers.
            . . . . **Cercospora leaf spot**
      iii. Primarily on centipedegrass. . . . **Anthracnose**
   b. Leaf spots not present.
      i. Grass covered with an easily removed crusty and/or sooty growth. . . . . **Slime mold**
      ii. Slippery green-to-brown growths covering soil and turf. . . . . **Algae**
      iii. Chlorosis or mottling of leaves associated with general decline. . . . . **Pythium root rot**
         . . . . **Nematodes***

* Request nematode information from County Extension Office.

Collecting and Submitting Turf Samples for Disease Identification

G. W. Simone

COLLECTING

Follow these steps, in order, to collect a turf sample for disease identification.

1. Sample problematic turf areas *before* the application of pesticides—especially fungicides.

2. Sample each symptomatically distinct turf area separately. Do not mix these samples together.

3. Take two samples from any turf areas expressing symptoms of wilt, poor color, slow thinning, or melting-out. One sample should be collected and submitted according to these instructions, while the second sample should be taken according to instructions listed in this manual for the Nematode Assay Laboratory. Both diagnostic services are charge services *only*.

4. The appropriate sample for plant disease identification is a 3- to 4-inch plug of turfgrass which is dug, not pulled, from the turf area.

5. Always sample from the marginal area of symptomatic turfgrass, not from the central dead zone. The marginal area is more likely to allow the isolation, identification, and interpretation of the causal organism(s). Each sample should have both living and dead (affected and unaffected) portions.

6. Plant disease identification procedures do not utilize soil. Excessive soil can be hand shaken from each plug but leave enough soil on the plug to keep the roots moist.

7. Do not add any additional moisture to the sample. All samples should be submitted at field moisture levels.

8. Before leaving the sampling site, note the recent pesticide history (7-10 days) and other relevant information such as disease incidence, severity, etc.

9. After collecting good samples, do not ruin them by allowing them to sit out in the sun or bake on the front dash or back seat of the car prior to submission.

SUBMISSION

Follow these steps, in order, to submit a turf sample for disease identification.

1. Samples arriving from sites in Florida that are 2 days or less mailing time from Gainesville, can be sealed in plastic bags for shipping. *Do not* add moisture to the sample.

2. Samples from distances greater than 2 days mailing time from Gainesville should be packed tightly in a box with dry paper. Do not seal in plastic because samples could deteriorate during the mailing period. Do not add moisture.

3. Mail samples early in the week to avoid a weekend layover at the post office.

4. For emergency samples, use overnight courier services to deliver samples to Gainesville.

5. All samples must be accompanied with a completed Plant Disease Diagnostic Form (IFAS Form # 2901). Forms are available at all county Extension offices and in this book at the end of the "Disease Problems" chapter.

6. Remember to note the recent pesticide history on the Specimen Data form with the sample.

7. Mail the completed Plant Disease Diagnostic Form *along with* the turf sample *but not in the soil and plant material*. This will keep the form dry, clean, and readable.

8. Plant disease identification is a charge service only. Current cost is $15.00. The Florida Extension Plant Disease Clinic is open from 8:00 am to 5:00 pm Monday through Friday at the following address:

Florida Extension Plant Disease Clinic
Bldg. 78, Mowry Road
P O Box 110830
Gainesville, Florida 32611-0830
Telephone: (352) 392-1795
FAX: (352) 392-3438

Algae

G. W. Simone

CAUSE AND SYMPTOMS

Algae are not pathogens of turfgrass, but are other life-forms that compete with turfgrass in specific landscape sites (Plate 86). Like all plants, algae prefer certain environmental conditions for optimal growth. Landscape sites where algae proliferate are characterized by partial shade, poor air circulation, a readily available nitrogen source, and either a high water table, poor drainage, or frequent surface/overhead irrigation.

Turfgrass areas where algal competition exists appear to "thin out" and decrease in vigor. Algae of various shapes and colors begin to colonize "thinned" areas of turfgrass. Most often these algae are green or brown in color and can be sheet-like, leaf-like, or cushion-like in appearance. Due to their high water content and the gelatin content of their vegetative form, turfgrass areas invaded by algae are often quite slippery. Algal growth may become so prolific that turf areas can become covered to the detriment of turfgrass. Many times various species of moss also invade those areas conducive to algae growth (Plate 87).

CONTROL

Improve air circulation and light exposure to affected turfgrass sites. Try to improve site drainage and/or lower water table. Reduce the concentration of freely available nitrogen at this site. Use of a topically applied mancozeb-based fungicide such as Dithane, Fore or Protect T/O will burn back the algae for a period of time. Be advised that professional brands of mancozeb are not normally labeled for homeowner use. Use of chlorothalonil (Daconil 2787) will aid in the control of certain algae for short time periods. Both fungicides are available in small package brands throughout Florida for small area treatment. Consult your local Cooperative Extension agent for current control recommendations.

Anthracnose

G. W. Simone

CAUSE AND SYMPTOMS

Anthracnose disease is primarily a problem on centipedegrass in the spring, but it is known to occur on bahia-, bermuda-, rye- and St. Augustinegrasses. Weather periods of high moisture and warm temperatures favor the causal fungus, *Colletotrichum graminicola*. Disease severity is often greater on insect-, nematode-, or fertility-stressed turfgrass, especially during springs following cold winters.

This fungal pathogen can infect leaves, sheaths, and tillers of centipedegrass. Leaf infection appears as reddish-brown to brown lesions that are often surrounded by a narrow chlorotic area (Plate 88). Single spots may span the blade width causing leaf yellowing and then death of the leaf. Tiller infection results in girdling of stems and the development of small, yellow patches of turf. The causal fungus can be observed with a hand lens. It will appear as dark, cushion-like reproductive structures (acervuli) with black spines (setae) extending from the cushion.

CONTROL

Maintain turfgrass areas optimally to avoid stress caused by either pests, fertility imbalances, or moisture extremes. Prevent thatch from accumulating. If spring severity of this disease warrants control, apply a fungicide containing either chlorothalonil (Daconil 2787, Thalonil), fenarimol (Rubigan), mancozeb (Dithane, Fore, Protect T/O), propiconazole (Banner), thiophanate methyl (Cleary 3336, Fungo, SysTec 1998), thiophanate methyl + mancozeb (Duosan) or triadimefon (Bayleton) as needed. Be advised that professional brands of mancozeb are not normally labelled for homeowner use. Small-sized packages of fungicides containing chlorothalonil, mancozeb and thiophanate methyl are available throughout Florida for home lawn use. Consult your local county Cooperative Extension agent for current control recommendations.

Brown Patch of Turfgrasses

G. W. Simone

CAUSES AND SYMPTOMS

Brown patch disease of turfgrasses is caused by the fungus *Rhizoctonia solani* Kuhn. It occurs in a great number of grass species, including the major turfgrasses grown throughout Florida: St. Augustinegrass, bermudagrass, bahiagrass, and centipedegrass. In southern Florida it is mainly a fall and winter disease, but in the northern part of the state it occurs primarily in spring and fall. Two other species of the Rhizoctonia fungus exist in Florida (*R. zeae* and *R. oryzae*). Both prefer the hot, humid season of summer when they cause Rhizoctonia Leaf and Sheath Blight, primarily on bermudagrass.

Foliage of affected grass may be killed in a few hours. The fungus infects parts of the foliage nearest the soil, disrupting transport of water and nutrients to the upper portions of the foliage, and causing death. Frequently, affected areas are invaded by weeds before regrowth of the grass can occur.

St. Augustinegrass (Plate 89) and centipedegrass are affected more severely than bermuda or bahia grasses. Overseeded ryegrass is especially susceptible to brown patch disease when temperatures are warm and the humidity is high (Plate 90). The first symptom of the disease is yellowing or chlorosis of the foliage. Wilting of the foliage can be associated with the chlorosis. Affected leaves dry and assume various shades of reddish-brown to straw brown. Under favorable conditions, an affected area may grow from a few inches to several feet in diameter. The affected area usually appears in a circular pattern, but mowing and other practices may alter the shape of the affected area by spreading the fungus. When diseased leaves are pulled, they separate very easily at the base from the rest of the plant. The basal portion of such leaves is rotted and brown. Tan to brown threads of the fungus are often visible. The grass in the outer margin of the circle is frequently wilted and darker, giving a "smoke ring" appearance. Surviving sprigs often grow and recover in the center of the patch so that the diseased area has a "doughnut pattern." In shady, moist locations a circular pattern may not occur.

CONTROL

Resistant varieties of grass are not available. A well-balanced fertilizer applied at moderate rates is important in reducing severity of this disease. Avoid application of freely available nitrogen when disease is active. Spread of this disease across turf areas can be slowed by less frequent mowings and the collection of fungus-bearing clippings.

Several fungicides effectively control Rhizoctonia brown patch. These products can include one or more of the following active ingredients: chlorothalonil (Daconil 2787), fenarimol (Rubigan), iprodione (Chipco 26019), mancozeb (Dithane, Fore, Protect T/O), PCNB (Defend, Engage, Penstar, Terraclor), propiconazole (Banner), thiophanate methyl (Cleary 3336, Fungo, SysTec 1998), thiophanate methyl + mancozeb (Duosan), or thiram (Spotrete). Be advised that professional brands of mancozeb are not normally labelled for homeowner use. Small package brands of fungicides containing benomyl, chlorothalonil, mancozeb, PCNB and thiophanate methyl are available in Florida for home lawn use. Apply fungicide treatments to the diseased area and a 1- to 2-foot border. A repeat treatment is sometimes necessary for complete control. Always follow directions on the label for best results and safety.

Contact your county agent for currently recommended fungicides. Or check the latest *Florida Plant Disease Control Guide* or Plant Pathology Plant Protection Pointer 29 (PP/PPP 29) for current brands.

Dollar Spot

G. W. Simone

CAUSES AND SYMPTOMS

Dollar spot disease is caused by the fungi *Lanzia* and *Moellerodiscus* spp. (previously *Sclerotinia homoeocarpa*). This disease can affect all turfgrasses grown in Florida but normally is more damaging on bermudagrass, bahiagrass, and zoysiagrass (Plate 91). These pathogens are favored by warm temperatures in spring and fall (60° to 80°F) although some higher temperature strains of these fungi apparently exist in Florida. Moisture from fog, dew, or irrigation is required to initiate disease. Turfgrass sites more susceptible to these pathogens are those with low soil moisture, high thatch buildup, and low nitrogen and potassium fertility.

Symptoms of dollar spot on fine textured grasses appear as 1- to 2-inch diameter spots that exhibit wilting followed by death with an accompanying straw-white color change. Infection of the coarser grasses results in larger diameter spots. During active disease periods, these discrete spots may coalesce into larger, irregularly killed areas. Discrete leaf lesions are also caused by the dollar spot pathogens. Leaf spots are typically marginal, irregular in size and shape, with light tan coloration and reddish-brown borders (Plate 92). Dollar spot on the coarser southern grasses can be confused with young Brown Patch except for the presence of leaf spots. Occasionally, under moist periods, the causal fungi may be observed as white mycelium on affected turf early in the morning.

CONTROL

Although all grass species are susceptible to this disease, dollar spot is primarily a problem on low vigor turfgrass sites. When disease is active, water deeply, but less often, and time irrigations for early morning. Try to collect clippings to reduce disease spread.

Applications of readily available nitrogen sources ($^1/_2$ pound nitrogen per 1000 square feet) will adequately control this disease on all turf except bahiagrass. If fungicides are needed, apply products containing chlorothalonil (Daconil 2787, Thalonil), fenarimol (Rubigan), iprodione (Chipco 26019), mancozeb (Dithane, Fore, Protect T/O), PCNB (Defend, Engage, Penstar, Terraclor), thiophanate methyl (Cleary 3336, Fungo, SysTec 1998), thiophanate methyl + mancozeb (Duosan), thiram (Spotrete), triadimefon (Bayleton), or vinclozolin (Curalan, Vorlan) for control. Remember to avoid thatch accumulation that serves as a food base and survival zone for the pathogen.

For small lawn areas, fungicides containing chlorothalonil, mancozeb and thiophanate methyl are available under various brand names in small sizes. Contact your nearest county Cooperative Extension Agent for currently available small-package fungicide brands or check the latest *Florida Plant Disease Control Guide* or Plant Pathology Plant Protection Pointer 29 (PP/PPP 29).

Fairy Ring

G. W. Simone

CAUSES AND SYMPTOMS

Many "mushroom" or "toadstool" type fungi cause fairy ring disease in turfgrass sites. These fungi are more apparent during warm-to-hot periods when ample rainfall exists and may cause the fairy ring symptoms several times a year. These fungi colonize quantities of buried organic matter (tree stumps, lumber, leaves, etc.) in the turfgrass site and may persist for many years.

As the various causal fungi colonize the organic matter and break it down, typical fairy rings will appear on the turf site (Plate 93). One important byproduct of organic matter breakdown is the release of available nitrogen which causes the initial, lush green fairy ring symptom. Depending on the fungal species involved, these green bands or partial ring patterns on the turfgrass may enlarge or shrink in size. Some fungi may release toxic metabolites in the turfgrass root zone causing death of rings or partial rings of turfgrass. Other fungi grow so vigorously in the turf root zones that areas of turfgrass may become impervious to irrigation causing turfgrass death.

All fairy ring fungi ultimately reproduce as mushrooms or puff balls within the ring of affected turfgrass.

CONTROL

Due to the type and variety of fungi involved in fairy ring formation, no presently labeled fungicides are recommended for treatment. Fairy rings will persist for as long as the buried cache of organic matter (food) remains. Fumigation is not recommended because these products are nonselective and only effective in the top 8 to 10 inches of soil. Fairy ring fungi can often arise from below this depth in the landscape.

To mask the lush green ring symptom, additional fertilizer can be supplied to adjacent turfgrass. If fairy rings begin to brown and die, aerify (puncture) the affected areas of turf to improve irrigation penetration. Remember to remove the mushroom stage of these fungi since many are poisonous to humans and pets.

Gray Leaf Spot of St. Augustinegrass

G. W. Simone

CAUSE AND SYMPTOMS

Gray leaf spot of St. Augustinegrass is caused by the fungus, *Pyricularia grisea* [Cke.] Sacc. St. Augustinegrass is the only important warm-season turfgrass that is seriously affected. The disease occurs throughout Florida during warm, humid weather. Spots (lesions) on the leaf blades are the most visible symptoms, but sheath and stem lesions also occur.

Leaf spots begin as olive-green to brown water-soaked dots smaller than a pinhead. These enlarge and form circular to elongate lesions that are brown to ash-colored with purple to brown margins (Plate 94). Under moist conditions, the fungus produces spores abundantly in the centers of the lesions, giving the spots a velvety-gray appearance. Many lesions may occur on a single leaf, and severely affected leaves wither and turn brown. A severely affected planting may appear scorched as though suffering from drought (Plate 95).

The disease occurs during moderate to warm weather accompanied by high relative humidity. However, disease development is most rapid during prolonged periods of 100% relative humidity and temperatures of 77° to 90°F. Severity of the disease is enhanced by application of readily available nitrogen fertilizer, and is proportional to the amount of nitrogen applied. Different cultivars of St. Augustinegrass have different levels of susceptibility to gray leaf spot. The most susceptible cultivars are the Bitterblue types, but susceptibility is greatest in all cultivars during the early coverage stage of newly sprigged or plugged areas. Cultivars become more tolerant of the disease after they are established. Susceptibility of the grass to the disease increases following application of herbicides such as atrazine.

CONTROL

Select fertilizers that are low in nitrogen or that release nitrogen slowly for use during wet summer months. Cultivars such as Floratam and others not in the Bitterblue group may be selected for a new planting to reduce gray leaf spot and other pest problems. Irrigation should be managed to water deeply but less frequently. This reduces the number of times the spore stage of this fungal pathogen can be splashed to unaffected areas of turf. Remember to irrigate early in the day to minimize the period in which the grass is wet. This will disfavor the infection cycle of this fungus. Mow less frequently during active disease and collect clippings to remove the reproductive structures of this pathogen from the lawn site.

Portions of a lawn may sometimes be temporarily disfigured by a disease outbreak. If conditions favoring disease are brief, resumption of drier conditions may make chemical treatment unnecessary. However, treatment with a fungicide may be required if the disease outbreak is severe and accompanied by a prolonged period of weather favorable for disease. Where chemical control is necessary, fungicides are available that contain either chlorothalonil (Daconil, Thalonil) or propiconazole (Banner). Only chlorothalonil is available in small package pesticide brands for urban lawn use.

Contact your county Cooperative Extension agent for currently recommended fungicides. Repeat applications may be necessary to maintain control during prolonged periods of high disease pressure. Use all chemicals with caution and follow label instructions.

Helminthosporium Diseases of Bermudagrasses

G. W. Simone

CAUSE AND SYMPTOMS

The fungus group *Helminthosporium* includes several species that cause diseases in various turfgrasses. Over the past two decades, this group of fungi has been reclassified as *Bipolaris, Drechslera,* and *Exserohilum* species. For convenience, the *Helminthosporium* designation will be used in this publication. Bermudagrasses are usually affected more frequently and seriously than other warm-season turfgrasses. Leaf spots are the most frequent symptoms but under favorable conditions some *Helminthosporium* species also cause stem and crown rots. This results in a gradual thinning and melting out, which may occur together. Both occur in irregular rather than distinct patterns.

Lesions in the leaf spotting phases of *Helminthosporium* diseases may vary depending on the *Helminthosporium* species. Eyespot lesions result from infection by *H. giganteum.* In general, spots caused by other *Helminthosporium* species, such as *H. cynodontis*, are brown to purple and range in size from smaller than a pinhead up to 0.2 inches in length (Plate 96). The spots frequently elongate to appear ellipsoidal or streak-like. The spots are often more numerous near the collar area of the leaf blade. During early stages of a severe attack the turf may develop an overall purple cast. Leaves with numerous infections turn reddish-brown before withering and drying to a light tan.

In the melting out phase, lesions on stems are dark purple to black. Stem and crown rot results in stunted, spindly shoots; stand thinning; or turf killed in irregular patches. In severe cases, the entire turf area may be affected.

The fungus spores are produced abundantly on lesions, dead leaves, and clippings in the turf. The spores may be carried by wind, water, mowers, tires, and shoes. One or more *Helminthosporium* species is active whenever turfgrass is growing actively. The leaf spot diseases occur mainly during wet, cool to moderate weather. Stem and crown rot may occur throughout the growing season. However, destructiveness is greatest during the periods when the grass lacks vigor. Lack of turf vigor may result from low to moderate temperatures, mineral deficiencies, or cultural practices such as low mowing height.

CONTROL

Since *Helminthosporium* fungi do not always cause serious damage, complete prevention of the diseases they cause is not necessary or practical. Severe damage to turfgrasses can be effectively controlled. Prevention of severe attack by *Helminthosporium* fungi is greatly enhanced by utilizing proper cultural management of fertilization, mowing, irrigation, and thatch control to promote turf vigor. Severe drying and wetting cycles may increase spore production, so maintain soil moisture at an even level. Removal of clippings when mowing reduces the source of spores.

Disease development during brief periods may be favored by combined environmental factors. Outbreaks of disease during such periods can be treated with temporary measures such as raising mowing height and reducing mowing frequency as much as possible. Light applications of nitrogen fertilizer will help to offset some of the visible damage. New leaves should be protected by fungicide applications until the disease outbreak subsides.

Fungicide application for control of *Helminthosporium* diseases usually must be to the entire planting in order to be effective. Several fungicide products effectively control *Helminthosporium* diseases. These contain either chlorothalonil (Daconil 2787, Thalonil), iprodione (Chipco 26019), mancozeb (Dithane, Fore, Protect T/O), PCNB (Defend, Engage, Penstar, Terraclor), propiconazole (Banner), or certain combination fungicide products. These trade name products are professional use products that are oversized and thus overpriced for homeowner needs unless accessed through professional lawn maintenance personnel. Many small package brands of fungicides with turfgrass use labels exist for chlorothalonil, mancozeb, and PCNB. Repeat applications may be necessary to maintain adequate control during periods of high disease pressure. Use all chemicals with caution, and follow label instructions.

Contact your county Cooperative Extension Service agent for recommended fungicides or check the latest *Florida Plant Disease Control Guide* or Plant Pathology Plant Protection Pointer 29 (PP/PPP 29) for names and manufacturers of these products.

Pythium Blight of Turfgrasses

G. W. Simone

CAUSE AND SYMPTOMS

Pythium blight is caused primarily by the fungus *Pythium aphanidermatum* (Edson) Fitzpatrick. The disease is sometimes called "grease spot," "cottony blight," or simply "Pythium." Grasses most affected are annual and perennial rye, bent, blue, fescue, and bermuda. The disorder is most frequently encountered on cool-season grasses that are overseeded on bermudagrass greens to maintain quality putting surfaces during the winter months.

The disease begins as small irregular patches 1 to 4 inches in diameter. The affected grass blades initially appear dark and water-soaked, but they later shrivel and eventually dry to a light brown (Plate 97). The patches may coalesce to form large diseased areas. However, the disease sometimes occurs in streaks rather than patches as a result of surface water or mowers carrying the fungus across the planting (Plate 98). The diseased leaves tend to mat together and feel slimy. The matting together of affected leaves is less pronounced in grasses maintained at low mowing heights, such as putting greens. During periods of high humidity, such as early morning or cloudy days, the diseased areas may have a cobweb appearance due to the fungus growing over the leaves.

Pythium blight can occur at temperatures as low as 68°F. Shaded locations where little air movement occurs tend to further encourage Pythium blight. Grass in the young seedling stage is the most susceptible. Leaf-to-leaf growth by the fungus allows it to spread short distances.

Spread to new sites occurs by movement of contaminated soil and grass clippings on tires, shoes, and mowing implements. Pythium also spreads in surface-water runoffs caused by rain or excessive irrigation (Plate 99).

CONTROL

Resistant varieties are not available; therefore, control must rely on cultural and chemical methods. Cultural manipulations that provide well-drained soil and promote rapid drying of moisture from turf foliage aid in reducing disease severity. For example, thinning of surrounding trees and shrubs will reduce shade and promote air movement and leaf drying. Irrigating early in the morning allows the foliage to dry before evening. When a disease outbreak occurs, traffic over the affected area(s) should be minimized to reduce spread. Reduce mowing frequency. Overseeding should be delayed as late as possible in the season because cool temperatures retard Pythium development. Also, use fungicide-treated seed when overseeding. Excessive thatch should be removed since Pythium can survive from season to season in thatch. Effective fungicides are available for control of Pythium blight. These fungicides include one of the following active ingredients: chloroneb (Terramec, Terraneb), etridiazole (Koban, Terrazole), fosetyl aluminum (Aliette), metalaxyl/mefenoxam (Subdue), or propamocarb (Banol). Contact your county agent for current fungicide recommendations.

Pythium Root Rot

G. W. Simone

CAUSE AND SYMPTOMS

All southern grasses grown in Florida are attacked by various *Pythium* spp. resulting in a nondescript thinning out or decline of turf areas due to root decay (Plate 100). Although the species involved with each turfgrass are still undefined, these species are collectively active in a temperature range between the mid-60s and mid-90s°F. Each species may be active at a different temperature range but collectively, they may cause Pythium root rot almost year-round in Florida. Conditions that favor this disease include high available moisture (fog, dew, rain, irrigation), poor air circulation, and poor soil drainage.

Symptoms of Pythium root rot are difficult to distinguish from those caused by soil insects or nematodes. Early symptoms may begin with small spots that appear dark, grayish green. These spots exhibit longer periods of daily wilt until the spots collapse and turn brown. Spots often streak into larger affected areas on slopes as surface water spreads the pathogen. Mechanical movement across wet turfgrass can also spread this pathogen. After prolonged moist periods, the cottony mycelium of this fungus may be visible early in the morning. Due to the confusing symptoms of turf browning and thinning, diagnosis of Pythium root rot should be done by a diagnostic laboratory.

CONTROL

Turfgrass areas with persistent Pythium root rot problems normally have problems with soil moisture. Improve aeration and water drainage in problem sites. Reduce frequent, shallow irrigation; and water only as needed. Avoid movement or maintenance activities across wet turf sites when disease is active. Apply the following fungicides as needed depending on the site conditions: chloroneb (Terraneb, Terramec), etridiazole (Terrazole, Koban), fosetyl aluminum (Aliette), metalaxyl (Subdue), or propamocarb (Banol). These fungicides are primarily marketed in large, professional use-sized quantities. Access to these active ingredients can be obtained through professional lawn care personnel when needed.

Newly installed lawns are particularly vulnerable to Pythium root rot. Much of Florida's sod production occurs on muck soils for a variety of quality and economic reasons. Muck-grown sod is an excellent product but irrigation management is critical on the part of the homeowner when installed onto a sandy soil type. Follow the recommendations presented earlier for proper irrigation duration and frequency for the turfgrass being installed. Resist the temptation to water 10 to 15 minutes every day for 2 to 3 weeks that can predispose the turfgrass to fungus invasion. This frequency/duration of watering will keep the muck soil saturated while the lower sand level is dry. This condition will cause root death from suffocation as oxygen becomes limiting in the root zone. Dead roots encourage soil fungi that cause further grass decline. Additionally, a wet sod zone over a dry native soil layer will slow root emergence and anchoring in this lawn site.

For very wet areas, apply products containing fosetyl aluminum as a foliar spray. In areas where soil moisture is not excessive, products containing either etridiazole, metalaxyl/mefenoxam, or propamocarb will be effective when drenched into the root zone within several hours of application. Contact your local county Cooperative Extension agent for the most current recommendations.

Rhizoctonia Leaf and Sheath Spot

G. W. Simone

CAUSE AND SYMPTOMS

A variation in the most common turfgrass disease has developed in Florida. Rhizoctonia brown patch disease has been a persistent disease across Florida turfgrasses affecting grass in the fall through the late spring period. In the 1990s, this disease appeared to extend its activity period through the hot, humid months of summer. Close examination revealed this disease to be caused by *Rhizoctonia* spp., but was different from *Rhizoctonia solani* that causes brown patch disease.

This new disease has been called Rhizoctonia Leaf and Sheath Spot. It can be caused by either *Rhizoctonia zeae* or *R. oryzae*, two species that cause disease under higher temperature periods than the classical brown patch pathogen *Rhizoctonia solani*. One or both of these fungi have been recovered from bermudagrass and St. Augustinegrass during hot, humid summer months. Symptoms produced include whole or partial necrotic rings ranging in size from several inches to several feet in diameter in affected turf areas (Plate 101). In addition to the rings, the causal fungi can produce a patch appearance (Plate 102) and a leaf and sheath spot with necrosis. This new disease can be confused with either brown patch or fairy ring on turf.

Rhizoctonia leaf and sheath spot can be distinguished from brown patch by the time of year (summer versus late fall through spring) and the absence of darkly discolored and rotted fascicles that are typical of brown patch disease. Time of year does not separate Leaf and Sheath Spot from fairy ring. However, turf plugs cut from affected turf areas will produce abundant mycelium of the fairy ring fungus when plugs are moistened and incubated for 24 hours in a plastic bag. Additionally, fairy rings often exhibit a band of lush green growth and either mushrooms or puff balls emerging in the ring. Leaf and Sheath Spot disease lacks these characteristics and does produce spots on foliage above ground (although these spots may be infrequent).

CONTROL

At present, there are no resistant turfgrass cultivars to this disease. It is assumed that a well-balanced fertility program will reduce disease severity. Spread of this disease can be slowed by less frequent mowing of infected turf coupled with the collection of diseased clippings. Several fungicides can effectively control both causal fungi. These products include one of the following active ingredients: chlorothalonil (Daconil 2787, Thalonil), fenarimol (Rubigan), iprodione (Chipco 26019), mancozeb (Dithane, Fore, Protect T/O), propiconazole (Banner), or thiram (Spotrete). Be advised that professional brands of mancozeb are not normally labeled for homeowner use.

Contact your local county agent for currently recommended fungicides or check the latest *Florida Plant Disease Control Guide* or Plant Pathology Plant Protection Pointer 29 (PP/PPP 29) for current brands. Apply fungicide treatment to the diseased area and a 1- to 2-foot border. A second application may be necessary for control. Always follow directions on the label for best results and safety.

Rust Disease

G. W. Simone

CAUSE AND SYMPTOMS

Several rust fungi (*Puccinia* spp.) affect turfgrasses in Florida. Rust disease, however, is a minor disease problem and usually only on ryegrass, St. Augustinegrass and zoysiagrass. Mild to warm, humid weather favors disease development fall through spring. Less vigorous turfgrass, like that in partially shaded or poorly managed areas, may exhibit more severe rust disease.

Symptoms of rust disease appear first as light-colored flecks on the leaves. These flecks enlarge rapidly into linear pustules, often along veins. These pustules rupture open, revealing red to orange spore masses. Leaf infection will result in general leaf yellowing (Plate 103). Severe infection can cause turfgrass to thin as well as generally appear chlorotic. The pustules (reproductive sites of the fungus) may produce dark brown to black spores later in the same season.

CONTROL

Rust occurrence is usually limited to cool, dry periods in spring and fall in turf areas that are partially shaded or unthrifty. Rust can be most rapidly controlled by mowing the turfgrass and collecting the infected clippings. If a situation arises where a fungicide is needed, apply a product containing one of the following fungicide active ingredients: mancozeb (zinc ion plus maneb complex), propiconazole, or triadimefon. All these fungicides are widely distributed throughout Florida in "professional use"-sized quantities that most often far exceed the needs of the average home lawn in both quantity and cost.

The fungicides propiconazole (Banner™) and triadimefon (Bayleton™) are systemic products that should not be needed by homeowners to control the level of rust disease that occurs in Florida. The active ingredient mancozeb represents a protectant fungicide that is effective and economical for homeowner use. Be advised that professional brands of mancozeb (Dithane, Fore, and Protect T/O) are not normally labelled for homeowner use. However, many small package pesticide companies do issue mancozeb- and maneb- containing products with turf disease labelling for home lawn use. Current availability of these small package products is available from your county extenion office, the current *Florida Plant Disease Control Guide* or Plant Pathology Plant Protection Pointer 29 (PP/PPP 29).

Slime Molds

G. W. Simone

CAUSES AND SYMPTOMS

Slime molds are not really disease-causing organisms on turf, but, due to their bright colors, are often mistaken as plant pathogens (Plate 104). These molds are primitive fungi that exhibit a motile or crawling stage. When sufficient food has been assimilated into the fungus colony and weather is moist and warm, entire colonies of these fungi turn reproductive. The reproductive stage "crawls" up and over anything that is above ground level, as with turfgrass blades. Off the ground, the orange to pink to purple, soot-like reproductive structures allow completion of the life cycle, dispersing spores into the air currents over 1 to 2 weeks. Slime molds use turfgrass as support structures for reproduction, producing no disease or injury.

CONTROL

Since no disease is produced, control measures are not needed. If the colors or density of these fungi on particular turf areas becomes unsightly, the fungi can be mowed off, raked, or brushed away, or dispersed with a strong stream of water.

St. Augustinegrass Take-all Root Rot

G. W. Simone

CAUSES AND SYMPTOMS

The soilborne fungus *Gaeumannomyces graminis* var. *graminis* (Ggg) causes St. Augustinegrass take-all root rot disease, bermudagrass decline disease, and is implicated in similar diseases of zoysiagrass and centipedegrass. This pathogen survives in the soil and parasitizes the root system of turfgrass through the root cortex and into the vascular tissue. Infection produces a water deficiency in the grass blades as well as starvation of roots, thereby causing turfgrass decline. Ggg has been diagnosed from at least 40 counties within Florida as well as from such states as Texas, Alabama, Georgia, and California. It is presently believed to be generally distributed throughout residential turfgrass areas in Florida as well as commercial sod production fields.

Disease development is subtle, occurring below ground in the root system. Symptoms above ground are delayed until sufficient root debilitation has occurred. Under environmental conditions of high moisture demand and/or other stress factors, large irregular patches develop, ranging from 3 to 15 feet in diameter (Plate 105). Affected turfgrass begins to yellow and then thins to bare ground during high temperature periods of summer and early fall. The root systems rot before the above ground symptoms develop. Affected St. Augustinegrass typically has short, rotted roots allowing the stolons to be pulled up from the ground easily. Crowns may be rotted with black lesions present on the stolons.

This fungus in considered a stress pathogen. When St. Augustinegrass is subjected to prolonged stress in the landscape, the lower vigor of the turfgrass can allow entrance and faster disease development by this soil fungus. Examples of turfgrass stress factors would include soil nematodes, insects, poor fertility, height of cut that is too low, scalping lawn areas, etc. Once the root system is invaded, the turfgrass becomes increasingly vulnerable to damage from other soilborne pests like nematodes, insects, or other fungi.

CONTROL

Management of take-all root rot is difficult at best. The first step is determining if this disease is present and responsible for an observed turfgrass decline. Symptoms provided by this fungus on St. Augustinegrass can mimic those produced by other diseases, nematode feeding, or insect damage. Sample symptomatic turf and submit this sample to a plant disease clinic such as the Florida Extension Plant Disease Clinic at Gainesville to confirm the presence of this disease.

When take-all root rot is clinically diagnosed, a series of management steps can be undertaken to moderate symptom severity on affected turfgrass sites. Do not rush to strip off affected turfgrass and replace it with new sod. Realize that at present no cultivar of St. Augustinegrass is tolerant or resistant to this fungus. In addition, no sod marketed in the Southeast is sold as Ggg-free by any company. Examine your maintenance practices for your lawn areas. Never mow St. Augustinegrass below the recommended height, and never remove more than one third of the leaf canopy in any mowing. Inspect lawn areas for insect pests, nematode injury, or damage from other plant diseases. Define these stresses and follow recommended management practices to reduce these stress factors. Finally, avoid irregular watering practices that will further stress diseased turf.

The use of fungicides to treat this disease is not strongly recommended at this time. Although such fungicides as Banner, Bayleton™, Cleary 3336, Fungo, Rubigan, and SysTec 1998 are recommended for management of this fungus on bermudagrass, there is no data to indicate their utility or effectiveness on St. Augustinegrass. Consider these fungicides as preventatives—not curatives. Apply them weeks to months before symptom expression. Remember that all of these products **must be irrigated** into the root zone within an hour or so of application to be effective.

 **UNIVERSITY OF FLORIDA**

COOPERATIVE EXTENSION SERVICE

Institute of Food and Agricultural Sciences - Plant Pathology Department
Florida Extension Plant Disease Clinic

PLANT DISEASE DIAGNOSTIC FORM

Please Print - Fill-in **ALL** relevant data; maintain office copy; submit original copy with specimen.
See reverse side for submission instructions.

DATE_____/_____/_____

Grower address   **Submitted by (if different)**

Name _____   _____
Company _____   _____
Address _____   _____
City/Zip _____   _____
County _____   Mail Results To: Grower ☐   Submitter ☐ _____
Phone No. (____)_____   (____)_____
FAX No. (____)_____   (____)_____

☐ Commercial Grower ☐ Consultant   ☐ Home Grower   ☐ Research

PLANT AND VARIETY _____

General Plant Appearance: ☐ wilted ☐ spotted ☐ yellowed ☐ abnormal growth ☐ stunted ☐ mosaic ☐ other_____

Part(s) of Plant Affected and Symptom(s) Expressed

☐ ROOTS: ☐ apparently normal ☐ poor growth ☐ discolored ☐ rotted ☐ stubby ☐ galls or swelling ☐ other _____

☐ TRUNK, ☐ STEM or ☐ BRANCH: ☐ galls or swellings ☐ cankers ☐ discolored internally ☐ dieback ☐ rotted

☐ abnormal pattern or number ☐ wilted ☐ other _____

☐ LEAVES: ☐ spotted ☐ blighted ☐ yellowed ☐ mosaic ☐ wilted ☐ galls or swelling ☐ rotted ☐ other _____

☐ FLOWERS or ☐ FRUIT: ☐ spotted ☐ blighted ☐ rotted ☐ discolored ☐ mosaic ☐ distorted ☐ other _____

☐ OTHER (specify) _____

Type Planting:		**Prevalence:**	**Symptoms Appeared:** (In Past)	**Recently Applied Chemicals:**
☐Field	☐Grove/orchard	☐Entire Planting	☐Days _____	Fertilizer _____
☐Interior	☐Landscape	☐Localized area	☐Weeks _____	Pesticide _____
☐Forest	☐Nursery	☐Scattered area	☐Months _____	_____
☐Garden	☐Greenhouse			
☐Other _____				

_____
COUNTY AGENT SIGNATURE (optional)

The Florida Extension Plant Disease Clinic (FEPDC) is a service provided to any Florida resident by the Institute of Food and Agricultural Sciences (I.F.A.S.), University of Florida in conjunction with the Cooperative Extension Service. The FEPDC is open from 8-12:00 am and 1-5:00 pm Monday-Friday (except for state holidays) and is located on the University of Florida campus at Gainesville. Submit sample and payment payable to:

Florida Extension Plant Disease Clinic
Building 78, Mowry Road

P.O. Box 110830
University of Florida
Gainesville, Florida 32611-0830
Phone (352) 392-1795 FAX (352) 392-3438

$15.00 PER SAMPLE

The primary role of the FEPDC is to determine if the plant dysfunction involves an infectious causal agent, e.g. fungus, bacterium or virus. This is done by associating causal agents with symptomatic plant tissue. The FEPDC does not test water or soil for plant disease causal agents.

It is FEPDC policy that:
1. All plant samples should originate within the geographical boundaries of the State of Florida or be accompanied by appropriate USDA/DACS plant importation permits.
2. Plant samples must be adequate in quality and quantity and be accompanied by a completed Plant Disease Diagnostic Form (#2901) or equivalent information. Obtaining the appropriate sample <u>before</u> submission will save both time and shipping expense. **NOTE:** FEPDC staff reserve the right to immediately discard any sample not meeting the submission criteria listed below.
3. Samples can be submitted to the FEPDC in either of the following manners:
   Mail or deliver samples directly from grower (e.g. homeowner, farmer, nurseryman, etc.) to the FEPDC. Samples must be accompanied by payment to insure timely release of disease determinations and recommendations. Clientele can arrange for monthly invoicing by contacting FEPDC staff. Sample charges may vary.
4. Samples are processed on a first come first served basis in most cases.
5. Plant disease determinations and associated control options are direct mailed or sent by FAX. Results of these samples are electronically mailed to the county faculty in the county of sample origin to keep them informed of plant disease problems in their county of responsibility. Exceptions to these procedures are made for research and service samples for university personnel who can receive either an electronic mail response or hard copy mail directly from the FEPDC. No recommendations will be sent without complete identification and crop situation.

GENERAL SAMPLE SUBMISSION GUIDELINES
1. Submit generous amounts of plant material representing a range of symptoms.
2. Don't add water or pack a sample that is wet.
3. Keep samples refrigerated after collection until they are submitted. After collecting good samples, do not ruin them by allowing them to bake in the sun or on the back seat of a car prior to submission.
4. Do not mix samples in the same submission bag. Moisture from root samples will contribute to the decay of foliage samples if they are mixed together.
5. Plant disease identification procedures do not utilize soil or water. Excess soil can be hand shaken from root systems but leave enough soil to keep roots at field moisture levels.
6. Please mark sample packages with a "Warning" if sample has thorns or spines.
7. All samples must be accompanied with a completed Plant Disease Diagnostic Form. These are available at all county Extension offices. Give complete information on the form and <u>keep the form separate from the sample</u>. Limit sample information to one (1) sample per form. You are encouraged to include any other pertinent information in addition to that on the form.
8. Remember to note recent pesticide history on the Plant Disease Diagnostic Form accompanying the sample (last three weeks).
9. Samples arriving from sites in Florida that are 2 days or less mailing time from Gainesville, can be sealed in plastic bags for shipping.
10. Samples arriving from distances greater than 2 days mailing time from Gainesville should be packed tightly in a box with dry paper. Do not seal in plastic because of the likelihood of sample deterioration during the mailing period. Do not add moisture.
11. Mail samples early in the week to avoid the weekend layover in the post office.
12. For emergency samples, use overnight courier services or US overnight mail.
13. See guidelines for specific type of plant dysfunction. (Sample Collection and Submission PP/PPP1).

SERVICES NOT PROVIDED
Presently, the FEPDC does not routinely provide the following services to clientele:
1. Pathogen determination from water sources;
2. Pathogen determination from soil or other growing media;
3. Diagnosis of lethal yellowing disease of palms, other mycoplasma or mycoplasma-like organisms, and other fastidious procaryotic pathogens except by symptoms;
4. Pesticide residue determinations in or on plants and soil;
5. Soil nutrient levels, soluble salts, soil pH, or plant tissue analysis for macro or minor elements;
6. Speciation of all pathogens isolated from plant disease samples;
7. Microbe identifications from <u>non-plant</u> samples;
8. Toxic plant identifications and mycotoxin analysis.

CHAPTER EIGHT

Nematodes

Nematodes: What They Are, How They Live, and What They do to Turf

R. A. Dunn

Newcomers and Florida natives alike are often dismayed at the many pests and diseases that can damage their lawns. In much of Florida, nematodes are among the most important and least well understood of those pests. Nematode damage to turf is more common in Florida than in most other places. Sandy soils and a long growing season favor development of very high nematode populations and also create conditions in which grasses are especially sensitive to their effects.

NEMATODE BIOLOGY AND ECOLOGY

Morphology and Anatomy

Nematodes are tiny, unsegmented round-worms, generally transparent, and colorless. Most are slender, with bodies from $1/100$ to $1/8$ inch (0.25 to 3.0 mm) long. They are essentially invisible to the unaided eye.

Nematode bodies are covered with a multi-layered cuticle that often has surface marks that are used to help identify them. The cuticle is usually transparent, so that sufficient internal anatomy can be seen using a low-power (generally 20 to 60 magnifications) "dissecting" binocular microscope to identify most nematodes to genus. Much higher magnification (900 times or more) is often needed to identify them to the species level.

Life Cycle and Reproduction

Plant parasitic nematodes have a fairly simple life cycle which has six stages: egg, four juvenile stages, and adult. Inside the egg, the embryo develops into the first stage juvenile. The first stage juvenile molts inside the eggshell to become a second-stage juvenile, which hatches from the egg, and in most species, must feed before continuing to develop. The nematode molts three more times to become a fully developed adult.

Male and female nematodes occur in most species, and both may be required for reproduction. Reproduction without males is common, however, and some species are hermaphroditic ("females" produce both sperms and eggs). With the production of eggs by the individual, the cycle is complete. The length of the life cycle varies considerably with each species, its host plant, and the temperature of its habitat. Rates of activity, growth, and reproduction increase as soil temperature rises, from about 50°F (10°C) to about 90°F (32°C). Minimum generation time is about 4 weeks for many nematodes under optimum conditions (about 81°F or 27°C for many nematodes).

The number of eggs deposited by a female varies among species and is affected by the habitat. Most species produce between 50 and 500 eggs, but a few sometimes produce several thousand eggs per female. Eggs of some species can survive without hatching for years but hatch quickly when a host plant grows near them.

WHERE NEMATODES LIVE AND HOW THEY AFFECT PLANTS

Plant nematodes are **aquatic animals** that live in soil water or in plant fluids. They are **obligate parasites** that must feed on living plant tissues. All have some form of hollow oral stylet or spear, much like a hypodermic needle, which is used to puncture the host cell wall. Many (probably all) plant nematodes inject enzymes into the host cell before feeding. These enzymes partially digest the cell contents before they are sucked into the gut. Most of the injury that nematodes cause to plants is related in some way to this feeding process.

Root galling is caused by growth-regulating chemicals in the saliva of some nematodes. Feeding of others stops growth of roots, causing **stubby, swollen root tips** and lateral root proliferation. As they move through roots, endoparasitic nematodes can cause open **wounds** which allow **rot and wilt disease** organisms to invade them. The wounds and other effects of feeding often cause **physiological changes** in plants, making them **more susceptible** to many plant diseases, sometimes even **breaking plant resistance** to diseases. Some plant nematodes can store and **transmit some plant viruses.**

Nematodes may feed on plant tissue from outside the plant (**ectoparasitic**) or inside the tissue (**endoparasitic**). If the adult females move freely through the soil or plant tissue, that nematode species is said to be migratory. Those species in which the adult females become permanently immobile in one place in a root are termed **sedentary.**

Ectoparasitic nematodes are nearly all **migratory.** Most feed superficially at or very near the root tip or on root-hairs, although a few have stylets long enough to reach several cells deep. The ectoparasites which cause the most widespread and severe turf injury in Florida are the sting (*Belonolaimus* spp.), stubby root (*Trichodorus* and related spp.), and awl (*Dolichodorus* spp.) nematodes. These feed at or near root tips and usually inhibit root elongation. Ectoparasites which rarely cause severe injury to their plant hosts include the ring (*Criconemella* and related genera) and spiral (*Helicotylenchus* spp.) nematodes. Centipedegrass is one kind of plant that is particularly susceptible to ring nematodes.

The stubby root nematodes and their close relatives, the dagger (*Xiphinema* spp.) and needle (*Longidorus* spp.) nematodes, are the only plant nematodes known to transmit plant viruses. The corky ringspot disease of potatoes, a problem in the Hastings area, is caused by a virus which is carried and transmitted by stubby root nematodes. However, no virus diseases of turf are presently known to be transmitted by any nematodes.

Migratory endoparasites at any stage of development (except the egg) can move into, through, and out of their host tissues. Migratory endoparasites generally live and feed in tender tissues such as the root cortex. They burrow through the tissue, breaking open many cells after they have finished feeding on them. The cells immediately around the feeding area often are killed by toxic materials released from the disrupted cells. These dead cells usually turn brown, and become small spots or lesions visible to a careful observer, and often are colonized easily by fungi which cause root rots. Premature root rot is often associated with infection by migratory endoparasitic nematodes.

A migratory endoparasitic nematode that is widespread in Florida turf is the lance nematode, *Hoplolaimus galeatus*. Although this large nematode may often feed on root cortical tissue from the outside and thus introduce only part of its body into smaller roots, it commonly burrows completely into the coarser roots of St. Augustinegrass, and is thus a true endoparasite in those cases. Other examples of migratory endoparasitic nematodes in turf include *Scutellonema* spp. and *Peltamigratus* spp., both related to, but apparently much more pathogenic to turf than, the spiral nematodes, *Helicotylenchus* spp. Lesion nematodes, *Pratylenchus* spp., are often recovered from turf, especially centipedegrass, but their importance is not known.

Ectoparasitic and migratory endoparasitic nematodes generally deposit their eggs singly as they are produced, wherever the female happens to be in the soil or plant tissues.

Sedentary endoparasitic nematodes include the root-knot (*Meloidogyne* spp.), and cyst (*Heterodera* spp.), nematodes. In most of these species, the second-stage juvenile is the "infective" stage which moves through the soil and roots to seek a suitable site for colonization. Once a feeding site is selected, the nematode injects growth-regulating substances into the cells immediately adjacent to its head, causing some of those cells to enlarge. These "giant" or "nurse" cells become specialized food sources for the nematode. At the same time, the nematode becomes immobile, and the body swells to a round, lemon, kidney, or ovoid form.

Mature females of the sedentary endoparasitic nematodes generally produce large numbers of eggs which are retained in the body or accumulated in masses attached to their bodies. The nematodes and the giant cells on which they feed are very dependent on each other. If the nematode dies, the giant cells die or lose their highly active condition. If the giant cells die, the nematode dies of starvation, because it cannot move to another site. Sedentary endoparasites cause serious disruption of the vascular system of the root by the giant cells.

Externally, the effect of root-knot nematode parasitism on roots of many of its hosts is overgrowth of the cortical (fleshy) tissues of the root, resulting in formation of a **visible swelling of the root which is commonly called a gall or knot**. Grass roots may sometimes become somewhat swollen, although they rarely react as strongly as some of their broad-leafed hosts such as many vegetables. Roots severely galled by root-knot nematodes usually rot much earlier than roots which are not galled. The gall tissues remain succulent, poorly protected from invasion, and very rich in nutrients so fungi grow rapidly. Finally, these nematodes apparently cause significant disruption of normal plant metabolism by redirecting the flow of nutrients to maintain their giant cells and themselves.

The living and feeding relationships that nematodes have with their hosts affect both sampling methods and the success of various management practices. Ectoparasitic nematodes which never enter roots may be recovered only from soil samples. Some endoparasitic nematodes may be detected most easily in samples of the roots in which they feed and live (lesion nematodes), while others are more easily detected as the migratory stage in the soil (root-knot nematodes). Endoparasites which are inside root tissues may be protected from nematicides which are active only in the soil, such as the soil fumigants. The root tissues may also shield them from many microorganisms which attack nematodes in the soil. Ectoparasites are fully exposed to pesticides and natural control agents in the soil.

NEMATODES IMPORTANT AS PESTS OF TURF

Many kinds of nematodes damage Florida turf; their feeding may alter root growth, cause small dead spots in the soft root tissues, or even kill the roots. Fungi often cause extensive rot of roots which have been injured by nematodes, and turf weakened by nematodes may be more susceptible to many kinds of diseases.

Nematodes important as turf pests in Florida are described briefly below, with indications of the lowest numbers of each kind of nematode expected to cause significant damage. Properly maintained turf can often stand much higher populations than the minimal action levels (AL = number of nematodes/100 cc soil) cited.

Sting Nematode (*Belonolaimus longicaudatus*): Damages all grasses commonly grown in Florida; generally found only in very sandy soils. Where conditions favor this nematode, it is the most damaging nematode pest of turf in Florida. AL = 10.

Lance Nematodes (*Hoplolaimus* spp.): Common turf pests because they attack all commonly-grown grasses, are easily distributed with sod and sprigs, adapt readily to many soil conditions, and are difficult to control with nematicides; the most important nematode pests of St. Augustinegrass in Florida. AL = 40.

Ring Nematodes (*Criconemella* spp., etc.): Widely distributed on most turfgrasses, but rarely considered to be a major pest on any but centipedegrass and occasionally on others when they are under extreme stress from other factors such as cultural practices. AL = 150 for centipedegrass, 500 for most others.

Root-knot Nematodes (*Meloidogyne* spp.): Widely distributed, found most frequently in St. Augustinegrass, zoysiagrass, and bermudagrass; assumed to be injurious when numerous, but their effects on turf grasses are poorly known. AL = 80.

Stubby-root Nematodes (*Paratrichodorus* spp. and related genera): Live in most soils in the state; damage similar to that of sting nematodes. AL = 40.

Spiral Nematodes (*Helicotylenchus, Scutellonema,* and *Peltamigratus* spp.): Frequently found on all grasses; *Helicotylenchus* is rarely a serious pest, but the other two apparently cause significant injury to many kinds of turf when they are very numerous. AL = 300?

Awl Nematode (*Dolichodorus heterocephalus*): Very damaging to turfgrasses in wet locations such as low land near lakes, ponds and canals. AL = 10.

St. Augustinegrass Cyst Nematode (*Heterodera leuceilyma*): Normally attacks only St. Augustinegrass, and high populations occasionally damage St. Augustinegrass; most commonly found on the lower east coast and central Florida. AL = 80.

Other nematodes may damage turf when especially numerous or when other pests, pathogens, or environmental conditions stress turf. Occasional turf pests include lesion (*Pratylenchus*), stunt (*Tylenchorhynchus*), dagger (*Xiphinema*), sheath (*Hemicycliophora*), and sheathoid (*Hemicriconemoides*) nematodes. Most would have to occur at levels above 80 to be of concern.

Diagnosis: When Nematodes Should be Suspected as Plant Pests

R. A. Dunn

It can be very difficult to decide if nematodes are causing, or are likely to cause, a plant growth problem. Nematode diagnosis, determining the role of nematodes in unsatisfactory plant growth, is often especially difficult because few nematodes cause distinctive diagnostic symptoms or signs. Do not depend on symptoms alone when trying to tell if nematodes are hurting turf. Since many other factors can cause similar symptoms, diagnosis should be based on most or all of: symptoms above and below ground, field history, and laboratory assay of soil and/or root samples.

AVOID BLAMING NEMATODES FOR PROBLEMS CAUSED BY OTHER FACTORS

"Nematodes" sometimes become a scapegoat for other things that are actually more responsible for poor plant performance. Avoid the temptation to seize upon the first positive diagnosis made, or one for which you have formal lab results on a printed form, as the sole explanation for a problem. It is very tempting to jump to the conclusion that nematodes are the ONLY reason that turf (or any other kind of plant) is growing poorly when there is an official-looking piece of paper with numbers on it indicating that nematodes could be responsible for the problem. However, many other factors (several are listed below) can cause symptoms in plants similar to those caused by nematodes, and it is quite normal to have more than one of those factors affecting a particular planting at any given time.

Even when high levels of nematodes are found in association with a problem, be cautious; it is not unusual for increased nematode reproduction to be a **result**, as much as **cause**, of increased plant stress. When nematode populations are higher than normal as a result of crop stress caused by persistent environmental factors (cultural practices, other diseases or pests, soil conditions), temporary suppression of the nematodes by chemical means without correcting the fundamental cause of the problem will not provide a long-term solution. In other words, enter into nematode diagnosis with a completely open mind, and be as completely objective as possible in evaluation of the evidence.

Symptoms Above Ground

Aboveground symptoms are rarely, if ever, sufficient evidence to diagnose a nematode problem. However, they are important because problems that might be caused by nematodes are almost always first noticed because of abnormal top growth. Certain kinds of symptoms are typical of nematode injury to roots, and should make one consider nematodes as a possible cause of the inferior performance. They can also be used to help locate the most severely affected areas in the planting after the problem is diagnosed.

Since most plant nematodes affect root functions, most aboveground symptoms are the result of inadequate water supply or mineral nutrition to the tops, include **wilting** under moderate moisture stress, **slow recovery of wilted areas** after rain or irrigation, and **"melting out"** (thinning or gradual decline) of turf (Plate 107). Foliage is sometimes **yellow** or shows other **nutrient deficiency symptoms.** An area damaged by nematodes is usually more obvious during periods of stress such as extreme heat or drought. However, no above-ground symptom is clear proof of nematode injury; other causes of root stress, such as fungi or other pathogens, insects, deficiency or excess of some mineral nutrient(s), too much or too little water, too much shade, soil compaction, and chemical spills may all cause symptoms similar to nematode injury.

Turf weakened by nematodes is less able to compete with **weeds**; grassy and broad-leaved weeds often become more common in nematode-affected turf than in healthy turf. Among weeds that occur frequently in nematode-damaged turf include sedges, spurges, and Florida pusley.

The Pattern of Damage

This may be an important clue to nematodes in turf. Nematode populations are distributed very unevenly in soil (great variation in numbers within a few feet is common), so above-ground symptoms also appear in areas of irregular size and shape. Nematodes move very few feet per year on their own. In undisturbed turf, visible symptoms of nematode injury normally appear as round, oval or irregularly lobed areas which gradually increase in size. Nematode damage is often seen first and most pronounced in areas under special stress, such as heavy traffic, excessive or inadequate drainage, because of slope or soil structure, and outside the perimeter of regular irrigation patterns. Nematode damage rarely is uniform or ends abruptly; a problem that has distinct, sharp boundaries between good and poor turf is probably not caused by nematodes, unless the boundary represents the breaking point between areas treated/not treated with a nematicide or other manipulations that might affect either nematode populations and/or sensitivity of turf to them.

Root Symptoms

Below ground symptoms are more useful than top symptoms for diagnosis of many nematode problems. Roots injured by nematodes are usually **dark** and **short**, with **few lateral or "feeder" roots**. Root tips may be swollen, and there is often excessive root rot.

Short roots that **do not hold soil together** well when a core or plug is lifted from the sod are the most frequently recognized symptom of nematode injury to turf (Plate 108). Abbreviated root systems may be caused by several kinds of nematodes.

Feeding by many ectoparasites, such as sting, awl and stubby-root nematodes, may stop root growth. Injured root tips sometimes swell, and often become much darker in color than uninjured root tips. Lateral roots often emerge a short distance behind the injured root tip; if a series of lateral roots are injured as they emerge, the end of the root acquires a bunchy or bushy arrangement of very short roots that is very characteristic of sting or awl nematode injury.

Abbreviated roots can also be caused by migratory endoparasites. When lesion or lance nematodes cause extensive wounds in the fleshy cortex of host roots, fungi which could not ordinarily penetrate the intact root often can colonize the injured tissues and, from there, move through the entire root. Rotted mature tissues at the tip of the root are a clue that endoparasitic nematodes and/or root-rot fungi rather than ectoparasitic nematodes may have shortened the roots.

Root-knot nematodes injure and reproduce in many grasses, including bermudagrass, St. Augustinegrass, and zoysiagrass, but may not cause such obvious galls on turf roots as they do on many broad-leaved plants. Absence of large galls does not rule out root-knot nematodes as a possible primary cause of turf decline. Slight swelling and distortion of root growth sometimes result from root-knot infection of turfgrasses.

The only turf nematode that can be readily seen without magnification is the St. Augustinegrass cyst nematode (*Heterodera leuceilyma*). The adult females are visible as tiny white beads about the size of the period at the end of this sentence, attached to the roots of its host. Each is a small, lemon-shaped egg capsule which will become tan, then deep brown, after the female has died. With experience, one can diagnose cyst nematodes on St. Augustinegrass without further aid.

Previous History

The history of an area should not be ignored. Specific nematode, disease, and insect problems identified earlier may suggest pests likely to be affecting the turf now. If you know from previous experience that a particular nematode pest was found in a site, continue to take steps to avoid damage by that species. It probably is still present, and can again become a problem if conditions favor it. Prolonged rotation to nonhost plants (a management option rarely available in turf culture) may reduce the population by starving them, but rarely eliminates them entirely.

SOIL SAMPLES

The relative importance of many nematodes to the various turfgrasses has been established through many years' experience, and a scale of approximate action levels has evolved (Table 1). However, these action levels often vary because of the effects of cultural conditions and turf vigor on turfgrass' sensitivity to a specific level of injury. There is also wide variation in how much injury is acceptable, depending on use of the grass, personal aesthetic standards, and maintenance budget. Also, the specific numbers used as thresholds for one laboratory may differ from those of another laboratory because of differences in the laboratory methods used by each.

The Florida Nematode Assay Laboratory, operated by the Florida Cooperative Extension Service, charges a fee of $12 per sample for its service. Several private laboratories also provide nematode assay service in some areas of Florida. Consult with their representatives about services they offer and their fees.

Since most nematode control treatments are expensive, enough nematode samples should be processed to determine if treatment is justified and what prospects for correcting the problem might be expected from those treatments and changes in cultural practices. We do not presently have good controls for all common nematode problems.

Collecting and Handling Nematode Samples

When taking nematode samples, the objective is to take a sample or samples that accurately represent a specific area and to deliver them to the laboratory in as nearly as possible the same condition in which they existed in the field. The following instructions for collecting a nematode sample are taken from the Florida Nematode Sample Kit. The Kit is a package available at all county Extension offices for anyone who wishes to use the services of the Florida Nematode Assay Laboratory. It is a 9" x 12" envelope which contains instructions and packaging materials for taking a soil sample and submitting it to the lab.

Table 1. Approximate action levels (numbers/100 cc soil) commonly associated with turfgrasses in Florida, as used by the Florida Nematode Assay Laboratory. Control is usually suggested when the number of a particular nematode exceeds the level shown in the table and is strongly urged when numbers are more than twice the levels in the table. Control may be suggested at lower population levels if more than one serious nematode pest species is present, or if other stresses such as diseases or insects are also excessive. There are other nematodes which cause problems on turf less frequently which are not included in this table.

| Nematode names | | Action level |
Common	Scientific	
sting	*Belonolaimus longicaudatus*	10
awl	*Dolichodorus* spp.	10
lance	*Hoplolaimus* spp.	40
stubby-root	*Paratrichodorus* spp. and related genera	40
root-knot	*Meloidogyne* spp.	80
stunt	*Tylenchorhynchus* spp. and relatives	80
spiral	*Helicotylenchus, Scutellonema, Peltamigratus* spp.	300
ring	*Criconemella* spp. and relatives	500*
*More than 150 ring nematodes/100 cc soil may injure centipedegrass; other turfgrasses tolerate levels up to about 500 under most circumstances.		

Collecting: The sample should be composed of a mixture of 10 to 20 "cores" of soil. Cores are most easily taken with a soil-sampling tube, auger or trowel. A shovel may be used by cutting a 1-inch thick slice of soil through the soil profile and discarding all but a 1- to 2-inch vertical band from the slice. Sample when soil moisture is favorable for plant growth; do not sample extremely dry or wet soil.

Where to Sample: When diagnosing a problem of growing plants, always sample near living roots of the plants for which diagnosis is needed. Avoid bare spots and weeds. Sample cores should be at least 3 to 4 inches, down to 8 inches if turf roots are growing that deep. It may be helpful to submit an additional sample from an adjacent area of good growth for comparison. Sample only when soil moisture is good for plant growth; avoid extremely dry or wet soil conditions for best results.

Each sample should represent soil and roots from <u>only one plant species</u>. A sample composed of cores or subsamples from several different species may contain nematodes from only one, several, or all of the species sampled; there is no way to know if a particular nematode in the mixed sample came from any one of those plants, or from many, so it is not possible to assess the risk from that nematode species to any plant included in the sample.

Mixing: Mix cores together carefully, then place 1 to 2 pints of the mixed soil in the plastic bag enclosed with the kit. Include as many fine roots as possible (up to ¹/₂ cup) mixed in with the soil sample. A 1-quart sample in the plastic bag will just fit into the box in the kit. Seal the sample in the bag with a rubber band or twist-tie. Label the *outside* of the bag with your name and a sample number or other identification so that the lab cannot confuse your sample with that of someone else. Label the

bag by writing directly on it with a *permanent black* felt-tip marker or with a permanent pen or pencil on masking tape stuck to the bag. Do not place a paper label inside the bag with soil, as it will decompose rapidly and may be unreadable when opened in the lab.

Handling and Submission: Nematodes may die from overheating, freezing or drying. Do not leave samples exposed to sunlight or carry them in a hot car trunk or on the dashboard. Do not add water to the sample, even if it seems dry. Just package and send it so it is received in the same condition as when it was collected. If nematodes are killed in handling, they can not be recovered in the laboratory, and assay results will be false.

Completing Form: Complete the Nematode Assay Record form with all requested information. Print or write clearly and be sure that your information is clearly legible on the form. Be sure that your sample numbers and the information on the form are correctly matched. Complete information about cropping history and plans, symptoms, etc., will help the laboratory make a more accurate diagnosis and recommendation. *Accurate identification of the plant* species (and variety, if possible) for which a diagnosis is needed is *absolutely necessary* to make a recommendation.

Packing and Payment: Use the two pieces of gummed tape to assemble the preaddressed box. Put the Assay Form, any correspondence about the problem, and payment for running the samples in the envelope and put it in the box with the plastic bag of soil. Each sample costs $12.00. Please do not send cash. Make check or money order payable to "Florida Nematode Assay Service." *Results will not be returned to you until the fee is paid.*

Delivering: Mail, ship or deliver samples to the Nematode Assay Laboratory as quickly as possible. The mailing address is printed on the sample box and on the Nematode Assay Record Form. For those preferring to deliver samples to the laboratory, it is located on Mowry Road, south of Lake Alice on the University of Florida campus. The telephone number is (352) 392-1994. Please deliver samples during the periods of 8:00 am - noon and 1:00 - 4:30 pm.

Results: The sample will be analyzed to identify to genus and determine the number of each kind of plant parasitic nematode. These results and the appropriate recommendations will be written on the Nematode Assay Record form or in literature sent to you with it. You and your county Extension agent will each be sent the results in 10 working days or less after receipt of the sample in the laboratory.

Nematode Management

R. A. Dunn

What can be done when nematodes are identified as a serious problem in turf? Choices include: ignore the problem; improve turf management and hope to live better with the nematodes; plant a different kind of grass to try to escape the problem; remove the grass, treat the soil with a chemical that will kill the pests, then replant; or treat the turf with a chemical that will reduce some kinds of nematodes without harming the grass.

TURF MANAGEMENT PRACTICES AFFECT NEMATODES

Grasses can withstand a few of most kinds of nematodes if given sensible care. **Watering deeply and less frequently** encourages deep root growth so turf can draw water and nutrients from more soil than can the short roots that result from shallow daily watering. However, turf already damaged by nematodes must be watered more frequently than this ideal; seriously wilted turf should be watered enough to wet soil to the depth that roots penetrate.

Avoid excessive nitrogen fertilization that encourages unusually succulent root growth, which may encourage high nematode reproduction.

Minimize other stresses to reduce susceptibility of turf to nematodes. Mow grass at the recommended height; turf that is **cut too short** cannot make enough carbohydrates to support normal root vigor and growth. **Soil compaction** and **nutrient deficiencies** can make turf more sensitive to root damage caused by nematodes. **Plant diseases**, especially root rots, are often associated with nematode injury and it appears that each may make the other more serious.

Soil amendments can affect the ability of turf to grow despite potentially injurious nematodes. In research done at Ft. Lauderdale, colloidal phosphate incorporated into a fine sand before planting enabled bermudagrass to tolerate several nematodes better. Adding composted municipal sludge to the same soil before planting apparently reduced numbers of some nematode species. Soil amendments that improve soil composition may help reduce nematode damage to turf on sandy soils throughout the region.

Plant A Different Kind of Grass

This may help if the new grass provides acceptable turf quality. No varietal resistance to any nematode has yet been found in turfgrasses, but turf species differ in the kinds of nematodes which affect them most and reproduce on them most readily.

If turf is to be replaced because of nematode damage, reducing nematode populations before planting usually will encourage most turfgrasses to become established faster and with more complete coverage. Chemical treatment of the planting site with Dazomet (Basamid® Granular Soil Fumigant), for example, (see text below) may satisfactorily reduce nematodes as well as some soilborne fungi which can cause turf diseases and some weeds. In some cases, removing several inches of the surface soil along with all turf roots is the most acceptable option.

Bahiagrasses generally tolerate nematodes better than other common grasses and are less likely to support high nematode populations. Sting nematodes sometimes injure bahiagrasses; sheath nematodes do so more rarely. However, not even bahiagrasses can be expected to become established in soil that already has high nematode populations. Their susceptibility to nematodes also is greater when watered and fertilized badly and cut shorter than recommended.

Centipedegrass is very susceptible to ring nematodes, and high numbers of these nematodes often develop on it. It can also be damaged by sting, sheath, and stubby root nematodes.

St. Augustinegrasses are susceptible to sting and lance nematodes, especially when over-fertilized and watered excessively. Other nematodes are less frequently serious.

Bermudagrasses may be damaged by sting, lance, stubby root, and several other nematodes. The close clipping and intense management programs under which bermudagrasses often are maintained increase their susceptibility to nematode injury.

Zoysiagrasses are susceptible to most nematodes which injure other turfgrasses. Sting nematodes injure zoysia most often; root-knot nematodes are found more frequently and in higher numbers with zoysiagrass than with other common turfgrasses.

BIOLOGICAL CONTROL

Nematologists in Florida and elsewhere are working hard to identify and learn to manipulate natural enemies of nematodes that could be used as biological control agents. Many different bacteria and fungi have reduced populations of some kinds of nematodes under laboratory conditions, but successes at the full-scale field level are few. Most organisms considered to be promising for biological control of one or more nematodes are quite specific in which nematodes they will attack, or have been very difficult to culture in sufficient quantities to be useful for field application, or both. The conditions under which each is most effective are often quite specific and limited. In all, then, commercially effective biological control as a means to reduce the effects of nematodes on lawns still appears to be many years away.

CHEMICAL CONTROL

In some cases, use of a chemical nematicide is the most practical way to reduce unacceptable nematode populations in turf. There are both **fumigant** and **non-fumigant "contact"** chemicals registered for use on lawns in some situations. There are some turf nematode problems for which there presently is **no** legal, effective nematicide.

Effects of Nematicides Are Only Temporary

Nematicides do not make turf grow new roots: both fumigant and non-fumigant nematicides provide only a limited period of relief from nematodes. Therefore, it is critical to provide for all cultural needs of the turf after treatment to give it the best chance to replace damaged roots during that limited period of relative freedom from nematodes. Failing to do so may result in the work, expense, and inconvenience of the treatment being wasted.

Fumigants have no residual effect: nematodes that survive or escape treatment (e.g., are too deep in the soil or are protected inside root tissues) or are in contaminated soil or sod brought in after fumigation can begin to re-infest the turf root-zone immediately.

A non-fumigant nematicide applied to living turf may remain in the root-zone for several weeks, but **eventually will dissipate** through the combined effects of leaching and natural degradation. Such products rarely kill all nematodes, but "inactivate" or paralyze many of them; some nematodes usually become active again after the chemical is gone.

Soil Fumigation Before Planting

Treating soil with a soil fumigant before planting new turf may help promote rapid and uniform turf establishment. Seed, sprigs, or sod planted into soil where nematodes damaged a previous planting are not likely to grow as well as desired. Soil fumigants may be used before planting to reduce populations of nematodes, weeds, and soil-borne fungi, but usually can not be applied to living plants.

When applied to soil, a fumigant produces toxic gases that spread through the soil. Soil physical conditions determine how well a fumigant works. A loose, open-pored soil permits more rapid and uniform spread of its vapors than a compacted or cloddy soil. Soil with a moderate moisture level is best; vapors do not spread well when soil pores are filled by water but may escape too rapidly from dry soils. Nematodes also are less susceptible to nematicides in very dry soils. Soil temperature must be within the range specified on the product label. Fumigants vaporize poorly and move more slowly in cold soils, and evaporate from hot soils too quickly to get adequate control.

Dazomet (Basamid® Granular Soil Fumigant) is a granular product which, when incorporated into moist soil within the temperature range specified on the label, produces gases that are toxic to most living things. Thus, when used carefully, it can control many kinds of soil-borne pests, including many nematodes, soil-borne diseases, and weeds. It now can be used to treat a wide range of turf and landscape ornamental planting sites.

The Basamid label gives specific instructions for use on turf planting sites. We have limited experience with dazomet in Florida, particularly for turf uses. Since its fumes spread slowly and only a few inches, uniform distribution throughout the volume of soil to be treated will be critical for maximum efficacy. Therefore, soil preparation and product incorporation are extremely important for successful use of Basamid.

Areas treated with fumigants should not be re-infested with nematodes in soil on tools, in run-off water, or as fill, or by using sprigs or sod from heavily infested soil. Pests introduced into partially sterilized soil often reproduce very rapidly, sometimes causing more serious damage than would have happened without treatment.

Nematicide for Living Turf

A non-fumigant "contact" nematicide may be available—consult current pesticide recommendations. The active ingredients of all such products known at the time of this revision (December 1996) are dissolved and carried into the soil profile by irrigation or rain water: too little water will not get them into the root zone, but excessive rain or irrigation may leach them too deep or carry them into environmentally-sensitive situations. To a great extent, home lawn nematode management must depend on the cultural practices discussed above, since chemical controls are temporary, not equally effective against all nematode problems (Table 1) and expensive.

Factors That Affect Success of Contact Nematicides: Physical treatments that improve penetration of water into the soil, such as mechanical thatch removal, vertical mowing, and core aeration should be done before applying nematicides; soil should be moist but not saturated when treated.

Table 1. Lowest numbers of nematodes that may justify chemical control of nematodes in turfgrasses in Florida, and expected effectiveness of nematicides that can be applied to living turf.

Nematodes	No/100 cc	Control expected from nematicides
Sting, Awl	10	G[1]
Lance	40	P - G
Stubby-root	40	M
Root-knot	80	P
Sheath	80?	M
Spiral	300	G
Ring	500[2]	M

[1] G = Good; M = Moderate; P = Poor.

[2] More than 150 ring nematodes/100 cc soil may injure centipedegrass; other grasses tolerate more.

Maintenance After Nematicide Treatment: Turf care immediately after nematicide treatment is important. No nematicide can assure better turf performance if other factors also limit its growth. The investment in nematode control may be substantially wasted if soil fertility, drainage, disease and other pest control, etc., limit turf growth, especially root growth.

Do not expect turf to respond instantly to nematicide application. After the chemical reduces nematode activity, the plants need time to grow new roots which can, in turn, support improved growth of foliage. If soil fertility or physical conditions limit root growth during that period, the above-ground response will be delayed and/or reduced, and the over-all effect of the treatment will be disappointing.

Over-using Any Nematicide May Reduce Its Effectiveness: **No nematicide is equally effective against all nematodes.** When one is used frequently, nematodes that are least affected by it will have a distinct advantage over those that are most affected by it. For instance, over-use of a product that affects lance nematodes less than other species enables lance nematodes to become dominant in that population. In other words, relying only on chemical control with one product and without changing fundamental cultural practices that affect the relationship of nematodes to turf is likely to result in reduced effectiveness of the chemical.

"Enhanced biodegradation" can reduce the effectiveness of a nematicide that has been used a lot on the same site. Repeatedly applying the same chemical to soil encourages build-up of bacteria and other microbes which can metabolize ("digest") that chemical, so they can destroy it much more quickly than was the original case. The net effect is a shorter period of control from a given treatment. Enhanced microbial degradation has been reported for over 200 soil-applied pesticides, including many nematicides, which have been used too frequently on a particular site. Use chemical controls as little as necessary, and rotate or alternate among all products that are legal and effective for a particular problem, to avoid prolonged selection for microbes that can build up on any particular pesticide.

SUMMARY

Many kinds of nematodes can damage turf in Florida. Although their effects can easily be mistaken for those caused by many other problems, their diagnosis is possible by combined evidence from symptoms, history of the site, and laboratory analysis of soil samples. Chemical control options are limited and biological controls are not yet available. Thus, it is prudent to employ the best integrated program of cultural practices to minimize nematode populations and sensitivity of turf to it, to make it possible to use nematicides little or not at all, and to maximize the benefit of their use when they are necessary and available.

CHAPTER NINE
Other Pests

Armadillos

J. M. Schaefer

Armadillos are rather unusual looking animals that belong to a family of mammals found primarily in Central and South America. The earliest fossil ancestor of our North American armadillo is from the Paleocene; it was as large as a rhinoceros. Our present-day nine-banded armadillo, *Dasypus novemcinctus*, is much smaller; adults normally weigh from 2 to 7 pounds. This species ranges from Texas eastward throughout the South; its range has expanded northward into Missouri and eastward into South Carolina. However, cold weather limits the further expansion of the northern boundary of the armadillo's range.

DESCRIPTION

Armadillos have a shield-like shell covered with horny scales (Figure 1). Joints in the shell are flexible, which enable the animal to bend and twist. Only the ears and belly of the armadillo are without bony armor. These peculiar animals have 28 to 32 peg-like teeth in simple rows well back in the mouth. There are no front teeth. Armadillos have poor eyesight and hearing, but a keen sense of smell. Both males and females are about the same size (2 to 7 lbs), look alike, and have similar habits.

REPRODUCTION

Although armadillos breed in late July, the 5-month gestation period is delayed which results in the young being born in February or March. Only one litter is produced each year, and it always includes four identical

Figure 1. Armadillo.

young of the same sex. The young look like the adults except that they are smaller and their armor coat remains soft and leathery for some time, becoming harder with age.

TYPICAL HABITAT

Armadillos inhabit dense shady cover, such as brush, woodland or pine forests. They typically rest in a deep burrow during the day and become more active during the late evening, night, or early morning. Burrows, which are located under brushpiles, stumps, rockpiles, or dense brush, are usually 7 to 8 inches in diameter and up to 15 feet long. Armadillos usually have several burrows and depend upon their ability to escape danger by running to the nearest burrow. Despite their awkward appearance, armadillos are agile runners and good swimmers, and even have the ability to walk underwater across small streams.

FEEDING HABITS

These animals feed primarily on insects and invertebrates, including ants, grubs, and earthworms. Armadillos usually root or dig in ground litter in search of food, but will occasionally eat berries and mushrooms. Reports of armadillo damage to birds' nests on the ground are rare.

DAMAGE CAUSED

Armadillos are, to some degree, beneficial because they eat insects and larvae. But to most people, these animals are a nuisance to private properties. Feeding armadillos dig numerous burrows and holes in lawns, flower beds, gardens and pastures (Plate 109). The burrowing in pastures poses a potential hazard to cattle. Armadillo damage, which is both costly and unsightly, has caused increasing concern for homeowners, farmers, and ranchers. There are a number of ways of controlling damage by armadillos.

METHODS OF CONTROL

Preventive and control methods suggested include:

❑ chemical treatment of soils to reduce the local food supply,

❑ erection of barriers (e.g., fences),

❑ use of live traps, and

❑ shooting of offending individuals.

Using insecticides that act to restrict the food sources (i.e., reduce the insect population) may help to reduce but will not stop armadillos from digging. It is important to realize that no chemical treatment will eliminate all of the armadillo's potential food source and all chemical treatment will have to be reapplied periodically on a permanent basis to have any impact. Before applying any insecticide, first identify the actual insect larvae in the soil. Refer to the chapter on insect problems or contact your local county Cooperative Extension office to determine the appropriate chemicals. As with any pesticide, read and follow label instructions for safe use.

Where highly valued plantings are in need of protection, small fences may be used to keep the animals out. These fences should be approximately 24 inches high with half of the fence buried below the surface of the ground.

Armadillos can be trapped in live traps (such as available from Havahart, P.O. Box 551, Ossining, NY 10502) or in homemade box-type traps. Traps should be located near the entrance of armadillo dens or burrows and baited with live earthworms and surrounding soil placed in bags made of old nylon stockings so the odor of the earthworms can be sensed by the armadillo. Trapping is most effective when leaf litter or soil is placed over the entrance to the trap to create familiar surroundings. If other species of animals get into these live traps, they can be released unharmed.

Other methods of trapping include:

❑ firmly inserting a 4-inch diameter PVC pipe into the entrance of an active burrow (regular-sized armadillos will get stuck in the pipe as they try to exit the burrow) or

❑ a nylon throw net used for fishing can also be staked down so it covers the burrow entrance (some armadillos will get tangled in the nets after they emerge).

Because armadillos are nocturnal, PVC pipe and net techniques should be applied late in the afternoon and checked several hours after darkness.

Relocating problem animals to another area is not recommended. This approach only transfers the problem somewhere else, can enhance the spread of diseases and upsets the balance of nature in the receiving area.

Armadillos can be discouraged from returning to burrows if you fill the hole with a mixture of dirt and mothballs after you are sure that they have left for the night.

Shooting is another method frequently used to control nuisance armadillos. Should you choose to control armadillos by shooting, be sure it is legal in your specific vicinity. Remember that it is illegal to use artificial lights to aid in the shooting of armadillos at night. Also, remember that armadillo meat is edible if properly prepared and there is no bag limit or season on them. Poison baits are illegal and ineffective.

A combination of control methods will likely be most effective.

Moles

W. H. Kern, Jr.

DESCRIPTION

The eastern mole, *Scalopus aquaticus*, occurs throughout Florida. Moles are not rodents but belong to the mammalian Order Insectivora. Insectivora means insect eater, and this group includes moles, shrews, and hedgehogs. The most notable aspect of the mole is its large, powerful front feet, designed for pushing soil out of its way (Figure 1). The eastern mole has an average total length of 5 to 6 inches and a short, sparsely haired tail 1 to 1¹/₂ inches long. The fur is very soft and differs from that of most mammals because it does not project toward the tail. With their fur pointing up, moles can move forward or backward within their tunnels without rubbing their fur the wrong way and trapping soil in their coats. The coat is so fine and dense that it keeps out water and dirt. The fur is slate gray with a velvety sheen. Moles living in red clay soils sometimes appear rusty in color. Their bellies may be slightly lighter in color, and some individuals may have tan or orange blotches on their bellies.

The star-nosed mole, *Condylura cristata*, has been collected in the Okefenokee Swamp in Georgia and has been reported in Florida. It is identified by numerous fleshy, fingerlike projections around the tip of its nose. This mole is normally found in wet soils, in marshes, and along streams, so it rarely causes problems in yards and turf. Because of its rarity in Florida, the star-nosed mole will not be discussed further.

HABITAT AND FOOD

The eastern mole prefers loose, well-drained soils. It has been found in dune sand and rich forest humus. The characteristic mole ridges that lie just below the surface are foraging tunnels (Figure 2). These tunnels are created as the mole searches among the plant roots for the

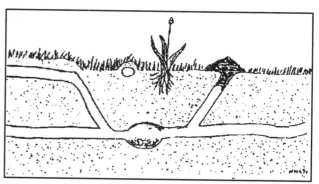

Figure 2. Mole tunnel system with shallow foraging tunnels, deep tunnels, nest, and mole hill.

earthworms and insects on which it feeds. Moles are beneficial because they eat mole crickets, beetle larvae (white grubs, wireworms, etc.), ants and ant brood, moth larvae and pupae (cutworms and armyworms), and slugs. They also help to loosen and aerate the soil. In loose soil, moles can tunnel up to 18 feet per hour. Their living space is in tunnels and chambers 6 to 12 inches below the surface. Soil from these deep burrows is pushed to the surface in small mounds.

REPRODUCTION

The mole's nest chamber is 4 to 6 inches in diameter and lined with fine grass and leaves. Moles have one litter of 2 to 5 young per year. The young are born in March after a 45-day gestation period. They are large at birth relative to the size of their mother and are able to fend for themselves in about 4 weeks.

DAMAGE AND CONTROL

The damage caused by moles is almost entirely cosmetic. Although moles are often falsely accused of eating the roots of grass and other plants, they actually feed on the insects causing the damage. The tunneling of moles may cause some physical damage to the root systems of ornamental or garden plants and may kill grass by drying out the roots, but this damage is usually minor.

When mole tunnels become an intolerable nuisance, moles may be captured and removed without a permit by homeowners, renters, or employees of the property owner. If a lawn service or pest control technician is hired to

Figure 1. Eastern mole with prey.

trap nuisance animals, that person must have a Nuisance Wildlife Permit issued by the Florida Game & Fresh Water Fish Commission. No poison (bait or fumigant) may be used on native wildlife without a Poison Permit issued by the executive director of the Florida Game & Fresh Water Fish Commission. Because suitable traps are available for mole control, it is extremely difficult to justify the use of poisons.

Flooding the tunnels with water may force moles to the surface, but this method rarely works in deep, sandy soils like those common in Florida.

Moles can be live trapped using a simple pitfall trap (Figure 3). Find an active surface tunnel. Collapse a tunnel with your foot, then come back in an hour or two to see whether the tunnel has been reopened. If the tunnel has been pushed back up, it is an active tunnel. Dig a hole through the tunnel large enough to insert a large coffee can, wide-mouth quart jar, or similar con-

tainer. Sink the can into the ground so the top of the container lies just below the bottom edge of the tunnel. Cover the area with a piece of cardboard or a board and the soil from the hole to keep light and air currents from alerting the mole to the trap. When the mole falls into the trap, the whole container can be pulled out of the ground and the mole carried to a forested area and released. Check your live trap often (several times a day). If this is not done, trapped moles may die from starvation or thirst.

Commercial mole traps are available in two main types: the choker-loop and the harpoon. The harpoon trap impales the mole with steel spikes when the animal pushes up on the trigger (Plate 110). To improve soil penetration, the spikes should be worked into the soil prior to setting the trap. Step on the tunnel to partially collapse it and set the trap so the trigger is over the collapsed section of tunnel. A plastic bucket can be

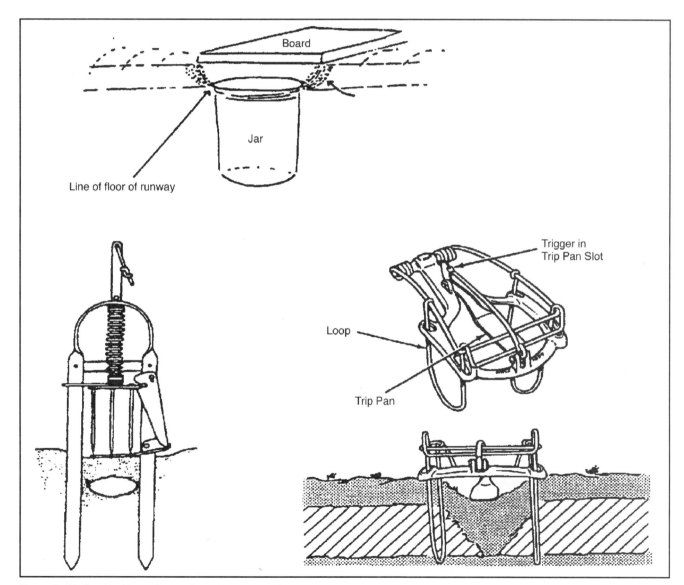

Figure 3. Methods of trapping moles using a live pitfall trap, a harpoon trap, and a choker-loop trap.

placed upside down over the trap to keep children and pets from disturbing the trap. The choker-loop trap kills the mole by squeezing it between the loop and the trap body. Lay the trap next to the mole tunnel. Make two slits across the tunnel with a spade. Step on the tunnel between the slits to partially collapse it. The choker loops are inserted into the slits, and the trigger is positioned over the collapsed tunnel. Read and follow the instructions that come with the trap you purchase. Set traps in active tunnels. If the trap is not sprung within 3 days, move it to a new, more active location.

Small, sensitive areas can be fenced to keep out moles, gophers, and pine voles (Figure 4). The barrier should be made with small-mesh galvanized hardware cloth, brick, or concrete. The barrier should extend at least 6 inches above the ground and 2 feet below the ground, with an outward projection extending 3-6 inches.

Moles can be discouraged from digging foraging tunnels in turf by controlling the populations of insects on which they feed. Elimination of white grubs, mole crickets, and other soil insects will make an area less attractive to moles. Identify the insect pests so the appropriate control method can be used. Ask your local county horticulture extension agent to recommend insecticides for your particular insect problem. Always follow label directions when using any pesticide. Nematodes or bacteria that parasitize insects can be used instead of chemical pesticides to control turf insects. If your soil is rich in organic material and supports a large earthworm population, insecticide treatments will not necessarily discourage moles. Also, be aware that insecticide treatment of an area may cause moles to tunnel more to seek out a diminishing food supply.

The use of vibrating devices to drive away moles has not been proven effective in scientific trials. In fact, the presence of mole tunnels next to highways would seem to be evidence against the effectiveness of these devices. The same is true for the use of mothballs to repel moles. The mole just blocks off the treated tunnels and moves to a different part of the yard. Many people claim that putting sticks of Wrigley's Juicy Fruit gum into moles' tunnels will eliminate the moles. This is another method that has not been proven in scientific tests.

SELECTED REFERENCES

Hamilton, Jr., William J. and John O. Whitaker, Jr. 1979. *Mammals of the Eastern United States.* Cornell University Press, Ithaca, NY.

Lowery, Jr., George H. 1974. *The Mammals of Louisiana and its adjacent waters.* Louisiana State University Press, Baton Rouge, LA.

Olkowski, Helga. 1988. "Much ado about moles." *Common Sense Pest Control* 4(2): 4-8.

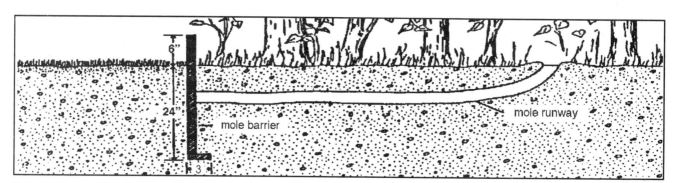

Figure 4. Use of a barrier fence to keep out moles. Fence can be made with brick, concrete, or fine-mesh hardware cloth.

Southeastern Pocket Gophers

W. H. Kern, Jr.

DESCRIPTION

The southeastern pocket gopher, *Geomys pinetis*, is also known as the sandy-mounder or salamander. The pocket gopher is a rodent that is well adapted for its life underground. It has very small eyes and ears and large claws on its powerful front legs. The term pocket refers to the fur-lined cheek pouches that the gopher uses to carry food (Figure 1). The old wives' tale that it carries soil from the burrow in these pouches is false. The lips close behind the protruding chisel-like front teeth so the gopher can chew through dense soil or large roots without getting dirt in its mouth. The southeastern pocket gopher is tan to gray-brown in color. The feet and naked tail are light colored. The average total length (tip of nose to tip of tail) for an adult gopher is about 10 inches, with a range of 9 to 12 inches. Its tail averages about 3 inches in length.

HABITAT AND FOOD

The southeastern pocket gopher requires deep, well-drained sandy soils. It is most abundant in longleaf pine/turkey oak sandhill habitats, but it is also found in coastal strand, sand pine scrub, and upland hammock habitats. Gophers dig extensive tunnel systems and are rarely seen on the surface. The average tunnel length is 145 feet and at least one tunnel was followed for 525 feet. The soil gophers remove while digging their tunnels is pushed to the surface to form the characteristic rows of sand mounds. Mound building seems to be more intense during the cooler months, especially spring and fall, and slower in the summer. In the spring, pocket gophers push up 1 to 3 mounds per day. Based on mound construction, gophers seem to be more active at night and around dusk and dawn, but they may be active at any time of day. The primary tunnels run parallel to the surface and most are 2 inches to 2 feet below the surface, but some tunnels may extend downward as far as 5 feet. Nests and food storage chambers are located in these deeper tunnels. As the gopher digs, it pushes the excavated dirt behind itself. It then turns around in the tunnel and pushes the dirt up a tunnel that ends at the surface, producing a mound. As the main tunnel progresses beyond the first tunnel, a new lateral tunnel is dug to the surface. Then the first lateral tunnel is backfilled to block it off from the surface. This behavior is a defense against the gopher's main predator, the Florida pine snake, which goes down the tunnel after its prey. The pine snake kills the gopher by pressing it against the wall of the tunnel, rather than wrapping it in constricting coils.

The pocket gopher feeds on the tap roots, crown roots, fleshy rhizomes, bulbs, and tubers of a wide variety of plants in its natural environment. Bahiagrass rhizomes appear to be a preferred food based on the contents of food caches. Gophers also have an unfortunate fondness for sweet potatoes, peanuts, sugarcane, alfalfa, and peas.

REPRODUCTION

Gophers reach sexual maturity at about 6 months of age. The southeastern pocket gopher usually has one or two litters per year. The average number of young per litter is 1.5 (1 to 3 young). Although gophers breed year round, breeding is most common in March and in July or August. They build nests of shredded grass in the deepest part of the tunnel system, 2 to 5 feet below the surface. The low reproductive rate can sustain gopher populations because the gopher has few natural predators, owing to its underground lifestyle.

DAMAGE AND CONTROL

The most common problem associated with gophers is the numerous large, sandy mounds they deposit on the surface. Occasionally, gophers will feed on the roots or tubers of garden, ornamental, or crop plants. In natural settings, gopher tunneling activities are beneficial. The soil gophers bring to the surface contains nutrients leached from surface soils. This natural fertilizer helps to maintain the sandhill ecosystem. The mounds of loose soil provide needed germination sites for some native plant seeds. Many amphibians and reptiles use gopher mounds as homes, including Florida's unique mole skinks.

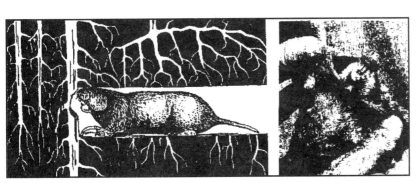

Figure 1. Southeastern pocket gopher. Closeup of fur-lined cheek pouches.

The gopher tunnels themselves serve as habitat for many unique invertebrates that are found nowhere else.

When pocket gophers are damaging lawns, golf courses, or gardens, it is legal for the property owners, tenants, or employees to trap them without a permit. Because the southeastern pocket gopher is a native nongame wildlife species, it is illegal to use any type of poison (bait or fumigant) to kill it without a Poison Permit issued by the Florida Game & Fresh Water Fish Commission. If a lawn service or pest control technician is hired to remove a pocket gopher, that technician must possess a Nuisance Wildlife Permit issued by the Florida Game & Fresh Water Fish Commission.

Trapping is the most effective method for controlling the few gophers that invade yards, gardens, golf courses, or crop fields. Gophers should be maintained in natural areas and can usually be tolerated along rights-of-way for roads and power lines. Traditional gopher traps are very effective but are less humane than choker-loop gopher traps (Figure 2). Because they do not always kill trapped animals quickly, traditional gopher traps should always be attached by a wire to a stake on the surface. In the morning, the trap can be gently pulled to the surface and the gopher killed quickly with a sharp blow to the head. Gophers are killed quickly when caught in a choker-loop trap. Regardless of which trap is used, the most important part of the trapping process is finding the tunnel. This is also the most difficult part of the process. One method depends on finding a mound in the process of being formed. This may require looking at night or around dusk. Push the mound of sand to one side and probe in that location with a trowel or stiff wire. When the tunnel is found and opened, insert the trap into the lateral tunnel (Figure 3). Cover the opening with a board or piece of cardboard and seal the edges with soil from the mound. This will block the light and prevent air movement that might alert the gopher to the trap. The next load of soil the gopher brings to the surface will place it in the trap. The other method of placing traps involves digging a hole down to the main tunnel and setting the traps in the exposed openings of the tunnel (Figure 3). The location of the main tunnel can be estimated to be under the line of mounds on the surface. When digging the hole down to the tunnel, put the excavated soil in a wheelbarrow or on a sheet of heavy plastic so it can be replaced after the gopher is captured. Again, cover the ends of the tunnels with soil after the

traps are set to avoid alerting the gopher to the traps. As a general rule of thumb, the larger the mounds, the larger the gopher. A larger gopher requires a larger tunnel, meaning that more soil must be excavated and moved to the surface. Choker-loop gopher traps were generally designed for western pocket gophers, which are smaller than our southeastern pocket gopher. These traps will work on smaller individuals, but traditional gopher traps may be required to capture large adult gophers.

Gophers can be excluded from small areas such as gardens, flower beds, and even small backyards through the use of underground fences made of ¹/₂-inch galvanized hardware cloth. The barrier should extend at least 2 feet

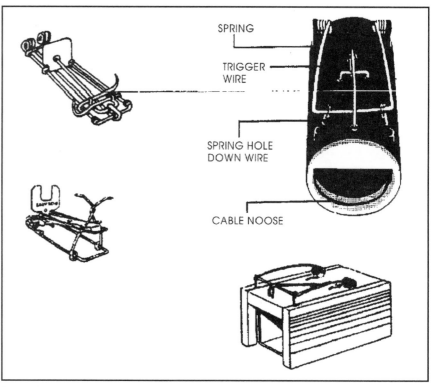

Figure 2. Traditional gopher traps (left) and choker-loop style traps (right).

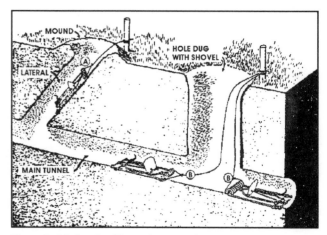

Figure 3. Methods of trap placement.

under the ground and at least 6 inches above the ground. Since gophers can burrow down to 5 feet, some may get under the fence, but this barrier will keep out the majority. Planting unpalatable plants such as oleanders around the edge of your property may deter gophers from entering. Unfortunately, there are no chemical repellents known to be effective against gophers. Vibrating devices have not been proven to repel gophers. Reports that Wrigley's Juicy Fruit gum kills gophers by blocking their digestive tracts have been proven to be false. Finally, tunnel flooding has been used successfully in other parts of the country. However, this method usually does not work here since the southeastern pocket gopher is restricted to deep, well-drained sandy soils in Florida.

SELECTED REFERENCES

Brown, L.N. and G. C. Hickman. 1979. "Tunnel system structure of the southeastern pocket gopher." *Florida Sci.* 36:97-103.

Case, Ronald M. 1983. "Pocket Gophers. Prevention and control of wildlife damage." Cooperative Extension Service, University of Nebraska, Lincoln. pp. B.13-B.26.

Daar, Sheila and William Olkowski. 1985. "Tips on gopher control." *Common Sense Pest Control* 1(3):18-19.

Wing, E. S. 1960. "Reproduction in the pocket gopher in north-central Florida." *J. Mammal.* 41:35-43.

Imported Fire Ants on Lawns and Turf

D. H. Oi and P. G. Koehler

Imported fire ants are aggressive, reddish brown to black ants that are $^1/_8$ to $^1/_4$ inch long. They construct nests which are often visible as dome-shaped mounds of soil, sometimes as large as 3 feet across and $1^1/_2$ feet in height (Plate 111). In sandy soils, mounds are flatter and less visible. Fire ants usually build mounds in sunny, open areas such as lawns, pastures, cultivated fields, and meadows, but they are not restricted to these areas. Mounds or nests may be located in rotting logs, around trees and stumps, under pavement and buildings, and occasionally indoors. When their nests are disturbed, numerous fire ants will quickly run out of the mound and attack any intruder. These ants are notorious for their painful, burning sting that results in a pustule and intense itching, which may persist for 10 days. Infections may occur if pustules are broken. Some people have allergic reactions to fire ant stings that range from rashes and swelling to paralysis, or anaphylactic shock. In rare instances, severe allergic reactions cause death.

In addition to stinging humans, imported fire ants can sting pets, livestock, and wildlife. Crop losses are also reported due to fire ants feeding on seedlings and even citrus trees. Harvesting machinery used on farms can be damaged by hitting hard fire ant mounds often found in clay soils. Electrical equipment and utility housings may serve as fire ant nest sites, sometimes resulting in short circuits.

The term **imported fire ants** generally refers to two species of ants: the black imported fire ant, *Solenopsis richteri* Forel, and the red imported fire ant, *Solenopsis invicta* Buren. The black imported fire ant was accidently introduced from South America into Mobile, Alabama, around 1918, and now infests a small area in Alabama and northern Mississippi. The red imported fire ant entered the United States probably in the 1930s. It was most likely introduced with cargo or in the soil used as ballast in ships from South America that were unloaded in the Mobile area. In the 1940s and early 1950s the red imported fire ant spread to Florida and other southern states in nursery stock and sod. Fire ants currently infest over 280 million acres in Alabama, Arkansas, Florida, Georgia, Louisiana, Mississippi, North Carolina, Oklahoma, South Carolina, Tennessee, Texas, and Puerto Rico (Figure 1). They have the potential to establish in other areas where average minimum temperatures are above 10°F and rainfall is greater than 10 inches a year, or in irrigated areas. Localized infestations have also been reported in Arizona and Virginia.

To limit the spread of imported fire ants, a federal quarantine restricts the movement of soil, potted plants, plants with soil attached, grass sod, hay, and used soil-moving equipment to uninfested areas of the United States. These items must be certified that they are free from infestation. While there are no restrictions on the

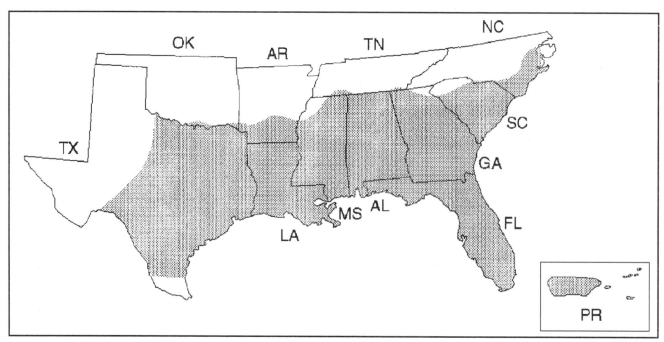

Figure 1. The distribution of well-established imported fire ant infestations in the United States includes 11 states and Puerto Rico.

movement of regulated articles within Florida and other quarantine areas, any shipments outside the quarantine areas require inspection and certification from the Florida Department of Agriculture and Consumer Services, Division of Plant Industry (FDACS-DPI). Information on specific laws and regulations may be obtained from any local office of the FDACS-DPI or the U.S. Department of Agriculture Animal and Plant Health Inspection Service/ Plant Protection and Quarantine, (USDA-APHIS/PPQ).

BIOLOGY

Red imported fire ants live in colonies that contain cream-colored to white immature ants, often called brood. The brood is comprised of the eggs, larvae, and pupae. Also within the colonies are adult ants of different types, or castes. The castes include winged males, winged females (which are unmated queens), workers of varying size, and one or more mated queens. The winged males and females fly from nests, usually in the spring and early summer, to mate in flight. Upon landing, mated females will shed their wings after finding a suitable nesting site. All the males die after mating. While thousands of winged males and females can be produced per year in large colonies, they do not sting, and fewer than 10% of the females will survive to produce a colony. Newly-mated queens can fly as far as 12 miles from the nest (or even farther in the wind), but most land within a mile.

New colonies do not make conspicuous mounds for several months. Once a colony is established, a single queen can lay over 2,000 eggs per day. Depending on temperature, it can take 20 to 45 days for an egg to develop into an adult worker. Workers can live as long as 9 months at 75°F, but life spans usually are between 1 and 6 months under warmer outdoor conditions. Queens live an average of 6 to 7 years.

Fire ants are omnivorous feeders, feeding on carbohydrates (e.g., honeydew, plant exudates, sugars, syrups), proteins (e.g., insects, meats), and lipids (e.g., grease, lard, oils from seeds). Their food preferences change depending on the nutritional requirements of the colony. In the spring and summer, when food is abundant, the colony produces new offspring, and the protein needs of the colony increase. Adult ants require carbohydrates and/or lipids to sustain themselves throughout the year. Fire ants are only able to ingest liquids. Solid proteinaceous foods are liquified by placing them on a depression in front of the mouth of the oldest larvae (the fourth instar stage), which then regurgitate digestive enzymes onto the food. Once liquified, the fourth instar larvae suck up the protein and regurgitate it to the workers, which pass it on to the rest of the colony.

Workers will forage for food more than 100 feet from the nest. They can forage during both the day and the night, generally when air temperatures are between 70° and 90°F. When a large food source is found, fire ants recruit other workers to help take the food back to the colony. Liquids are ingested at the food source, and stored within the ants until they are regurgitated to other ants within the colony. Liquids from solid foods are extracted at the source, or are carried back as solid particles. Large solids may be cut into smaller pieces so they can be carried back to the colony.

There are two types of fire ant colonies:

❏ single-queen, or monogyne, colonies, and

❏ multiple-queen, or polygyne, colonies.

Single-queen colonies have only one egg-laying queen, and may contain as many as 100,000 to 240,000 workers. Multiple-queen colonies have many egg-laying queens (usually 20 to 60), with 100,000 to 500,000 workers. Single-queen colonies fight with other fire ant colonies. Because of this antagonistic behavior, colonies are farther apart, resulting in a maximum of 40 to 150 mounds per acre. Multiple-queen colonies generally do not fight with other multiple-queen colonies. Consequently, mounds are closer together, and can reach densities of 200 to 800 mounds per acre. Multiple-queen mounds may also be inconspicuous, often times being clusters of small, flattened excavations, in contrast to the distinct dome-shaped mounds of single-queen colonies. Workers from single-queen colonies vary in size, ranging in length from 1/8 to 1/4 inch, and are usually reddish brown to black in color. Workers of multiple-queen colonies are generally smaller (1/8 to 3/16 inch), have only a few large workers, and are lighter in color (orangish-brown) than single-queen colony workers.

The large colony sizes, and the presence of numerous queens makes multiple-queen colonies more difficult to eliminate than single-queen colonies. Since 1973, multiple-queen colonies have been found in eight of the 11 fire ant infested states, including Florida. Multiple-queen colonies produce fewer winged, or alate, queens that will start new colonies after a mating flight than single-queen colonies. However, multiple-queen colonies can establish new colonies by budding, where a portion of the queens and workers splits off from a colony.

The spread of fire ants into new areas depends on many factors, such as climate, surrounding fire ant populations, and the native predators and competitors in the areas. Areas with an abundance of natural enemies and competing ant species may hinder colony establishment because the enemies prey upon newly-mated queens and compete for resources. However, if an area is disturbed, for example, by clearing land for pastures or urban development, natural enemies or competitors may be adversely affected and fire ants may colonize the area more rapidly.

It may take as long as 11 years for single-queen fire ant colonies to become the dominant ant species in a new area which has been disturbed by urbanization, and has not been treated with insecticides to control ants. Multiple-queen colonies may become dominant in new areas at a slower rate because they spread more by budding than by establishing numerous new colonies scattered throughout an area after mating flights.

In areas where native ants and fire ant populations have been reduced or eliminated with insecticides, reinfestation by fire ants may be noticeable within a month after treatment. Fire ants reinfest these areas more rapidly and outcompete other ant species because of their tremendous reproductive capacity and faster colony development. If fire ant control is not maintained, the subsequent reinfestation of an area may result in even greater fire ant populations than existed before the application of insecticides.

CONTROL STRATEGIES AND TECHNIQUES

Imported fire ants have been the target of innumerable methods of control. Unfortunately, there are no control methods that will permanently eliminate fire ants from an area. Four strategies are currently being used to control fire ants:

❑ broadcast bait applications,

❑ individual mound treatments,

❑ a combination of broadcast baiting and individual mound treatments, and,

❑ barrier and spot treatments.

The following discussion provides general descriptions of these strategies and guidelines for employing them. Suggestions for using these strategies in lawns and ornamental turf follow this section.

Broadcast Bait Applications

This strategy attempts to reduce fire ant populations by applying insecticides incorporated into an attractant, or bait, on an area-wide basis. Most bait products (eg. Amdro®, PT®370 Ascend™, Award®, or Logic®) contain slow-acting toxicants dissolved in soybean oil, which is a food source for fire ants. The toxicant-laden oil is then absorbed into corn grits, which makes the product easier to handle and apply, and more available to the ants. The small size of the corn grit allows the ants to either carry the grit back to the colony and extract the toxic oil within the mound, or extract the toxic oil from the grit immediately and carry it back to the colony internally. The slow action of the toxicants allows the ants to feed the toxic oil to other members of the colony before they die. When

the toxicant is fed to the queen(s), she either dies or no longer produces new workers and the colony will eventually die.

There are four different toxicants, or active ingredients, that are used in commercially available broadcast bait products specifically registered for use against fire ants. Hydramethylnon, which is used in Amdro® and Combat® outdoor ant killing granules, is a slow-acting poison that kills all members of a colony that ingest it. After 1 to 5 weeks, 80 to 90% of the fire ant colonies in the treated area will be killed. However, these areas are subject to reinfestation.

Two of the other active ingredients interfere with reproduction, and are often referred to as insect growth regulators, or IGRs. The active ingredient in Ascend is abamectin B_1 which, at broadcast application rates, prevents queens from laying eggs. Fenoxycarb is the active ingredient in Logic® and Award®, and it prevents queens from laying worker eggs. Because workers are no longer being produced, colonies treated with IGRs will eventually be eliminated because the queen(s) will not be cared for and will die as workers die off naturally. Abamectin and fenoxycarb products may take 5 to 10 weeks to eliminate 90% of the colonies, and large treated areas (>1 acre) may have control for as long as a year. Control in smaller areas is not as long lasting because these areas are more easily reinfested from adjacent areas.

Another bait product, Bushwhacker®, contains boric acid as the active ingredient. Boric acid will kill individual fire ants but its actual mode of action is not completely known. Published data on the effectiveness of this bait product under outdoor conditions are not available.

A broadcast bait application eliminates the need to locate mounds, because it relies on foraging fire ants to find and feed the baits to the rest of the colony. Thus, large areas can be treated more efficiently. To ensure baits will be fed upon, follow these guidelines for effective bait applications.

❑ *Use fresh bait.* Most available fire ant baits use soybean oil as a feeding attractant. Baits that are old (over 2 years old in an air-tight container), left in unsealed bags, or stored at high temperatures may become rancid and will not be fed upon by foraging workers.

❑ *Keep baits dry.* Wet baits are not attractive to fire ants. Apply baits when the grass and ground are dry or drying, and rain is not expected, preferably for the next 24 hours.

❑ *Apply baits when fire ants are actively foraging.* Foraging activity can be determined by spreading bait in a small pile in the area to be treated. If fire ants are actively foraging, you should see ants removing the bait within 10 to 30 minutes. This also will indicate that the bait is attractive, and not too old. Fire ants generally will forage when air temperatures are between 70° and 90°F. During hot, summer weather, apply baits in the late afternoon or evening because fire ants will forage at night under these conditions.

❑ *Follow the directions on the label.* It is against the law to apply baits in areas not listed on the label.

Bait broadcasting equipment (Figure 2) suitable for small areas such as lawns and playgrounds include hand-held seed spreaders (Scott's Handy Green®, Republic EZ Handspreader®, or Ortho Whirlybird®) and chest spreaders (Plant Mates Canvas®, Spyker Poly® model 75, Earthway Canvas EV-N-SPRED® 2700A, Cyclone Poly® model 1A1). The spreader should be set at the smallest opening, and the applicator should walk rapidly to apply approximately 1 ounce of bait per 2,000 square feet. Electric spreaders such as the Herd Model GT-77A®, Cyclone Spreader Model M-3, or other similar spreaders are suitable for broadcasting baits over larger areas (1 to 25 acres). These spreaders must be mounted onto vehicles that can maintain low speeds and be calibrated to apply 1 to 1.5 pounds of bait per acre. Walk-behind rotary spreaders generally apply excessive amounts of bait and are not recommended. However, some manufacturers may provide separate attachments (Spyker® models 44-22, 24-22) that result in application rates of 1 to 1.5 pounds per acre.

Individual Mound Treatments

This strategy attempts to eliminate colonies of fire ants by treating mounds individually. To eliminate a colony, the queen must be killed. If she is not destroyed,

she will continue to lay eggs and the colony will recover. In the case of multiple-queen colonies, all the queens must be killed, thus making effective treatments very difficult. Individual mound treatments are time consuming and labor intensive because the mounds must be located and treated one at a time. However, colonies treated individually may be eliminated faster than colonies treated with broadcast bait applications.

There are chemical and nonchemical methods of treating mounds individually. Chemical methods include insecticides that are formulated as baits, drenches, granules, dusts, and aerosols. Non-chemical methods include applying hot water, and physically excavating the nest. All individual mound treatments may cause the ants to relocate and create a new mound. Even if the queen is killed, surviving ants may still inhabit the treated mound or make a new mound until they die off naturally, which may take over a month. Thus it may be necessary to retreat remaining mounds that still contain ants.

Baits

Bait products used for broadcast bait applications can be applied to individual mounds. Sprinkle the recommended amount of bait around the base of the mound up to three feet away (Figure 3). In addition, follow the Guidelines for Effective Bait Applications given previously. As with broadcast bait applications, the use of baits for individual mound treatments may take one to several weeks to eliminate colonies.

Drenches

These products are solutions consisting of insecticides and water that are applied to mounds. To be effective, the drench needs to contact a majority of the ants. This

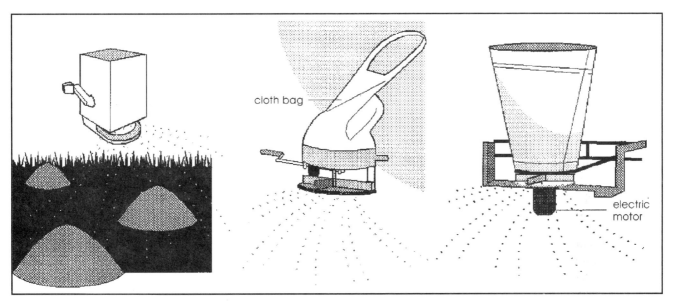

cloth bag

electric motor

Figure 2. Bait broadcasting equipment (from left to right): hand-held spreader; chest spreader and electric spreader.

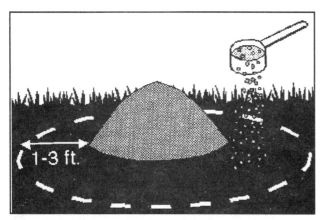

Figure 3. Application of bait to individual ant mound.

is best accomplished by applying the drench to an undisturbed mound on cool, sunny mornings. Under these conditions the ants, including the queen(s) and brood, are concentrated just under the top surface of the mound, where it is warm. If drenches are applied in hot, dry weather, most of the ants are deep within the mound, and the drench will not contact the ants. It is recommended that entire mounds be saturated by first wetting the top of a mound, then soaking a 12-inch swath around the base of the mound, and finally, pouring the remaining drench on top of the mound from a height of at least 3 feet to obtain penetration into the mound. Use about 1 gallon of drench per mound for mounds with bases up to 8 inches in diameter and 2 gallons for larger mounds (Figure 4). Colonies may be eliminated within a few hours to several days after treatment.

Granules

In general, these products contain an insecticide that is released and carried into the mound with water that is poured over the granules. As with the drenches, granules are effective only if the insecticide penetrates the mound

and contacts a majority of the ants and the queen(s). To apply, evenly scatter a measured amount (follow label directions) of granules over the surface and around a mound, without disturbing the mound. With a sprinkler can, sprinkle 1 to 2 gallons of water over the granules, gently, to avoid disturbing the colony and washing granules off the mound (Figure 5). Watering may not be necessary with some products (follow label directions). Treating mounds on cool, sunny mornings will help the treatment contact the colony. It may be several days before the entire colony is killed.

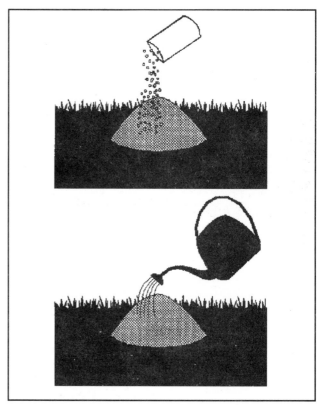

Figure 5. Application of granular insecticide: Top, scatter granules over mound; Bottom, water in with sprinkler can.

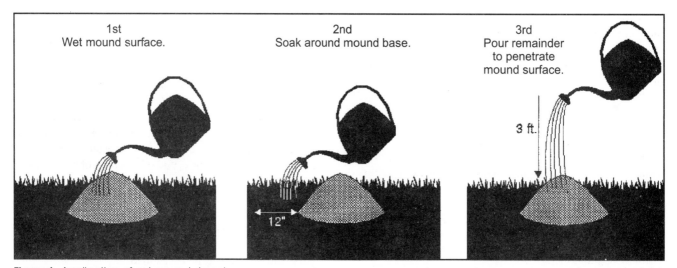

1st
Wet mound surface.

2nd
Soak around mound base.

12"

3rd
Pour remainder
to penetrate
mound surface.

3 ft.

Figure 4. Application of ant mound drench.

Dusts

Dusts are insecticidal products that are dry powders. The dusts stick to the bodies of ants as they walk through treated soil. Ants that contact the dust will eventually die. Dusts are applied by evenly sprinkling a measured amount of dust (follow label directions) over the mound. Avoid inhaling or touching the dust (Figure 6). Some dusts, such as those containing 75% acephate, should kill an entire colony within a week.

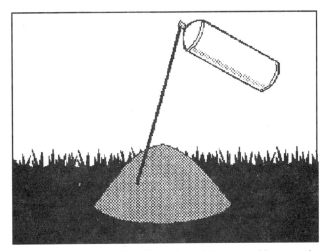

Figure 7. Inject pressurized insecticide into mound in several places according to label directions.

Figure 6. Sprinkle dust evenly over the entire mound. Avoid inhaling or touching the dust.

Aerosols

Some products are available in aerosol cans equipped with a probe, and contain insecticides that quickly immobilize and kill ants on contact. As the probe is inserted into a mound, the insecticide should be injected into the mound for a specified amount of time (follow label directions). Depending on the size of the mound, several insertions may be needed to distribute the insecticide. Aerosols generally disperse throughout the mound more quickly than drenches. However, as with other individual mound treatments, application on cool, sunny mornings will help maximize contact with the colony (Figure 7). While aerosols are more convenient to use than drenches, they generally are more costly and do not provide significantly better control than some drenches.

Organic Insecticides

Commercially available organic products that contain ingredients such as boric acid and diatomaceous earth are known to kill ants. However, their effectiveness in killing entire colonies when applied to mounds has not been consistently demonstrated. There are also several products which contain plant derived, or botanical, insecticides such as rotenone, nicotine sulfate, and pyrethrins. As with the other mound treatments, the product must contact and kill the queen(s) to control colonies.

Hot Water

Scalding or boiling water (190° to 212°F) has been used to eliminate colonies. Slowly pour about three gallons of hot water onto the mound. The water should drain into the vertical tunnels of the mound and eventually collapse the entire mound structure. Treatments may be more effective if applied on cool, sunny mornings. It has been reported that 20 to 60% of the mounds treated by this method have been eliminated. Several applications may be needed, and hot water may injure plants adjacent to treated mounds. One must be very careful when using hot water to avoid burning oneself.

Excavation

Fire ant mounds may be dug up and removed from an area. Apply talcum or baby powder to the handle of a shovel and the inside of a bucket to deter the ants from crawling up the handle or escaping from the bucket. The best time to excavate a mound is on cool, sunny mornings, when a majority of the ants and brood are near the mound surface.

Other Home Remedies and Control Devices

Many home remedies and mechanical control devices have not been scientifically proven to consistently eliminate fire ant colonies. Oftentimes these cures will kill many ants and the colony will abandon the mound, thus giving the false impression that the colony was killed. In actuality, the colony most likely just established another mound elsewhere, and elimination of the entire colony, or the queen(s) did not occur. Some home remedies also are dangerous to apply and can seriously contaminate the environment. These remedies include the use of gasoline or other petroleum products; battery acids; bleaches, ammonia, and other cleaning products. Such remedies should never be used.

Other ineffective home remedies include:

❏ soap solutions and wood ashes soaked into a mound, which supposedly remove the wax layer that protects an ant's body;

❏ applying grits to fire ant mounds in an attempt to get ants to eat the grits, which will then supposedly swell inside them and explode the ants (recall that ants can only ingest liquids, so they do not even eat grits); and,

❏ shoveling mounds together in an attempt to have different colonies fight and kill each other (this is not effective with either single or multiple-queen colonies).

Combining Broadcast Baiting and Individual Mound Treatments

This strategy utilizes the efficiency of broadcast baiting and the fast action of individual mound treatments. Baits must be broadcast first to efficiently reduce fire ant populations (see Guidelines for Effective Bait Applications). Wait a minimum of 3 days after broadcasting to allow fire ants to forage and distribute the bait before individually treating mounds. Treat mounds preferably with a dust, drench, granular, or aerosol insecticide specifically labeled for fire ant control. Treat only mounds that are causing immediate problems or are a potential hazard (e.g., mounds located in areas frequented by people or pets) (Figure 8). Most mounds that receive the slower acting baits will eventually be eliminated, and the presence of small populations of fire ants may help slow the reinfestation of an area.

Barrier and Spot Treatments

Products that contain active ingredients such as acephate, bendiocarb, carbaryl, chlorpyrifos, diazinon, isofenphos, propoxur, permethrin, and resmethrin,

immediately kill ants on contact. These products are usually sold as sprays or dusts. They may be applied in wide bands on and around building foundations, equipment and other areas to create barriers that exclude ants. They also may be applied to ant trails to eliminate foraging ants. Barrier and spot treatments do not eliminate colonies. Follow label directions for specific uses and application procedures.

OPTIONS FOR MANAGING FIRE ANT POPULATIONS IN LAWNS AND TURF

Fire ants infest lawns, school yards, athletic fields and parks. In these places they may pose a medical threat and affect human activity. Their mounds also detract from the aesthetic value of the landscape.

Treatment Options

Option 1: For Small Areas

For small areas (usually 1 acre or less) of ornamental turf or where preservation of native ants is desired. This option selectively controls fire ants, but reinvasion should be expected. It requires more labor and monitoring than other options.

Step 1. Treat all unwanted fire ant mounds using the individual mound treatment of choice.

Step 2. Selectively treat new or undesirable mounds as needed.

Option 2: For Long-term Suppression

For long-term ant suppression in ornamental turf and non-agricultural lands, including roadsides. This option is best suited to larger areas and will not eliminate all ant activity. Suppression of ants occurs slowly (weeks to

Figure 8. Combining broadcast baiting with individual mound treatments: (from left to right) 1) broadcast bait; 2) wait three days; 3) individually treat mounds.

months) and the cost is moderate. This option is not suggested for areas with large numbers of native ants and few fire ant mounds (15 to 20 per acre or fewer).

Step 1. Make an annual or semi-annual broadcast application of a bait-formulated insecticide (PT®370 Ascend™, Amdro® or Award®) in the spring and/or fall.

Step 2. At least 3 days after broadcasting the bait, begin treating individual mounds in sensitive or high traffic areas as needed.

In areas with excessively high numbers of mounds per acre (200 or more), two applications of bait may be needed within several months to result in a satisfactory level of ant suppression, since all mounds may not be affected by a single bait application. Reapply when the presence of ants justifies the cost of treatment.

If and when bait applications are terminated, fire ants can reinfest the area, sometimes with more mounds than were present initially. Mated queens may "seed" the treated area with new colonies and be unaffected by the earlier bait applications. Also, in low-lying flood prone areas, baits may be less effective because ants move in and out of these areas often.

Option 3: To Eliminate Mound Building and Foraging Activity

To eliminate all mound building and foraging activity in ornamental turf. Effects of this option are more rapid and dramatic than with Option 2, but this option may be more expensive and requires more contact insecticide.

Step 1. (Optional). Make an annual or semi-annual broadcast application of a bait-formulated insecticide in areas where there are many mounds (more than 20); or, individually treat fire ant mounds.

Step 2. Routinely broadcast or spray a contact insecticide every 8 weeks or so when ants are detected. Heed the re-entry or treatment-to-harvest intervals specified on product labels.

Option 4: Small Areas Needing Minimal Pesticide Use

For small areas (less than an acre) where minimal pesticide use is desired, such as areas frequented by young children. This option is very labor intensive, and may be practical if only a few mounds are present.

Step 1. (Optional) Broadcast a bait-formulated insecticide. Note that relative speed of population reductions from fire ant baits are from fastest to slowest: Amdro® or Combat®, Ascend™, and Award®. However, while all baits have low mammalian toxicities, relative toxicities for the three baits from highest to lowest are: Amdro®, Ascend™, and Award®. At the 1 to 1.5 lb per acre application rate for the above products, bait particles are widely scattered and difficult to find.

Step 2. At least three days after baiting (if baits were applied) individually drench mounds with hot (scalding) water.

Step 3. Excavate and/or reapply hot water to mounds that are still active. Repeat when necessary.

Step 4. (Optional) Make an annual or semi-annual broadcast application of a bait-formulated insecticide in the spring and/or fall to suppress reinfestations.

Commercial Turf Treatment Options

Option 1: Shipping Sod Within Quarantined Area

To treat sod to be shipped within the quarantined area use options 1, 2, or 3 listed for lawns and ornamental turf.

Option 2: Shipping Sod Out of Quarantined Area

To treat turf to be shipped out of the quarantined area (from Florida Imported Fire Ant Certification Procedure Manual, revised Sept. 1992).

Step 1. A Compliance Agreement and required shipping permits must be obtained from the Florida Department of Agriculture and Consumer Services.

Step 2. Apply granular chlorpyrifos or chlorpyrifos wettable powder (for details see the Florida Imported Fire Ant Certification Procedure Manual).

ACKNOWLEDGEMENTS

This article was adapted from the University of Florida, Florida Cooperative Extension Service bulletin "Imported Fire Ants and Their Management in Florida."

References to commercial products or trade names does not imply any recommendation or endorsement by the authors, the USDA or the University of Florida over any products not mentioned. Product names are used solely for the purpose of providing examples. All uses of pesticides must be registered by appropriate State and/or Federal agencies.

CHAPTER TEN

Pesticide
Application
and Use

Pesticide Use and Safety

L. B. McCarty and O. N. Nesheim

Pesticides are chemical agents which control pests. They include herbicides, fungicides, insecticides, nematicides, and others. The majority of pesticides are organic compounds which interfere with a physiological process in the pest organism. For desired control, a pesticide must be present at an effective concentration at the site of pest activity for a sufficient period of time. Desirable attributes of a pesticide include:

❏ effective pest control,

❏ no affect on nontarget pests,

❏ no persistence beyond the control period, and

❏ nonhazardous to humans and the environment.

When choosing the correct pesticide for a particular purpose, always follow these guidelines:

❏ Positively identify the pest to be controlled.

❏ If several pesticides are available, choose the least toxic one.

❏ Read and follow all directions before use. Note any statements on protective equipment needed to mix and apply the pesticide. Also notice if watering-in is required following application.

❏ Do not purchase more pesticide than can be used in one season.

❏ Keep written records on pesticide use (see sample form).

LABEL INFORMATION

The pesticide label is a guide to the safe handling and proper use of a pesticide. Certain information is required by law to be on the label, attached to the pesticide container:

❏ name and address of the manufacturer

❏ trade (product) name of the pesticide

❏ list of active ingredients

  ○ percentage of active ingredient

  ○ common name

  ○ chemical name

❏ type of pesticide (herbicide, insecticide, etc.)

❏ type of formulation (wettable powder, granular, etc.)

❏ EPA registration number

❏ Storage and disposal precautions

❏ Hazard warning statements (signal words are highlighted to indicate how much of the pesticide can kill if swallowed, inhaled, or absorbed by the skin)

  ○ *danger/poison* – these pesticides are highly toxic (It takes only a few drops to 1 teaspoon to kill a person. A red skull and crossbones will also appear on the label.)

  ○ *warning* – these are moderately toxic, and only 1 to 3 teaspoons can kill a person

  ○ *caution* – More than 1 ounce of these pesticides would be required to kill an adult

❏ directions for use (this includes information on legal use for specific crops and pests; proper application rates are also listed, as well as mixing instructions, necessary equipment, and proper timing of the application), and

❏ net contents.

Labels often list precautions to follow for safe use. Some of these precautions include:

❏ keep out of reach of children

❏ do not store with food or livestock feed

❏ remove and wash contaminated clothing before re-use, and

❏ wash with soap and water after handling.

SAFETY PRECAUTIONS

❏ Before opening the container, read and follow the label. It is illegal to use a pesticide in any manner that is inconsistent with the label.

❏ Wear the protective clothing that is indicated on the label. This may include coveralls, rubber boots (not leather), rubber gloves, a respirator, face shield, goggles, and a wide-brimmed waterproof hat. Wash protective clothes separately from other clothes after each use (Figure 1).

❏ Avoid mixing excess pesticide.

❏ Never eat, drink, or smoke while handling pesticides.

❏ Always wash with soap and water after handling pesticides.

❏ Store pesticides safely. Keep them locked up, away from children and animals.

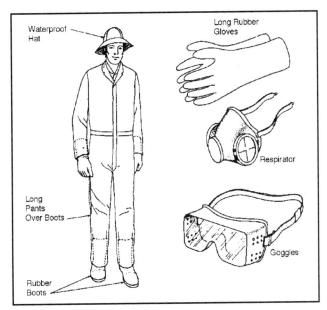

Figure 1. Protective clothing.

Always keep pesticides in their original containers, and store them in well-ventilated, cool, dry places.

PESTICIDE LICENSING

Certain pesticides are classifies as "restricted use." Restricted use pesticides must be purchased by and used by a licensed pesticide applicator. Over-the-counter pesticide products available at garden center or supply stores are not classified as restricted use. Homeowners who are not familiar with the correct manner to handle and apply any pesticide should use the services of a commercial pesticide applicator.

DISPOSAL OF CONTAINERS

Once a container that held liquid pesticide is empty, the container should be rinsed three times. Follow these steps, in order, to dispose of liquid pesticide containers.

1. Fill container one-third full with water.

2. Place cap on container and shake.

3. Pour rinse water into the spray tank (never down a drain or ditch) and spray on a labeled crop.

4. Repeat these steps at least two more times.

5. Punch several holes in the used container.

When using paper bags, empty all contents and dispose in normal garbage containers. Never reuse pesticide containers.

PESTICIDE APPLICATION RECORD

Commercial Applicator _____ Application Date & Time _____

Pesticide License Category _____ Number _____

Supervisor _____ Pesticide License Category & Number _____

Pesticide Name(s) _____

Active Material_____ Manufacturer_____

Pesticide Formulation_____ % Concentration _____

Safety Equipment Needed _____

EPA Registration No. _____ Restricted-entry Interval _____

APPLICATION INFORMATION

Type of Area Treated _____ Plant Species _____

Target Pest(s) _____ Total Treated Area _____

Application Rate _____ (per acre or per 1000 sq. ft.) _____

Amount of Pesticide Mixed _____ Per _____ Gallons of Water

Total Amount of Pesticide Used _____ Application Timing _____

Additive (Surfactant/Wetting Agent/Crop Oil, etc.) _____ Rate _____

WEATHER CONDITIONS

Air Temperature (°F) _____ % Relative Humidity _____ Dew Presence (Y/N) _____

Wind Velocity (MPH) _____ Wind Direction _____

Soil Temperature at 4 Inches (°F) _____ Soil Moisture _____ % Cloud Cover _____

APPLICATION EQUIPMENT

Method of Application _____ Speed (mph) _____ Motor Speed (RPM) _____

Nozzle Type _____ Nozzle Height _____ Nozzle Spacing _____ Boom Width _____

Gallon Per Acre (GPA) _____ Spray Pressure (PSI) _____

Other Comments:

Signature _____ Date _____

Spray Additives and Pesticide Formulations

L. B. McCarty

SPRAY ADJUVANTS

Spray adjuvants (additives) are added to pesticides to enhance the performance or handling of that pesticide. Adjuvant is a broad term and includes surfactants, crop oils, antifoaming agents, stickers, and spreaders. Adjuvants are usually classified according to their use rather than their chemistry.

Adjuvants are not under the same guidelines for registration as are pesticides. Anyone can mix up a nonpesticidal concoction, give it a name and sell it as an adjuvant.

The best way to avoid a "snake oil" is to buy a recognized name-brand product from a reputable dealer. If the claims sound too good to be true, they probably are not.

Surfactants (Surface-Active Agent)

Surfactants are chemicals which modify the surface properties of materials they contact. Surfactants are often added to herbicides to increase the activity on weeds. However, surfactants may also increase crop injury. Three major surfactant types are emulsifiers, wetting agents and stickers.

Soaps and household detergents are essentially surfactants. However, these are not generally as effective because:

❑ they contain low concentrations of surfactant (10 to 20%) compared to agricultural (50 to 95%)

❑ they combine with hard water to form scum and precipitants affect sprayer performance, and

❑ they make too much foam in the spray tank.

Emulsifiers. Emulsifiers promote the suspension of one liquid in another. Emulsifiers are most commonly used to disperse oil in water.

Wetting agents. Wetting agents reduce interfacial tensions between normally repelling substances. Normally the *non-ionic* group of surfactants are used as wetting agents due to their compatibility with most pesticides and low toxicity to plants and animals.

Stickers. Stickers are adjuvants that cause the pesticide to adhere to the plant foliage and also to resist wash-off. Spreader-stickers are combined products to provide better spray coverage and adhesion. These are more commonly used with fungicides and insecticides.

Crop Oils and Crop Oil Concentrate

These are nonphytotoxic light petroleum-based oils that contain surfactants. Crop oils contain 1 to 2% surfactant and are used at a concentration of 1 gallon in 20 to 25 gallons of spray solution. Crop oil concentrates contain 17 to 20% surfactant and are used at approximately 1 quart per 20 to 25 gallons of spray.

Utility modifiers allow a given formulation to be used under a wider range of conditions.

Antifoam agents (foam suppressants). Antifoam agents suppress the foam formed when tanks are agitated.

Compatibility agents. Compatibility agents are adjuvants used to reduce incompatibility (lack of mixing) of pesticides or pesticide and liquid fertilizer mixtures.

PESTICIDE FORMULATIONS

A formulation is a pesticide preparation supplied by the manufacturer. The formulation includes all contents inside the container active ingredient plus inert ingredients (such as solvents, diluents, and various adjuvants).

Purpose of Formulating a Pesticide

Ease of application. Formulating a pesticide allows a small quantity to be mixed with a larger quantity of carrier so that the pesticide can be more easily applied more uniformly to a large area.

Improves pesticide performance. Formulating a pesticide aids in application, aids in mixing, improves coverage, aids in uptake, etc.

Stability of product. Formulating a pesticide provides better stability in shipping and storage and a longer shelf life.

Safety. Formulating a pesticide dilutes the active ingredient and its acute toxic effect; the user is exposed to lower concentrations.

Compatibility. Formulating a pesticide aids mixing with carriers.

Types of Formulations

Sprayable Formulations

❑ Water soluble liquids

○ are designated as S or SL or SC

○ form true solutions when mixed with water; nonabrasive, and

- will not separate or settle-out upon standing; requires no agitation once initially mixed.
- example: Vantage.

❑ **Water soluble powders**
- designated as SP
- finely divided solids that dissolve completely in water; form true solutions when mixed with water, and
- will not separate or settle-out upon standing; require no agitation once initially mixed.
- example: Dowpon M.

❑ **Emulsifiable concentrates**
- designated as E or EC
- oil-soluble herbicide containing emulsifiers
- form emulsions when mixed with water
- require mild agitation to keep properly mixed in spray tank, and
- can have normal emulsions and invert emulsions.
- examples: Basagran 4EC and Roundup 4EC.

❑ **Wettable powders**
- are designated as W or WP
- finely ground solids consisting of a dry carrier (a finely ground hydrophilic clay), pesticide, and dispersing agents
- forms an unstable suspension when mixed with water, and requires continuous vigorous agitation; without agitation, a solid precipitate forms at the bottom of the tank
- need to make a slurry before adding to a spray tank, and
- causes rapid nozzle wear.
- examples: Rubigan 50WP and Aatrex 80WP.

❑ **Water dispersible liquids**
- frequently designated as liquids or flowables; WDL, L, F, AS
- finely ground solids suspended in a liquid system
- form suspension when added to water in spray tank
- particles smaller than a WP, agitation requirement intermediate between that for WP and EC
- nozzle wear intermediate between WP and EC, more similar to WP, and
- tend to settle out in storage; container must be vigorously shaken before use.
- examples: Sencor 4L, Surflan 4AS, and Aatrex 4L.

❑ **Water dispersible granules**
- also called dry flowables; designated as WDG or DF
- dry formulations of granular dimensions
- granules made up of finely divided solids (a size similar to that in flowables) that combines with suspending and dispersing agents
- easy pouring advantage over WP and F, and
- other properties (such as nozzle wear and agitation requirements) similar to F.
- examples: Sencor DF and Princep Caliber 90 WDG.

Dry Formulations (for direct application)

These formulations are applied directly from the package ("straight out of the bag") to the field without dilution in a liquid carrier. Usually comes as a low concentration formulation (2 to 25% active).

❑ **Granules**
- are designated as G
- consists of a dry material in which active ingredient is impregnated on small dry carrier particles of uniform size; the carrier can be clay, sand, vermiculite, or corn cob; granule size less than 0.61 cubic inches
- applied with granular applicators; in general, they are more difficult to apply uniformly than a sprayed material
- may be moved from applied area by wind or rain (for example, a banded application can be blown or washed off the top of the bed), and
- in general, requires slightly more rainfall for activation than a sprayable formulation; on the other hand, rate of pesticide loss by volatilization is somewhat slower.
- examples: Balan 2.5G and Ronstar 2G.

❑ **Pellets**
- are designated as P
- dry formulation of pesticide and other components in discrete particles usually larger than 0.61 cubic inches
- frequently used for spot applications, applied by hand, from shaker cans, or with hand spreaders, and
- low concentration, usually 5 to 20%.

Proper Order for Tank Mixing

When mixing two or more compatible pesticides, the order in which they should be added to the spray tank varies with the formulations. In general, the proper order is:

$$WP \rightarrow DF \rightarrow F \rightarrow EC \rightarrow S$$

Agitate after each addition.

General Information

❑ Definition of a **solution**: a physically homogeneous mixture of two or more substances; cannot be separated by mechanical means; transparent, but may be colored; nonabrasive.

❑ Definition of a **suspension**: a mixture containing finely divided particles dispersed in a liquid. Particles retain identity, can be physically separated from liquid.

❑ Definition of **emulsion**: one liquid dispersed in another liquid; each liquid maintains original identity.

Example: **Normal emulsion** (oil-in-water emulsion): water is continuous phase, oil is discontinuous phase.

Example: **Invert emulsion** (water-in-oil emulsion): oil is continuous phase, water is discontinuous phase.

Carriers

Carriers serve as the diluent for the pesticide formulation. The carrier is the material to which the formulated pesticide is added for field application. Primary purpose of carrier is to enable uniform distribution of a small amount of formulated pesticide to a large area. There are three types of carriers: liquid, dry, foam.

Liquid. Liquid carriers for spray applications include water (most widely used), liquid fertilizers, vegetable oils, and diesel oil.

Dry. Dry carriers are used to apply herbicides without further dilution and are the major components of granules and pellets. Includes attapulgite, kaolinite, vermiculite, starch polymers, corn cob, others.

Dry fertilizers can also be carriers. Herbicide can be impregnated on dry fertilizer, and is used for some soil-applied herbicides. Label will have details. Some fertilizers cannot be used. From 200 to 450 pounds fertilizer per acre is necessary to have enough volume for uniform application. A major problem is uniformity of application. Spreader trucks (or the drivers) often do a poor job of uniform application.

Foam. Used only in special applications. Special equipment is needed.

COMPATIBILITY TESTS

Tank mixes of two or more pesticides are commonly applied. Sometimes these pesticides may not mix well in the tank even though each product alone mixes well. Also, there are situations where it is desirable to use a fluid fertilizer or liquid nitrogen as the carrier. Some pesticides are compatible with fluid fertilizers and some are not. By conducting a simple compatibility test before adding the pesticides to the tank, one can usually avoid making "jello" in the tank. Every batch of fluid fertilizer or liquid nitrogen should be tested for compatibility. Batches can vary in pH, salt concentration, or even temperature. Minor differences may affect compatibility.

Materials Required for a Compatability Test

❑ Two 1-quart jars with lids (mark one "with" and the other one "without")

❑ Teaspoons

❑ Fluid fertilizer or liquid nitrogen to be tested

❑ The pesticide(s) to be tested

❑ A compatibility agent.

Procedure

The procedure for a compatability test is often outlined on pesticide label. Follow these steps, in order, to perform a compatability test.

1. Add 1 pint of the fluid fertilizer to each quart jar.

2. To the jar marked "with," add teaspoon of compatibility agent. Gently shake for 5 to 10 seconds.

3. To each jar, add the following appropriate amount of pesticide(s) (Table 1). Shake gently for 5 to 12 seconds.

4. Let the jars sit for 5 minutes, then look at them. See if there are any flakes, sludge, gels or other precipitants. Also see if there is any separation or layering, or small oil particles in solution.

If incompatibility occurs in "without" jar but not in "with" jar, use a compatibility agent.

Table 1. Amount of pesticide to add for a compatability test.

Type of Pesticide	Rate/Acre	Teaspoons to Add
WP or DF	1 lb	1.5
	2 lb	3.0
	3 lb	4.5
	4 lb	6.0
EC, F, L, or S	1 pt	0.5
	1 qt	1.0
	2 qt	2.0
	4 qt	4.0

If incompatibility is observed in the "with" jar, this combination is not compatible and should not be used.

5. If separate layers are formed after sitting up to 30 minutes but can be resuspended by shaking, commercial application is possible. Use agitation in the sprayer.

If there is layering, an emulsifiable concentrate will normally go to the top. Wettable powders will either settle to the bottom or float on top, depending upon density of the fertilizer carrier.

Sprayers for Homeowners

L. B. McCarty

The correct use of pesticide application equipment is important to the success of the pest-control job. Select the right kind of application equipment. Use and maintain it properly. Here is some advice about choosing, using, and caring for equipment.

There are three types of application equipment: hand sprayers, hose-end sprayers, and wipe-on applicators. In each case, the sprayer should be:

❑ designed to do the necessary job

❑ durable, and

❑ convenient to fill, operate, and clean.

HAND SPRAYER

Hand sprayers are for professional application of pesticides for small jobs around the home and garden. They can be used in restricted areas where a power unit will not work (Figure 1).

The **advantages** of hand sprayers are:

❑ economical

❑ simple, and

❑ easy to use, clean, and store.

The limitations of a hand sprayer are:

❑ frequent lack of good agitation and screening for wettable powders (WPs) (keep WPs in suspension by shaking the sprayer)

❑ only practical for treating small areas, and

❑ difficult to obtain uniform coverage.

HOSE-END SPRAYERS

Many homeowners prefer buying and applying pesticides which are packaged for garden hose-end type application. A small amount of pesticide is mixed with water, usually no more than a pint, and placed in the receptacle attached to the hose. A tube connects this concentrate to the opening of the hose. When the water is turned on, the suction created by the water passing over the top of the tube pulls the pesticide concentrate up and into the stream of hose water. The stream can reach into trees of medium height, if water pressure is high.

The **advantages** of hose-end sprayers are:

❑ economical

❑ easy to use, clean, and store

❑ light weight, and

❑ versatile.

The **limitations** of hose-end sprayers are:

❑ limited number of pesticides available in this form

❑ difficulty in obtaining uniform application

❑ only practical for treating small areas; hose must be able to reach these

❑ constant refilling, and

❑ difficult to calibrate.

WIPE-ON APPLICATORS

Wipe-on applicators are designed to provide selective placement of herbicides to weeds above the desirable plant. Commonly used types include the rope wick, sponge wick, and carpet roller applicators.

The initial cost of the wipe-on applicator is generally low. However, herbicide delivery is gravity fed and usually two passes are frequently required for complete coverage.

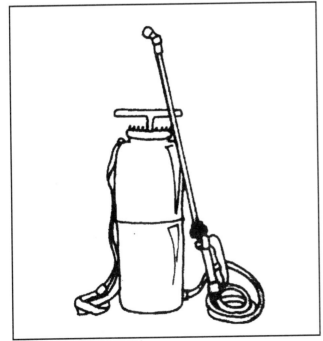

Figure 1. Portable hand sprayer.

Currently, glyphosate (Roundup) is the herbicide primarily used in the wipe-on application process. Care must be taken to ensure that the wipe-on applicator does not come into contact with desirable plant foliage when using glyphosate and that the applicator is not so saturated that it drips.

The **advantages** of wipe-on applicators are:

❑ low cost

❑ simple to operate

❑ no drift, and

❑ reduces amount of pesticide used.

The **disadvantages** of wipe-on applicators are:

❑ applicable only in special situations; difficult to calibrate

❑ several passes are usually necessary to ensure complete coverage, and

❑ weeds must be physically taller than the desirable plant.

CHAPTER ELEVEN

County Cooperative Extension Service Offices

County Cooperative Extension Service Offices

Alachua
2800 N.E. 39 Avenue
Gainesville, FL 32609-2658

Baker
Rt. 3, Box 1074-B
Macclenny, FL 32063-9640

Bay
324 W. 6 Street
Panama City, FL 32401-2616

Bradford
2266 N. Temple Ave.
Starke, FL 32091-1612

Brevard
3695 Lake Drive
Cocoa, FL 32926-8699

Broward
3245 College Ave.
Davie, FL 33314-7798

Calhoun
340 East Central Ave.
Blountstown, FL 32424-2206

Charlotte
6900 Florida St.
Punta Gorda, FL 33950-5799

Citrus
3600 S. Florida Ave.
Inverness, FL 34450-7369

Clay
2463 State Rd. 16 W.
P.O. Box 278
Green Cove Springs, FL 32043-0278

Collier
14700 Immokalee Rd.
Naples, FL 33964-1468

Columbia
P.O. Box 1587
Lake City, FL 32056-1587

Dade
18710 S.W. 288 Street
Homestead, FL 33030-2309

DeSoto
P.O. Drawer 310
Arcadia, FL 34265-0310

Dixie
P.O. Box 640
Cross City, FL 32628-1534

Duval
1010 N. McDuff Avenue
Jacksonville, FL 32254-2083

Escambia
3740 Stefani Road
Cantonment, FL 32533-7792

Flagler
150 Sawgrass Road
Bunnell, FL 32110-0308

Franklin
33 Market Street, Suite 305
Apalachicola, FL 32320-2310

Gadsden
2140 W. Jefferson St.
Quincy, FL 32351-1905

Gilchrist
P.O. Box 157
Trenton, FL 32693-0157

Glades
P.O. Box 549
Moore Haven, FL 33471-0549

Gulf
200 E. 2 Street
P.O. Box 250
Wewahitchka, FL 32465-0250

Hamilton
P.O. Drawer K
Jasper, FL 32052-0691

Hardee
507 Civic Center Drive
Wauchula, FL 33873-1288

Hendry
P.O. Box 68
Labelle, FL 33975-0068

Hernando
19490 Oliver St.
Brooksville, FL 34601-6538

Highlands
4509 W. George Blvd.
Sebring, FL 33872-5803

Hillsborough
5339 State Rd. 579 S.
Seffner, FL 32584-3399

Holmes
201 N. Oklahoma St.
Bonifay, FL 32425-2295

Indian River
1028 20th Pl., Suite D
Vero Beach, FL 32960-5360

Jackson
4487 Lafayette St.
Marianna, FL 32446-3412

Jefferson
275 N. Mulberry
Monticello, FL 32344-2249

Lafayette
Rt. 3, Box 15
Mayo, FL 32066-1901

Lake
30205 State Rd. 19
Tavares, FL 32778-4052

Lee
3406 Palm Beach Blvd.
Ft. Myers, FL 33916-3719

Leon
615 Paul Russell Road
Tallahassee, FL 32301-7099

Levy
P.O. Box 219
Bronson, FL 32621-0219

Liberty
P.O. Box 369
Bristol, FL 32321-0368

Madison
900 College Avenue
Madison, FL 32340-1426

Manatee
1303 17th Street West
Palmetto, FL 34221-2998

Marion
2232 N.E. Jacksonville Rd.
Ocala, FL 32670-3615

Martin
2614 S.E. Dixie Hwy.
Stuart, FL 33494-4007

Monroe
5100 College Road
Key West, FL 33040-4364

Nassau
P.O. Box 1550
Callahan, FL 32011-1550

Okaloosa
5479 Old Bethel Road
Crestview, FL 32536-5513

Okeechobee
458 Highway 98 North
Okeechobee, FL 34972-2303

Orange
2350 E. Michigan St.
Orlando, FL 32806-4996

Osceola
1901 E. Irlo Bronson Hwy.
Kissimmee, FL 34744-8947

Palm Beach
559 N. Military Trail
W. Palm Beach, FL 33415-1311

Pasco
36702 State Rd 52
Dade City, FL 33525-5198

Pinellas
12175 125th St. N
Largo, FL 34644-3695

Polk
Drawer HS03
PO Box 9005
Bartow, FL 33831-9005

Putnam
111 Yelvington Rd., Suite 1
East Palatka, FL 32131-8892

St. Johns
3125 Agri. Center Dr.
St. Augustine, FL 32092-0572

St. Lucie
8400 Picos Rd., Suite 101
Ft. Pierce, FL 34945-3045

Santa Rosa
6051 Old Bagdad Hwy., Rm. 116
Milton, FL 32583-8944

Sarasota
2900 Ringling Blvd.
Sarasota, FL 34237-5397

Seminole
250 W. County Home Rd.
Sanford, FL 32773-6197

Sumter
P.O. Box 218
Bushnell, FL 33513-0218

Suwannee
1302 11th St., S.W.
Live Oak, FL 32060-3696

Taylor
203 Forest Park Drive
Perry, FL 32347-6396

Union
25 N.E. 1st Street
Lake Butler, FL 32054-1701

Volusia
3100 E. New York Ave.
DeLand, FL 32724-6497

Wakulla
P.O. Box 40
Crawfordville, FL 32326-0040

Walton
732 N. 9 Street, Suite B
DeFuniak Springs, FL 32433-3804

Washington
1424 Jackson Avenue, Suite A
Chipley, FL 32428-1615

Plate 1: Too much shade to grow most turfgrasses (p. 2).

Plate 2: Bahiagrass (note V-shaped seedhead) (p. 5).

Plate 3: Bermudagrass (p. 6).

Plate 4: Common bermudagrass (right) texture and density compared to an improved hybrid (left) (p. 6).

Plate 5: Buffalograss (p. 8).

Plate 6: Carpetgrass (p. 10).

Plate 7: Centipedegrass (common) (p. 11).

Plate 8: St. Augustinegrass (p. 12).

Plate 9: Bitterblue (left) and Floratam (right) St. Augustinegrass (p. 13).

Plate 10: Seville (left) and Raleigh (right) St. Augustinegrass (p. 13).

Plate 11: Delmar (left) and FX-10 (right) St. Augustinegrass (p. 13).

Plate 12: Zoysiagrass (p. 14).

Plate 13: Smoothing the surface of a well-prepared seedbed by raking (p. 19).

Plate 14: Firming the seedbed with a roller (p. 20).

Plate 15: Using a cover for fumigation (p. 20).

Plate 16: Applying seed with a drop spreader (p. 22).

Plate 17: Newly seeded area mulched with straw or hay (p. 22).

Plate 18: Laying sod in a "brick-like" pattern for an instant greening effect and minimal soil erosion (p. 22).

Plate 19: Individual pieces of turf plants used as sprigs (p. 23).

Plate 20: Establishing a new lawn by plugging (p. 23).

Plate 21: Turf overseeded with ryegrass to provide winter color (p. 56).

Plate 22: Poor fertilizer coverage, resulting in striping effect (p. 58).

Plate 23: Cyclone/Rotary/ Centrifugal spreader (p. 58).

Plate 24: "Foot-printing" pattern indicates the need for water (p. 61).

Plate 25: Folded St. Augustinegrass leaf blade due to water (drought) stress (p. 61).

Plate 26: Calibrating the output of a sprinkler system by placing cups throughout the irrigation pattern and measuring the amount of water applied over a certain time period (p. 62 and 64).

Plate 27: Proper mowing height for most St. Augustinegrass and bahiagrass varieties (p. 67).

Plate 28: Excessive clippings from too infrequent mowing (p. 68).

Plate 29: Front deck, walk behind type rotary mower often used by lawn maintenance firms (p. 68).

Plate 30: Reel mower used on high quality, low cut turf such as bermudagrass or zoysiagrass (p. 68).

Plate 31a and b: Ragged St. Augustinegrass leaf (left) following mowing with a dull blade compared to using a sharp blade (right) (p. 68).

Plate 32: Mulching mower. Note the absence of discharge chute (p. 68).

Plate 33: Scalping turf due to improper mower height and excessive thatch development (p. 69).

Plate 34: Thatch layer between the green top grass and gray-colored soil underneath (p. 70).

Plate 35: Core aerifier which enhances soil-to-air oxygen exchange and increases water penetration and drainage (p. 71).

Plate 36: Topdressing to add a thin layer of quality soil to encourage thatch decomposition (p. 71).

Plate 37: Scalped bermudagrass (left) in an attempt to remove thatch (p. 71).

Plate 38: Vertical mowing (or verticutting) to remove thatch (p. 71).

Plate 39: Bahiagrass following proper vertical mowing (p. 71).

Plate 40: Southern Sida (*Sida acuta*) (p. 97).

Plate 41: White Clover (*Trifolium repens*) (p. 97).

Plate 42: Alternanthera (*Alternanthera paronychioides*) (p. 97).

Plate 43: Garden Spurge (*Chamaesyce hirta*) (p. 97).

Plate 44: Ground-ivy or Creeping Charlie (*Glechoma hederaces*) (p. 97).

Plate 45: Brazilian Pusley (*Richardia braziliensi*) (p. 97).

Plate 46: Asiatic Hawksbeard (*Youngia japonicá*) (p. 97).

Plate 47: Slender Amaranth (*Amaranthus viridus*) (p. 97).

Plate 48: Hairy Beggar's-tick (*Bidens alba*) (p. 97).

Plate 49: Spreading Dayflower (*Commelina diffusa*) (p. 97).

Plate 50: Pennywort or Dollarweed (*Hydrocotyle umbellata*) (p. 97).

Plate 51: Creeping Indigo (*Indigofera spicata*) (p. 97).

Plate 52: Cutleaf Evening Primrose (*Oenothera laciniata*) (p. 97).

Plate 53: Yellow Woodsorrel (*Oxalis stricta*) (p. 97).

Plate 54: Matchweed or Match-head (*Phyla nodiflora*) (p. 97).

Plate 55: Niruri or Chamberbitter (*Phyllanthus urinaria*) (p. 97).

Plate 56: Florida Pusley (*Richardia scabra*) (p. 97).

Plate 57: Florida Betony or Rattlesnake Weed (*Stachys floridana*) (p. 97).

Plate 58: Puncturevine (*Tribulus terrestris*) (p. 97).

Plate 59: Coast Sandbur (*Cenchrus* spp) (p. 97).

Plate 60: Crowfootgrass (*Dactyloctenium aegyptium*) (p. 97).

Plate 61: Blanket or Rabbit Crabgrass (*Digitaria serotina*) (p. 97).

Plate 62: Goosegrass (*Eleusine indica*) (p. 97).

Plate 63: Thin or Bull Paspalum (*Paspalum setaceum*) (p. 97).

Plate 64: Nutsedge (*Cyperus* spp.) in turf (p. 97).

Plate 65: Perennial or Green Kyllinga (*Cyperus brevifolia*) (p. 97).

Plate 66: Globe Sedge (*Cyperus globulosus*) (p. 97).

Plate 67: Purple Nutsedge (*Cyperus rotundus*) (p. 97).

Plate 68: Two tawny mole crickets (left) and two southern mole crickets (right) (p. 111).

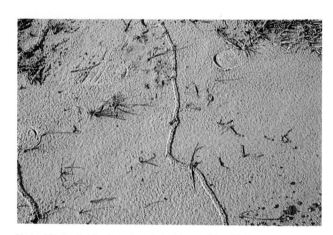

Plate 69: Individual mole cricket tunnel (p. 111).

Plate 70: Typical mole cricket damage in turf (p. 111).

Plate 71: Adult chinch bugs on St. Augustinegrass (p. 111).

Plate 72: Chinch bug damage in St. Augustinegrass (p. 112).

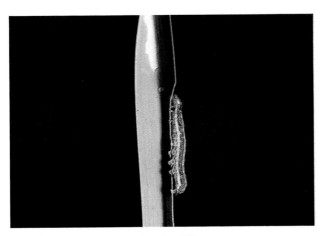

Plate 73: Armyworm feeding (p. 112).

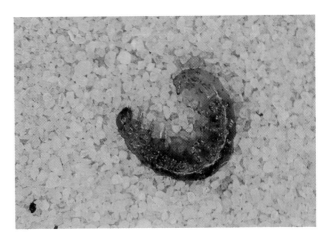

Plate 74: Tropical sod webworm larvae (p. 112).

Plate 75: Notched leaf damage from sod webworm feeding (p. 113).

Plate 76: Hunting billbug larvae (left) and adult (right) (p. 113).

Plate 77: Hunting billbug damage (p. 113).

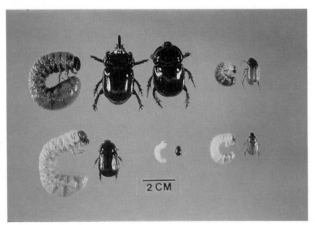

Plate 78: Various white grub larvae and adults (p. 113).

Plate 79: White grubs feeding on turf roots (p. 113).

Plate 80: Bermudagrass mite damage (p. 113).

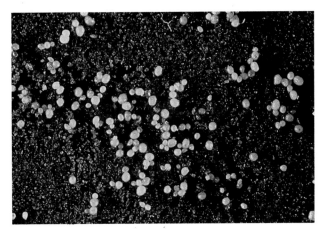

Plate 81: Ground pearl adults found in centipedegrass (p. 114).

Plate 82: Bermudagrass scale (p. 114).

Plate 83: Two-line spittlebug found in centipedegrass (p. 114).

Plate 84: Spittlebug mass on centipedegrass (p. 114).

Plate 85: Centipedegrass leaf striping damage from spittlebug feeding (p. 114).

Plate 86: Algae on poorly drained, continuously wet turf (p. 134).

Plate 87: Moss in a lawn due to excessive shade and water, and poor soil drainage (p. 134).

Plate 88: Anthracnose lesion on centipedegrass (p. 135).

Plate 89: Brown patch disease in St. Augustinegrass (p. 136).

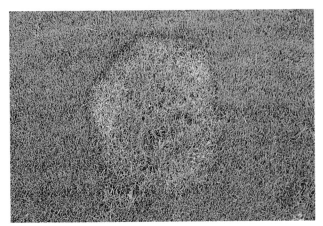

Plate 90: Brown patch disease in overseeded ryegrass (p. 136).

Plate 91: Dollar spot disease in bermudagrass (p. 137).

Plate 92: Dollar spot lesion in centipedegrass (p. 137).

Plate 93: Fairy ring (p. 138).

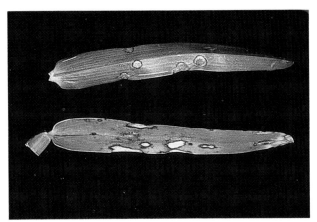

Plate 94: Gray leaf spot disease in St. Augustinegrass (p. 139).

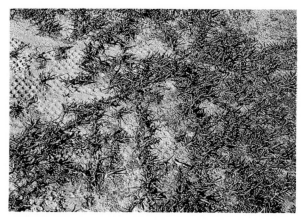

Plate 95: Severe gray leaf spot disease in St. Augustinegrass resembling drought damage (p. 139).

Plate 96: Helminthosporium leaf spot disease lesions in bermudagrass (p. 140).

Plate 97: Patches of *Pythium* blight in overseeded ryegrass (p. 141).

Plate 98: Streaking of *Pythium* blight in overseeded ryegrass (p. 141).

Plate 99: *Pythium* or cottony blight in a harvested St. Augustinegrass sod field (p. 141).

Plate 100: *Pythium* in bermudagrass (p. 142).

Plate 101: Rhizoctonia leaf and sheath spot symptoms (p. 143).

Plate 102: Patch appearance of rhizoctonia leaf and sheath spot (p. 143).

Plate 103: Rust in zoysiagrass (p. 144).

Plate 104: Slime mold on turf (p. 145).

Plate 105: St. Augustinegrass Take-all Root Rot (p. 146).

Plate 106: Centipedegrass decline (p. 45).

Plate 107: Thin bermudagrass due to sting nematodes (p. 153).

Plate 108: Sting nematode damage (right) in bermudagrass (p. 154).

Plate 109: Damage from an armadillo digging in search of food (p. 162).

Plate 110: Tunneling from ground moles and trap placement for control (p. 165).

Plate 111: Dome-shaped fire ant mounds (p. 170).

Plate 112: Dog urine injury on bahiagrass (p. 27).

COOPERATIVE EXTENSION SERVICE, UNIVERSITY OF FLORIDA, INSTITUTE OF FOOD AND AGRICULTURAL SCIENCES, Christine Taylor Stephens, Director, in cooperation with the United States Department of Agriculture, publishes this information to further the purpose of the May 8 and June 30, 1914 Acts of Congress; and is authorized to provide research, educational information and other services only to individuals and institutions that function without regard to race, color, age, sex, handicap or national origin. The information in this publication is available in alternate formats. Information on copies for purchase is available from C.M. Hinton, Publications Distribution Center, University of Florida, PO Box 110011, Gainesville, FL 32611-0011. Information about alternate formats is available from Educational Media and Services, University of Florida, PO Box 110810, Gainesville, FL 32611-0810. This information was published December 1990 as SP 45, Florida Cooperative Extension Service. Revised March 1997.